The
Ripple
Effect
Our Harvest

Also by Betty J. Eadie

Embraced By The Light

and

The Awakening Heart

The

Ripple Effect
Our Harvest

BETTY J. EADIE

njinjinkta Publishing

Onjinjinkta Publishing, a division of Gleska Enterprises
P.O. Box 25490, Seattle, WA. 98125

ISBN: 1-892714-00-0

First Onjinjinkta Publishing hardcover printing September 1999
Gleska Enterprises.

10 9 8 7 6 5 4 3 2 1

Printed in the U.S.A.

This book is dedicated:

To the many ripples in my life.
First, to my Heavenly Father,
the creator of my soul. He is my reason for living,
my purpose for life. To Him I dedicate all that I do.

To my husband Joe,
who continues to be my rock in spite of my many changes.
He supports and loves me unconditionally.

To my children,
our love as a family has grown because of the many
challenges my work has brought them. As God
continues to reside in our home, we will endure all things.

To my Grandchildren, my Earth Angels,
Kurt, Jessica, Zach, Natalie, Stephanie, Meggan,
Jennifer, Keona, Brandi, Lauren, Tommy, Joseph,
Hannah, Jonah and Jacob.

To my many friends and readers,
especially those who shared from their heart in this book.
Because of their ripples we are taught, through lives,
the powerful effect of the Spirit of God.

Acknowledgments

My love and appreciation to my son Thomas. He stands behind me through thick and thin as an energy of light. He supports all my efforts with radiant hope, as he serves me not only as a son, but as the business manager of my press. He designed the cover of this book, using my picture and his superb instincts, to create an image of serenity and strength. His love for me and his dedication to business extends our natural bond to fulfill what I believe is our higher Spiritual purpose in serving God.

Great appreciation to my editorial staff, without whose skills this finished product would have been impossible: Jay Davis, Curtis Taylor, Stan Zenk, and Peter Orullian.

My love to Georgia Carpenter, Michelle Freyer, and to all the staff members of Onjinjinkta Publishing and Distribution. Congratulations! Your sacrifices have made this happen and have meant a lot to me. God's eternal blessings as your tremendous efforts continue to "Ripple On."

Contents

Author's Note

his year I will celebrate the twenty-sixth anniversary of my death and rebirth. In some ways, the events I experienced then are more vivid now than they were immediately after coming back. I knew upon returning that I was to share the experience at the appropriate time and that the message of God's unconditional love would reach many people around the world. The message went out in 1992 with the publication of *Embraced By The Light*, and was increased and amplified by *The Awakening Heart*, which was published in 1996. The message now ripples out to millions who, in turn, share the power of God's love with others. This is the ripple effect at its finest, creating waves of positive energy that are full of love, going forward until one day that love will be experienced by all.

Everything we do ripples out; we affect others, and they in turn affect us. Sometimes the ripples create huge waves that wash over humanity, changing it forever, as Christ's life did. Sometimes they are so small that they remain relatively unknown in this lifetime. The ripples from *Embraced By The Light* and *The Awakening Heart* continue to go forth, and are now returning to me in the form of letters, e-mail and phone calls. I'm delighted, even overwhelmed, at how many lives have been touched. Each person received an answer to a prayer or question. Each received a response, through the Spirit, to a need in their lives. And as they read and felt encouragement, their spiritual growth and strength increased; as their strength increased, they felt the Lord calling them to a higher level of his work. People wrote to share how they had grown by applying universal principles to their lives. Some shared spiritual experiences, while others simply needed to share their pain. But, for whatever the reason, most people who contacted me did so, they said, because they felt compelled to write. If only a few people had said they were compelled, I might not have thought much about it. But when almost every letter began with the words, "I just had to write," it became clear that an important connection was being made. A similar reaction came at speaking engagements, when people told me how compelled they had felt to attend. Many said they felt as though they had always known me, and when we parted, genuine feelings of sorrow were expressed by us all. I know that love is contagious, but there seemed to be something else occurring, something borne of knowledge as well as love.

Truth is so powerful that, when we find it, we instantly feel the need to reach out to the person providing it. When that truth is an example of God's love, our desire to reach out can nearly overwhelm us. Spiritual experiences need to be shared. In my experience, Jesus told me that we are not to hide the truth; we are to share it with one another, to speak of the wonders and mysteries of God as they have been gifted to us.

We are all compelled by the Spirit to reach out, and I understand a little better why I have been given this desire so strongly. On my way to Washington D. C., surrounded by strangers on a jet traveling six miles above the earth, I was reading a letter from somebody I had never met, and the love I felt in the letter overwhelmed me. I sobbed uncontrollably; my heart could not help but give in to the waves of love and gratitude that I was feeling. Perhaps I should have been embarrassed, but the power of the words on the paper left me oblivious to my surroundings. I'm a passionate person and find it difficult to control certain emotions, especially feelings of love. Taking a minute to compose myself, I reread the letter.

Dear Betty,

Your book, *Embraced By The Light*, has been such a major part of my life lately, and I suppose it's only right that I explain how and why.

Not long ago, I found work at a convalescent home as an activities assistant. This is where my life began to change significantly. It was very difficult, at first, dealing with terminally ill people and even with the folks who weren't dying. So many were desperate to have company, a friend or just a little attention. I soon found that I could offer such things, and it felt great.

It was heart-warming to see the volunteers who gave their time to these folks. I remember one man in particular. He was a black man who looked as though he belonged on a professional football team, but even bigger than that was his heart. The first time I saw him he was traveling from room to room with your book in hand, reading certain parts to different folks. It really touched my heart, as the chemistry he had with even the very ill people was so strong and spellbinding.

That next payday I got myself a copy of *Embraced By The Light* and was instantly absorbed in its pages. I cannot express adequately what it has done for me and others. All I know is that it is always there, like a rainbow that travels at my side, no matter the distance . . .

After reading your book and closing its last beautiful page, an important question came to mind and heart, "Who would benefit most from this book right now?" Then there was a name that entered my thoughts as big as a billboard. I had been drawn to this new patient the first time she entered the facility. She was young, early sixties, and had lung cancer. I had been told that she didn't have long to live, as the cancer had entered her bloodstream.

I couldn't wait to give her your book. I came to work eager to get to her room, because I was sure God wanted the book in her hands as soon as possible. But when I reached her room, I stopped in my tracks and fell speechless. There in her hands was the book! She said her daughter had given it to her, and she proceeded to tell me all the things about it that I had planned to say to her! It blew me away—to say the least.

Later in the week, she revealed to me that she could no longer read. Her vision had become too obstructed. So I offered to come on my day off to read more of your book to her.

The day I arrived, she was on the patio outside her room, creating a picture out of the flower petals from a garden there. Her bookmark was at the chapter entitled, "Embraced By The Light," and I began to read. She listened while she continued working with the flower petals. With the last page and last words of that chapter, she stopped me. She said, "That's a beautiful place to end it." Not long after that time we spent together in the garden learning about God's most loving message, she died.

Only days later, a friend called me out of the blue, a friend I hadn't heard from for what seemed an eternity. She had been pretty wild in our younger days, a heavy drinker, and she frequented the nightclubs. That's what made what she had to say even more shocking, as well as meaningful.

"There's something I felt I had to tell you," she said. "I've read a book that's changed my life for the better."

She went on to explain how this book had made her appreciate life in a way she never had before. It had touched her so very deeply and she was very definitely "Embraced By The Light."

"I suggest you read it," she added before hanging up. "Maybe it can do the same for you."

"It has," was all I could say . . .

Love for each person in this letter filled my heart. I saw no passengers on the plane around me, heard no sounds, felt no sense of time or travel. If I had been able, I would have crawled into the letter at that very moment to give each of them the embrace my arms longed to share. This letter illuminates love—a beautiful gift shared by a godly woman. Jesus once said, "Let your light shine before men, that they may see your good deeds and glorify your Father in heaven" (Matthew 5:14-16). What an example this woman had been of letting her light shine! She had followed her heart, led by the hand of God, relentlessly giving of her time and love. She had become part of God's ripple effect, his love that washes over humanity to remove fear by the power of its purity.

Who am I, then, that the message I share touches so many lives? I don't know, and I don't worry about it as I used to. I am comfortable in the knowledge that I have a message to share, a message of Christ and his redeeming love. I know that for many God has used my light to guide them toward him. For that I am most humbled, and I accept that responsibility. The connections made are God given, God blessed. Some people he has prepared feel compelled to listen to my message; others do not. Some feel close to me, wanting to communicate and share their lives, and I rejoice in the oneness we experience. But I know that regardless of my reception, regardless of apparent success or failure, regardless of pain or sacrifice, I must share this message. I will create as many ripples within the family of mankind as God blesses me with. If it is His will, I will share His love until my voice is gone and my body stilled. And I invite everybody else who feels the call to do the same. It is the greatest gift we have to offer.

We are all shepherds to some degree. We are all compelled by the Spirit to seek his truth and do his will, each in our own way, creating waves that overlap others and resonate within their souls, inviting them to do better, to look to God, to live life to the fullest with joy.

Each letter reprinted here is precious to me, as are all I receive. And seeing how each individual has been profoundly touched by the power of God's love, I'm humbled, even awed, to have been a part of their lives. Now I'm humbled further to continue in some way to respond to the many questions and concerns.

My experience in the spirit world came as a gift to me, and though I am determined to share that gift with others, I am unable to answer each individual personally. I hope by sharing a few letters here that, perhaps, I can address the concerns and questions most often posed to me. In sharing these treasured letters, I feel a need to protect the writers' privacy. No names or locations are mentioned, except in special cases. And each letter easily represents hundreds similar to it.

And by sharing the letters, I feel that I am doing what the Lord asked us when he said: "Let your light so shine . . ." Each person in this book has a divine purpose, and by sharing their light, we can see how one person can make a difference in our life. If each of us shares our light, soon all dark corners will be reached, and we will begin the healing of the world by chasing out darkness. We, too, will begin the healing of our own souls. As we each find one person with whom to share our light, a wonderful miracle begins to take place: we find the Lord answering our individual prayers and preparing us to become the light, the answer, to yet many others.

In this world of billions of people, many lead lives of loneliness and desperation. Because of pain produced by others, some protect themselves behind walls of anger or fear, lashing out at or retreating from others. God has shown me that the precious cure for their pain lies within each soul. The cure, of course, is honest and pure love. God's love. Unconditional love. It resides within each of us naturally at our beginning. In the stories that follow, we see how others have begun to overcome their own fears and hurts to become the answer to others' prayers. We see that we are not alone, that everything we do touches everybody else in some way, and that as we release our love to others, we each become the vessel God has chosen from the beginning.

Letting our light shine, letting our love and truth emanate to as many people as possible, is a mission given to each of us. Allowing our goodness to ripple into the lives of others will not only bring us closer to the divine, it will create the spiritual Awakening of the world. This Awakening is now gathering momentum, leading many to come closer to God. This movement is universal and unstoppable. And it must proceed from our hearts, our lives, into the lives of others. It is not God's gracious work alone; it is our work, our opportunity, and it can only progress as we let our lights shine. As one reader declared, the time has come for us all to "Ripple on!"

—Betty J. Eadie
September 1999

The
Ripple
Effect
Our Harvest

Our Heavenly Home

During my near-death experience I was blessed with precious knowledge of life and death, but I remind people that I do not have all the answers. What I have was gifted to me, but it is still incomplete. Much of what I learned on the other side was removed from my memory when I returned to earth. God let me keep what knowledge I needed, and he restores a little more as time goes by.

He responds to everyone this way. Being a wise and impartial God, he blesses all who reach out to him, granting them knowledge and faith. All who are open to truth and are willing to live by it once they receive it, will receive more—by visions or visitations or, more likely, by quiet prompting and insights. Much about life will remain a mystery while we dwell in this earthly plane. But through faithful living and prayer, much may also be revealed.

Perhaps no subject interests people who write me more than that of our heavenly home. The idea that our spirits once lived with God before coming to earth surprises many, even though our pre-mortal life is mentioned in the Bible. I quote from the Bible from time to time, because, although some people dismiss it, in my opinion it contains most of the answers we desperately seek from God. In Jeremiah 1:5 God is speaking of the pre-existence of our spirits when he tells Jeremiah: "Before I formed thee in the belly I knew thee; and before thou camest forth out of the womb I sanctified thee, and I ordained thee a prophet unto the nations." The preacher in Ecclesiastes echoes the idea of this pre-life when he said, "Then shall the dust return to the earth as it was: and the spirit shall return unto God who gave it."

God created our spirits long before we were born on earth. I saw this clearly and repeatedly during my experience. In fact much of what I "learned" about heaven was actually a remembering of it from when I lived there before. I remembered it because, when we die, the veil of forgetfulness is removed from our minds. Being free from the body, we are able to recall the immensity of truth and experience we had before coming here. Among the things I remembered was counseling with our Heavenly Father before coming to earth. Each one of us made plans with him and set goals for our lives here. He agreed to bless us with the experiences we needed for our ultimate spiritual development. We were excited about being born in the flesh to parents who had preceded us to earth. We knew that birth would bring a forgetting of the previous life. And we knew why the forgetting would be necessary. It is because life here is to be a test, an examination of our spirits, similar to attending a university. By coming here without our eyes fully open, we are forced to follow the whisperings of our spirits—those quiet truthful impressions that spring from the subconscious. As we follow them, we begin to hear also the whisperings of God. If we want to grow to become all that we can be, we must be true to ourselves—to the spirit within us that came from heaven. However, knowing ourselves requires painful effort, and this is the test. We are sent here to walk in faith, believing we are going forward, all the while not quite knowing where "forward" is.

If it were different, if we could remember our former life and association with God, what test would that be? How could we foster our spirit's development if our mortal minds recalled every reason for good and every punishment for evil? These are things we surely learned about before this life. How could we learn who we are deep inside, if we are not required to rely on our spirits for guidance? This process of discovery is not only how we learn who we truly are, but it is how we gain experience necessary for our growth. As difficult as this life is, it is a perfect plan.

Memories of the former life have been removed from most of us, but, I am pleased to discover, not from everyone. There are some who remember. One woman writes:

> I've always recalled my before-birth experiences and my decision to leave my close companions to come here. I recall the place I was in, and those around me, and God. I knew it was "planned" that I be born, and that my life was "pre-selected," and that I "had to go" for growth reasons. Of course, my memories have faded, but there's a connection to them that's permanent.

Some individuals with these memories were unsure what to make of them until they read *Embraced By The Light*. One woman, a nurse, writes:

> While reading your book I began to notice that some of the things you experienced are things I have realized for a long time. For instance, the fact that we all have known each other forever and actually chose to come here for our growth. When I was younger, I would tell this belief to friends and family,

3

and they would joke about it and ask where I came up with such a crazy idea. I was elated to hear that this was your perception also and now I know that I was right! But how in the world could I have known these things without having a near-death experience? I thought our celestial lives were barred from our minds until that hour when we return home again.

Clearly, some do not to need to lose all their knowledge at birth. Be assured that God is in control. All knowledge ultimately comes from him, and if he sees a need to restore a pre-earth memory to you, he easily can. He may restore a portion to you, if you earnestly seek this gift, are true to the light you already possess, and are open to spiritual impressions. But most people must continue to walk—and grow—by faith.

Many readers of *Embraced By The Light* and *The Awakening Heart* have questions about what form we take as spirits in heaven. One man asked:

Does the spiritual body appear similar to the physical body, with faces and hands and feet and ears and hair? You speak in your books as though it did, but you really don't come out and say so. Did you look like your physical body in the spiritual body? Several times you referred to the spirits as male or female. All my life, I have always believed that the spirit had no gender. That we are distinguished male or female only by the body that housed our soul. How did you determine that a spirit was male or female?

In heaven we are our true selves. Our spirits are in the same image as our bodies, including heads, arms, hands and feet, but made of refined spirit matter and light instead of flesh and blood. Since we associate there with family, friends and other souls we have bonded with, our spirits appear in a form that is most recognizable to them. For example, if you were to meet your grandmother there, she would have the features you know her by. Her eyes, her hair, even her mannerisms would be instantly recognizable to you. And yes, she would most certainly be female. I saw distinctly that we do retain our gender. The three ministering angels who came to me—the ones I lovingly call my "monks"—were men. I saw both men and women in heaven. Their relations and distinctions were as loving and peculiar as they are here.

Our greatest identifier is our "presence," and this gives us our uniqueness and sets us apart from anyone else. When we die, our attitudes, demeanor, and personality remain with us. In heaven, who you truly are—your unique identity—is actually sensed by others. There's no need to "get to know you," because you cannot hide yourself. Both who you were at spiritual creation and who you are after creating your life on earth remain with you. You do not change merely because you die. It's just as in this life: what you are born with and what you have made of yourself, combined, are you. You are who you are, and all heaven will know you as such.

Embraced By The Light has raised another gender related issue. This writer sums it up:

> I'm far from being a radical feminist, but I do believe in equal rights for men and women. I was truly disturbed to think that you encountered a council made up entirely of men.

This part of my experience has generated response from radical and non-radical feminists. One woman wrote to say that my book's dedication to my husband did the world of women a lot of damage. I had thanked Joe for wearing each white shirt more than once to work, and for eating TV dinners so I could spend my time at the computer. Now, Joe is not a great cook or even a good one. And I would never dream of letting him touch an iron to one of his shirts. Garbage, nails and hammer, lawn mower and dishes are his more talented ways to serve our family. Joe and I function as a team, we divide our work. As I observed in the spirit world, the roles and relations of men and women are divided and distinct there, too. They are perfectly balanced and accepted. And more, they are enjoyed.

What I wrote in my book, I wrote because I experienced it. I understood that our Father in Heaven created man in his own image—which is that of a perfect and multifaceted man. Women, too, are in the image of God and are multifaceted. Women's bodies are co-creators of mortal life and this makes us Godlike in a literal sense. In heaven, women and men are perfectly balanced in their roles and are equal. Standing side by side they are perfect complements of each other.

Though to some it may seem unfair that I stood before a council of men, having been there I know that nothing more natural or right or fair could have occurred. Mankind's twist on relationships and roles here is something that was never meant to be. Change must take place soon for our sakes and for the sake of our society.

A number of people have questions about age in heaven:

How old is a person when he gets to heaven?

Do you stay the same age forever?

My dad was 55 when he died. Is he still 55?

You noted that you saw few children in heaven. If I was a parent who had lost a child, I would so much want to see them again.

In a similar vein, a woman who recently lost her father asked:

Is it true that there isn't a time concept in heaven? It seems like it will be forever before we see Dad again, but when we do, it will be like the same day to him as when he passed. Does this make sense?

As I went to the other side, I remembered the creation of earth, and I saw that all of God's creations are created spiritually before they are created in material form. The Bible speaks of God creating the earth in six days. These "days" are figurative, symbolizing a segment of time from the perspective of mortals. But heaven is timeless. The mortal body ages through time in hours, days, and years. But the spirit quickens or matures through its understanding and ability to master tasks required of it. In heaven a being's maturity isn't segmented into periods of time.

Imagine a high school reunion. It's been over twenty years since you last heard from a friend, but when the two of you meet and become comfortable again, it almost feels as though no time has gone by. Your bodies look different because they have aged, but your spirit identities are timeless and, though more mature, are as recognizable and hopefully as lovable as ever! In such a moment, twenty years doesn't seem all that long. In fact it is nothing.

Another popular area of questions about heaven is animals. For example: "You mention seeing pets going through the tunnel, but you never mention them again. Do they not possess some type of afterlife?" "Can you comment further on seeing animals in the tunnel? I should so much like to meet up with my favorite cats in heaven."

I don't recall much about animals in heaven, but I know most assuredly that all forms of life existed before and will exist after living on earth. Each of God's creations will return to its Maker. We love our pets, and through caring for them we learn more fully how to foster love. This love is binding, and I believe we will enjoy the comfort and love of our pets in the next life if we so desire.

Many people are curious for details about what heaven looks like. "Were there steps in Heaven? It's a strange question, I know, but it would clear up an old question of mine." "I always suspected that heaven would be structurally similar to earth with trees, water, flowers, etc., just as you saw. God wouldn't thrust us into a totally alien environment after being used to nature."

Everything we know in the beauties of nature can be found in heaven. Dwellings, too, are there—complete with stairs if needed for beauty or functionality. I remember vividly a room I was taken to. How my escorts and I arrived there I do not recall, but I remember that the room was beautiful beyond compare. Its walls seemed made of a very fine substance—similar to thin marble—that defined the room and yet let light flow through. But to describe the room completely is simply not possible. Our emotions are not grand enough to feel its magnificence, our intellect insufficient to comprehend its power and seeming life. Yes, life. All things have life and glory in heaven, and to describe them in terms of the deadness and stillness of this existence falls short. We will never feel in this life what we will find commonplace forever in our magnificent heavenly home.

Outside the room a glorious vista of mountains and valleys and rivers captivated me. The scene was filled with life and color and passion. I have heard the phrase "the mountains will sing at His coming." In heaven the mountains sing endlessly. Everything has energy and tone and love. Everything is alive and alert and full of joy.

If you want a taste of heaven's radiance, find the most serene and beautiful place you can. Reflect on it for a while and then imagine that it's only a colorless photo negative of what is real in heaven. Gradually the faintest idea of heaven's splendor will come through.

"Are there different levels in heaven?" is another common question. Another woman writes and asks, "Is there a hierarchy of goodness in heaven? My worry is that my mom, who was an angel on earth, will be in an elevated heaven, and we won't be reunited with her."

One of my favorite people in the Bible is Paul. He tells us that, "There is one glory of the sun, and another glory of the moon, and another glory of the stars: for one star differeth from another star in glory" (I Corinthians 15:41). I too learned that different levels or degrees of glory exist in heaven. Some spirits appear brighter and more glorious than others, yet it is important to note that no spirit judges another because of station or degree of growth. Individuals are who they are, and they are accepted and loved completely, regardless of personal development. Every spirit I saw was happy and engaged in loving service meant for the mutual growth of one another. This is how they receive their greatest joy and continued growth.

Here's a letter from another woman who visited heaven. She learned that spiritual growth on earth brings us to the next level and so on until we find our rightful position.

As I lay dying in the emergency room, I saw someone spiritual standing at the end of my bed. I left my body and went to the beautiful place that you describe in your book. I met such a wonderful person and although I believed in Jesus Christ, I would not say that it was Jesus who I met, but he showed me love and respect. I began to berate myself and show him pictures of my terrible life. He was very gentle and took each picture of my life and turned it around and said, "This is what really happened." I was so surprised at how things had truly unfolded in my life, in ways that I never dared to dream were possible.

I was shown how there was room in heaven for everyone ever created . . . something I could not have fathomed here on earth. I also saw that there were places in heaven that can only be filled by one particular individual and that each of us has a perfecting that is taking place so that we can "belong" or fit into that place when we go there. He showed me that there was no point in jealousy because each person had to have their own particular experience in order to be ready for heaven. I did not want to leave. I did not miss my children, and felt so much more developed and content there.

I was also shown places that were empty or not filled by the ones that were supposed to fill them, which saddened him briefly. But because there is no sin or sadness there, that passed. Then he said to me, "Do you know why those places are empty?" I supposed that it was because the people had sinned or were being punished. He said, "No, it is because they do not want to be there."

When we are able to expand our minds and hearts to accept the riches of heaven, we will receive them. This is our Creator's promise to us. To accept, we must believe. To receive, we must open. To gain more, we must share.

Although there exist many glories or "mansions" in heaven, I did not consider them greater or lesser, just different. They are levels of understanding and development, not of privilege. The painful lesson I learned was that I possessed a judgmental attitude that was not acceptable. I was not to judge a single soul, not to speculate on which spirit would dwell in which degree of glory, or on which spirit would receive which heavenly mansion. This very concept opposes the spirit of heaven. Although we may sense a greater or lesser development in people, we are not to speculate on their final judgment. Only God knows where we will be happiest. In his wisdom he will ensure us the opportunities to experience and enjoy all that is possible—which is far beyond what anyone can imagine for themselves.

Many readers are curious about angels—messengers who come to earth from heaven. Interest in angels is increasing because the presence of heavenly guardians and guides is being felt more often today. This is a sign of the spiritual Awakening of people throughout the world.

The following are similar questions from different readers:

Is it important to know who our guardian angels are?

Sometimes I feel someone is sending me messages and guiding me through a situation. How do I relate to these spirits or guardian angels effectively?

Does my mom become my guardian angel? Or does she leave that in the hands of others?

In heaven there is much work to be done, and various tasks are assigned to those who are best suited to accomplish them. It was the same with us before coming to earth. Our individual missions were assigned according to the talents and abilities God gave us at our creation. In performing our missions we magnify our talents beyond their original capacity. The Father wants all his offspring to expand their talents that they might grow in spiritual abundance, have a more perfect joy, and glorify him more completely. We continue developing our talents as spirits in heaven. Some spirits do this through service on earth as angels.

Guardian angels have been granted authority to guide individuals as God permits. These angels may have lived on earth previously, or they may not have come here yet. They may be relatives or best friends who have passed on, or they may be unknown spirits. If we are ever blessed to have an angel appear to us, we may relate with it by simply speaking to it. Angels understand us perfectly when we communicate with them. Angels may come to us in dreams since they are able to enter our thoughts when authorized by God to do so. We must not fear them, but receive their message with gratitude and humility. We can know if a message or an angel is from God because we will sense no darkness in them. No unclean thought or thing can come from God. We can test their spirits by remembering this.

Those who don't believe in angels will probably be unfamiliar with their voices. During my experience I saw many angels hovering over people on earth, attempting to communicate with them or to guide them. Most of the people, however, refused to hear them. If you are open to the gifts and words of God, you will receive answers and directions you need in life.

Sometimes guardian angels are permitted to do more than speak to us. At crucial moments they can attend us in physical ways. This woman shares an example:

> Benjamin is my guardian angel. I know there are others but he is the one that is always with me. I was made aware of him when I was five, and as I grew up, the wonder of having him has grown with me. I am now 44. There are numerous incidents in my life where Benjamin has acted as my protector. A car accident in which the police say I should have been killed, or at least seriously injured, was only one example. When I felt his wings/arms around me, I knew I was being protected. There was not a bruise, not a piece of glass on me—just an overwhelming sense of comfort. Many times I have felt that bump on the shoulder (which is his way) and have been helped in an instant.

Angels have whatever power necessary to assist us when God wills it. Another woman describes a car accident in which she felt a hand pressing her right shoulder firmly against the seat. Afterward her doctors couldn't figure out how she had survived, nor why she had a bruise on her right shoulder when she had been hit from the left.

Some kinds of angels perform tasks of a larger and more serious nature. I saw the Warring Angels of heaven. These beautiful and magnificent angels possess no weapons as we know them, but they possess the power of God to protect his creations from evil. God is a god of love, and these angels protect that love in heaven and earth. I saw a host of them rush to the earth to protect a person from the forces of Satan. God knows what is just and unjust. He knows what kind of temptations a person can withstand, and he will prevent Satan from tempting anyone beyond their power to endure. Warring Angels protect us from evil forces, from destructive thoughts, and from the unfair tactics of Satan. They see to it that our course is clear to do God's will. However, we are always to exercise our own faith. God will bless us with a clear path to do his work only after a trial of our faith and after we have prayed for protection and guidance.

I have many letters from men, women and children alike who express their desire to experience the embrace of Christ as I did. They long to receive a portion of God's love here on earth, and there was no greater joy for anyone than this love. By describing it in my book, the energy of Christ's love went out to bless many people. Heaven in all its glory could be summed up in one word: Christ. He is the light of creation, the joy of all life, and above all, the deepest love of our souls. To embrace him is to embrace the meaning of life and the eternal power of God. As long as I live I will never forget his embrace, and I will never cease sharing the wonder and magnificence of it with others. But here is the great secret, the great truth: we will all know him and feel his miraculous and healing love. Whatever our glory or mansion or mission, we will all embrace him and love him again.

And another secret: we can each experience a taste of his embrace by opening ourselves to his unconditional love and then by giving that love away to everyone we meet. The ripple effect, from its very source, is available to all who are willing to pass it along to others. Heaven can be anywhere.

I do not have words to describe the perfection of our heavenly home. No mortal language can convey the smells, sounds, colors, and emotions, nor transmit the love and joy pervading every heavenly creation. But a portion of heaven's experience is available to each of us. As we allow ourselves to believe in God and to accept his love, a quiet joy will rekindle our souls, a joy we will instantly want to share with others. And as we share it lovingly, that spark of joyful heaven will begin to swell within us, filling our entire souls. Then we will begin to discover the truth that heaven is everywhere we allow it to be, and it resides in us just as we once resided in it. Then, each of us will be blessed to know for ourselves, what words can never convey.

Searching For Meaning

I was always looking for the missing pieces in my life, not knowing what it was that was missing.

A great Awakening has begun. People around the world are opening their eyes to their own spiritual natures. They are beginning to see who they truly are and what they have always been—beings with an eternal past and a glorious future. In my near death experience I was told the Awakening would happen soon, and I am deeply grateful that *Embraced By The Light* and *The Awakening Heart* have played a part in it. Many readers have written suggesting that this was my mission in life—to help create this Awakening through my books and lectures. I can now accept this as part of my mission, but I know that my entire mission is not complete; Jesus promised me that I would be taken home as soon as it was done.

As long as there is life, God wants us to do more.

Our individual missions are important, whether we are to reach out to millions or, like the drunken man I saw in my experience, to reach only one. God may make our missions known to us, or he may not. Regardless, they are still our works to be done—works we helped plan and agreed to perform before we came here. Two readers ask:

> If we are here to love fully, to expand and to magnify our lives, what is the purpose? How will these things help or hinder us on the other side?

> Were we not content to stay in heaven with God and be near him? Why would we choose to be here when we could be safe and happy in heaven with God and all our friends?

Searching for meaning in this life is often painful, especially when experiencing a tragedy or crisis. I am often asked why, if we already had the answers in our prior existence, do we have to come to earth to search for them? The following letter provides a few answers to these universal questions:

> I first read your book about a year ago, and I've referred to it frequently ever since. It has meant so much to me and my family. I am profoundly grateful to you and others who have been willing to be open and generous in sharing messages of comfort and hope from the "other side."
>
> So many things in your book touch me deeply because of the specific trials and heartaches I have had. The things you were taught in the spirit world about the meaning and purposes of this school we call mortality have reinforced beliefs I already held. They opened the way for me to understand much more deeply how we exercised our free agency in designing our individual mortal courses of study. (I sometimes say, "Why didn't I just sign up for French?!") This fuller understanding is very sustaining as I struggle to meet my life's challenges. It helps me to be more truly patient and to appreciate the soul's progress—which is often unrelated to merely worldly or easily visible change and accomplishment.
>
> I also feel less guarded about loving where there is risk of much pain. I remember you saying in a television interview that the rose you communed with in the heavenly garden grew when you loved it. You related that principle to each of us. The truth the heart knows—so much more readily

than the mind!—is exquisitely simple, isn't it? And so beautiful! We only fear to trust that truth because we wish for pain-
free lives. But in fact pain is a teacher without compare, when
we will accept its lessons. I'm not suggesting we seek pain—
heaven forbid! But if we suffer because we love, then the
purpose is worth the sacrifice. Christ is our Great Example
in this, isn't he?—as he is in all things good.

I can scarcely think about your loving reunion with our
Savior, and your feelings of being home at last, without being
filled with longing and homesickness myself. But your experience helps me feel confident of his perfect love. Your book
also helps me know that I'm still here—in a place that isn't
my home—because I have not yet completed my mortal mission, and I would not want to go home without completing
it.

Leaving the peace and security of heaven to come to the earth
was a willing sacrifice on our part. We agreed to the sacrifice for
the same reasons we spend thousands of dollars and years of
effort to graduate from college. And as long as we have life here,
we are learning, our spirits are growing, and we are coming closer
to the divine, even by the things we suffer. We may not always
know what to do in our lives, we may be troubled and in pain,
but be assured, as long as we are here, we are growing. We are
only here for divine purposes, and the greatest divine purpose of
all is to love. Even when we are confused or imprisoned by choices
we have made, we can always learn to love.

Although I cannot imagine what I am to do, I can love, and I
will continue to think positively, and this may help me with
my purpose. No longer does life look routine, but filled with
great possibilities. I may never know if I accomplished my
goal—like the drunken man in *Embraced By The Light*—but I
understand that we are all here for a reason.

Yes, each one of us came to earth on a personal mission to be
loved or to give love. We are to learn the value and price of love.
Other parts of our mission include learning patience, humility,

self-discipline, and other virtues. These attributes are parts of love. I saw in heaven that those spirits who were to become slaves on earth knew it before coming. I understood that they may have chosen to teach compassion or to learn humility in this life, even though it would come in such a degrading way. They volunteered for their terrible stations in life, sacrificing much else they might have accomplished for the sake of a deeper spiritual growth born of the offenses they would suffer. I recall Christ's words in the New Testament: "Woe unto the world because of offenses! for it must needs be that offenses come; but woe to that man by whom the offense cometh!" (Matthew 18:7). It is not God's will that we enslave one another, or beat or kill or hurt one another. But the facts of this life are known to God before they happen, and in his foreknowledge he helps us plan those missions in life that best meet our needs. Surely there are more positive, more noble ways to teach compassion or to learn humility than through slavery, but slavery is what mankind made available to God to work with on earth. Children are born—some into slavery, some into wars, some into starvation—but all come with a mission to fulfill.

Our sufferings come not only with a price, but with a reward. How far will we grow in God's love through the benefit of our trials? Some may be here to break a family's cycle of addiction. Others, to support a family member or friend in their difficult mission. Some come to earth only briefly, but in their few minutes or hours may touch a life for eternity. One reader writes:

> If we all have a mission, why do some of us die through murder or accident at an early age? What mission could a six-month-old have fulfilled?

Babies and young children embody unconditional love. Having not yet been conditioned to fear, they trust absolutely, allowing themselves to be cared for, or hurt, by those with power over them. For some spirits, to surrender all their love unconditionally in the arms of a loving parent is all that is required. After sharing their innocence and pure love briefly, they are taken home. Other spirits may be here to assist another child at a particular point in its life. Some may come to gain bodies in order to provide organs which allow other children to fulfill their missions. Our purposes are countless but always include serving one another and glorifying God.

I received a phone call from a bereaved mother of an eighteen-year-old son. After graduating from high school he had enthusiastically prepared for the ministry. She said he had often set an example for his peers, showing them how to behave as the Lord would want them to. He had told his mother his graduation would come and go quickly, that his remaining time with her would be short, and they should treasure it. She had not realized how true his words were. Two weeks after his graduation, in an early-morning drive home from a friend's house, he was killed by a drunk driver. His mother now understood with a broken heart that the ministry he had prepared for was of a higher order—service to our Heavenly Father and to his children in the spirit world. A few months later, the mother learned that the man who had killed her son was seen clutching a Bible in his cell, crying in grief over what he had done. It seemed God used the return of her son to Him to fill another purpose for Him as well.

Even in our finite awareness we can see how the young man completed his mission in his last few weeks. His spirit was in tune with God's as he prepared himself for his transfer into the spirit world. Then, being in tune, he helped prepare his mother for his departure. And, in giving of his life, he gave of himself two-fold. First, he gave himself back to his Heavenly Father, and two, he helped bring a soul, the drunken man, to his knees in humility before his Creator. Even as Christ gave of himself that others might live, this young man blessed another in his final moments on earth. We are entering a period of difficult but wonderful changes soon to take place in the world. During this time God will call home many elite spirits—such as this young man— to better serve us from there.

Here is a letter illustrating that we may never know who we are called to help in this life:

> For many years I have struggled with low self-esteem. While I have made a lot of progress from time to time, I have episodes where I still feel very unlovable. One day, in terrible emotional pain I cried out to God in prayer. I asked him to take this cross from me and to help me to love myself. Prior to this cry for help, I had been invited to the wedding of a person I knew from high school. We hadn't been real close in recent years, so I kind of wondered why I had been invited. I had a feeling, though, that there was a reason I should go. Well, that reason appeared in the form of two people who, quite out of the blue, shared with me the reasons why they felt I was a wonderful person. I was deeply touched by their comments, particularly from a person I had hardly seen or spoken to in twelve years. Suddenly I remembered my prayer! I truly believe God used these people as his "conduits." He spoke through them to remind me of my worth as a person and of his deep, abiding love for me. What is even more amazing is that he had all this planned out for me before I even asked for his help.

Every encounter we have, even if brief and seemingly unimportant, may have more significance than we know. A brief encounter may begin a greater ripple that reaches its intended purpose years later. Everyone who comes into our lives may be part of our mission, and we, a part of theirs. Understanding this can give meaning to the common events of life. By being positive and helpful towards others, even in casual moments, we can make the most of our time on earth.

Occasionally we find people who seem to know the chief purposes for their lives. Some seem to know from childhood, while others discover it later. A letter from a high school junior who knows her mission is to be an actress:

> It makes me happy just thinking about it. I pray to God with all my heart and soul for his guidance to assist me in making

people happy in my own little way. Nothing has happened yet, but I have a hopeful feeling that something is going to. Deep down I know my prayers are being answered.

She may be right. One way to discern if we are on the correct path is that it brings us great joy and fulfillment. This is how one third grade teacher in a Catholic school came to realize the nature of her mission.

I truly believe that my mission on earth is teaching the young children about the path they need to follow to be with Jesus, how they need to treat others kindly and do good deeds for others, and how we need to love others with all of our hearts. I couldn't imagine living on this earth without teaching children about Jesus and God and the Holy Spirit. The gleam in the eyes of the children I teach is the reason for my mission. Carrying on the message of God to future generations is my gift to God.

For others, the knowledge of their mission, or one of their missions, is more intuitive. It comes to them as a "knowing" or a glimpse of the future. A man now retired from the Air Force wrote this about his mission:

I want to say thank you for putting my life in perspective. I was not sure what I was to accomplish upon my retirement. However, I felt that whatever it was, I knew it would be for God. This premonition was because of some deep-set knowledge of my destiny.

Because our spirits remember the plan we chose for this life, we are often drawn to people or situations that impact us in important ways. This is often the force behind "chance" encounters. I was told there are no coincidences. However, making the most of these opportunities is up to us as we exercise our free will.

There is nothing wrong with not knowing our missions. We are not always meant to know. Some people seem preoccupied with trying to figure out their mission and they waste valuable time. Instead, they should live into their purpose by following their hearts. I was told it is best to follow God's promptings, to be flexible and moldable. He can make better use of our lives that way. Each person's life is multifaceted, and we should trust the power of God and his angels to give us every opportunity we need to succeed. Our part is to seek to improve ourselves and, above all, to love others more fully. By praying for guidance and letting love rule our hearts and minds each day, we will eventually accomplish our many purposes. One woman shares her insights this way:

> My life now has a sense of purpose, although I am unsure, as yet, what that is. My outlook has changed overnight. I have always believed God loved me. But even with this knowledge of his love, I have been focusing on negative things, like what I haven't accomplished. Someone recently told me to be more positive in my life and think about what good I have done, and you have reinforced this. I know it's a message from God. I am putting my energies into being a cheerful, giving and loving person, and asking for his direction in my life. My children are grown—they've turned out wonderfully—and now it's time to move into another capacity. Hopefully, I will know what it is when the time comes.

God desires that we accomplish our missions and return to him spiritually stronger than when we left. But free will causes many people to spend their lives missing the very opportunities they chose in the pre-mortal life. Some are distracted by materialism and worldly appetites. Some let themselves be ruled by fear or negativity—two of Satan's greatest tools. And if we fail to love as we should, we will certainly fail in our greatest mission—to mature into beings who are more like God. But who hasn't failed in some way? We all fall short virtually every day. One reader from Chicago asked:

> If a person fails at his earthly mission and dies, will the spirit receive another chance to grow? And where? With all the

21

struggles on earth, I would imagine that there are many, many humans who never realize their potential or actualize their life mission.

Even failing is a part of our mission. It brings valuable experience and knowledge that facilitates our growth. We need to be careful in judging whether or not someone has fulfilled his mission. A person who appears to be failing may in fact be learning more quickly than a person who appears successful. Our Creator knows which weaknesses we come with and which experiences we require for spiritual growth. The young man who sent the following letter from prison faced obstacles most will never see. Some may judge him as "failing" in life, when in fact he is making enormous progress.

> Let me tell you a little bit about myself and why your book interested me so much. I was thirteen before I realized we were the poorest people in the ghetto. I watched my father and mother use drugs every day and listen to them tell me how I'd never amount to anything. I was the oldest of four children. After the drugs, my parents would fight every day. My father would beat my mother, and then he'd get on his motorcycle and leave. My mother would run outside yelling, "I hope you get on your motorcycle and die!"
>
> Over the next three years I got tired of the verbal and physical abuse. At the age of sixteen, I ran away from home. I went to a nearby park and slept. I remember my mother laughing as I walked out the door, saying, "You'll be back. You don't have anywhere else to go." The park was dark and scary. I'd never prayed in my life, but I prayed then. I was one of the top athletes in the state and was too ashamed to ask for anyone's help. I went to school every day. That's where I got my meals and my showers.
>
> Before I knew it, school was out and it was summertime. The first couple weeks were hard because I had no money. My little brothers and sisters would sneak me food down to the park, but when my parents found out they put a stop to it. I had never stolen anything in my life, but I was

starving. I went into a store and put a box of Little Debbies in my shirt. A security guard grabbed my arm and took the cakes out of my shirt. He yelled, "Get out of here, you thief!" I was so embarrassed I walked out trying to pretend he was speaking to someone else. I went for two days without eating, but I was still praying. After the third day, I decided to steal again. I was so hungry I didn't care if I got caught. I just prayed to God that I wouldn't. I was almost to the store when I looked down and saw a book of food stamps. I ate good the whole summer, but I didn't thank God.

School started again and I was still too ashamed to tell my basketball coach I was sleeping in the park. When it was real cold outside I'd sleep in the restroom. I eventually caught pneumonia and spent three days in the hospital. On another occasion a bad storm came up with freezing rain, and I decided to walk to try to stay warm. I was praying that it would stop raining when a car pulled up beside me. A young lady was driving. She said, "Get in, Steve." My name wasn't Steve but I got in anyway. She said, "Steve, what are you doing out here in the rain? You'll get sick." I said, "I got mad at my mother and ran away from home." She asked me if I was hungry, and I said yes, so we went to a pancake house. After we ate she said, "My parents are out of town for a week. You can stay at our house." Being young, you know the first thing I thought of, but it wasn't like that at all. I ate and slept good for the next week, and then it was time to go. I thanked her but I felt an obligation to tell her who I was, that I wasn't Steve. She just stood there as I spilled my guts. She smiled and said, "I know you're not Steve. I knew that when you sat in the car, but God said you needed my help." Still, I continued to ignore God's presence.

I didn't attend my high school graduation, although I graduated with honors. I got a football scholarship to a university. My first month there my thirteen-year-old sister called me and said she was pregnant. I told her I'd get the money for her to have an abortion so my parents wouldn't find out. It took me two weeks to get it, and I planned to leave that Friday to take my sister to get it done. But on Wednesday, I received a phone call from her saying, "Daddy was killed in a motorcycle accident after he and

Momma had their usual fight. He lost control of his motorcycle and ran into a tree." After that, I told my sister if she'd have the baby, I'd take care of it. I quit school and came back home and got a job.

My two little brothers always wanted to follow me. I'd always tell them no and they would cry. One brother was fourteen and the other was eleven. They were too young to be with, and I was busy chasing girls. Over the next few years everything went well. I noticed all of my brother's friends around, but I didn't pay any attention to the clothing they were wearing. I realized not long after that one of my brothers was in a gang. I stopped speaking to him completely. I'd just go see my youngest brother. He was my baby.

At this time I was working at a mental health facility in the adolescent department. I was on my way home when I got a call on my car phone. It was my sister, and she told me that my brother had just got shot. I kept driving, thinking that's what he gets for being in a gang. Then my phone rang again. This time it was my brother on the phone. He told me it was my baby brother who had been shot. I drove home hoping he would be all right. When I got there the paramedics were pumping his heart. He was a fifteen-year-old victim of a drive-by shooting.

For the next three years I blamed my other brother for our baby brother's death. Now I was working in the sheriff's department and making good money, legally and illegally. I was talking to a kid one day about why he joined a gang. He said, "My big brother never wanted to spend any time with me, so I picked my friends. They were just into the wrong things." That night I prayed because I knew it was just as much my fault about my baby brother's death as it was my other brother's. I called my brother the next day and told him to come over to my house. I told him I felt it was just as much my fault and I didn't blame him. We cried together and he told me how he had prayed for the day I could forgive him. Through my family's adversities, we are as close as ever. And my little niece is now ten and I love her to death. I'm glad we made the decision against abortion.

I've never used drugs, but I've sold plenty. I left the sheriff's department and started working at a treatment center, and that's where I was arrested. In the two years I've been locked up, all my buddies who were involved in selling drugs have received life in prison. And many are dead from drug-related violence. I wonder where I'd be if God hadn't saved me. I thought God punished me when I was sent to jail, but actually he saved my life.

Thank you and God bless you.

The well-known saying comes to mind: "There, but for the grace of God, go I." Who can say they would have done differently if they had been born into this young man's family? What if God had placed your spirit into his body? Would you have run away from home? Would you have stolen? Would you have sold drugs? As we seek our purpose in life, I pray that we do it in the Lord, that we are very careful in judging the hearts of others. No one knows what God wills for each of his children. No one can judge character or intent but him.

If we could glimpse the mind of God, the truth about some people's missions would absolutely amaze us. For years the renowned professor and scientist, Charles Camp, debated religious leaders on the radio. He also traveled nationwide advocating the facts of science as opposed to the concepts of Creationism. Over the years he lost faith in God and became known as an outspoken and articulate atheist. Then, as he lay dying in a hospital, all that changed. He discovered the beauty and intricacy of God's plan for him. He was astounded that—despite his atheism—God had been using him all along for His loving purposes. Here, Charles Camp's widow, Joanna Camp, shares the story:

Dear Mrs. Eadie:

My husband died in 1975. Before his actual death, his doctors pronounced him dead three times. They were astonished to witness his return to life each time with a clear mind and filled with energy, even though he was dying of terminal cancer and old age. At the hospital, the nurses began to call him among themselves "the man who wouldn't die." All this is recorded in the hospital records.

During the times he was dead, my husband experienced things, some of which were exactly as you wrote about in your book.

Charles was a professor at the University of California at Berkeley and was written up as the "father of paleontology." For years he taught medical students. When the subject of near-death experiences would come up in class, Charles would explain that there is no life beyond the grave, that everything ends there, that the body gradually changes to become nourishment for other forms of life. The experience of going through a dark tunnel to see "God" at the end as a bright light was just an illusion. For when the body is undergoing the hard stress of dying, he said, certain chemical reactions are triggered in the brain, and this is nature's way of providing ease from the stress, nothing more. So imagine his great surprise when he found himself separated from his physical body at the hospital. He told me that he began to analyze everything carefully, taking nothing for granted. But soon he had to admit to himself, that this was certainly not an illusion. He'd never felt more alive! All of his many senses seemed to surface, to come alive in him, he said.

Next he found himself in the dark tunnel, before the bright light and God! God received him with the same unconditional love that you experienced, Mrs. Eadie. He said his entire body vibrated with God's wonderful love. From head to toe, God's love flooded him, and once you have experienced God's love, he said, you'll want to remain forever by his side, never to be far from his love ever again. He learned that though he had not believed in God on earth, God believed in him! God had loved him tremendously, since the very beginning.

Charles had been an atheist on earth, but he was not a person who fought good, nor was he against humanity. He was known for his genuine humility, gentleness of spirit and his great love for people. His goal in life had been to aid humanity in any way possible, to help mankind evolve and get on the right path mentally. He dedicated his life to help remove some of the ugly racial and religious prejudices. For seventeen years Charles was a spokesman for the university and a radio debater. His job was to deal with the radical preachers who were constantly challenging the science departments of the nations' universities, demanding that they shut down or teach science only according to the Bible—or according to their own interpretations of it.

Charles was well prepared for this. He had studied the Bible for many years in the original languages. He said his aim was to make the church leaders realize how far they had strayed from the true master that they claimed to follow: Jesus Christ. Charles soon gained great fame for this, but because of the dark works found in the Christian churches then, he turned further and further away from the Bible—and he eventually wanted no part of the God that these churches followed.

Then, when he died and stood before God's bright light in heaven, he learned this had been his major mission on earth—to debate with religious leaders who were taking the world into a dark path. He learned that the only way he could do this was as a scientist! He was reminded that Jesus Christ came to earth to chastise the religious leaders of his time, who were also leading their people in the wrong path.

Who would ever have believed that Berkeley's famous atheist would be the person to teach me about God! And who would have believed I would look deeply into the eyes of an atheist to see the spirit of Christ in those eyes! Life has never ceased to amaze me.

It may take a lifetime of following our hearts before learning that we've been doing what God sent us to do in the first place. Charles Camp reminds me of Saul in the Bible. What passionate men! They knew what they believed, and they taught it with all their hearts. In *The Awakening Heart* I told the story of my brother-in-law Tom, who had been an atheist most of his life. I told him of my experience in heaven with God, and he dismissed it outright. Then God redirected his life by giving Tom his own near-death experience. What a gift and a blessing! Tom was instructed to tell everyone he met that God lives both in heaven and in the hearts of all mankind. Today, as he speaks of his knowledge of God, he shares his precious message with passion and love. God can especially use people who throw themselves into what they love, who walk forward confidently committed to a cause. In Revelation 3:15-16, we read: "I know thy works, that thou art neither cold nor hot: I would thou wert cold or hot. So then because thou art lukewarm, and neither cold nor hot, I will spue thee out of my mouth."

Following one's heart with passion, direction, and determination is giving life to life. Could any father ask for more?

On the other side I was told that each person's life is like a river. The destination is set, but the method of our journeying is up to us. We can cruise down the middle of the river at top speed, or we can hug the shore and spin around in eddies. We can crash over rapids or chart a safer path between obstacles. We can slum along the bottom in the mire and slime of sediment, or we can glide along the sparkling surface where the air is clean. The river is ours from birth to death. How we navigate it is determined by the hundreds of small choices we make each day.

God can especially use people who will throw themselves passionately into what they love, who walk forward confidently committed to a cause.

To discover our mission in life we must see challenges as opportunities for growth and then face them head on. Each challenge measures our strengths and progress. Even when trials cause pain or sorrow, we must look for new lessons in the pain and ask God for the power to learn and to grow from it. Suffering focuses our attention on what matters most, and with God's help, we can strengthen our spirits by learning patience, tolerance and love. These lessons learned, we become co-navigators with God. But when unlearned, we go into the eddies, spinning around, making little progress, even blaming God for our unremitting suffering. One reader wrote:

Life just seems so hard—so demanding—I can't keep up. Is this it? Can I not expect any more? Is my total existence here just to complete a mission? I'm not to have any happiness, just wait for the job to be up so I can "check out?"

28

This person despairs of ever finding joy. He's in a whirlpool, sinking to the troubled bottom where frigid darkness clutches him. He can wait there in misery until his air runs out, or, like the young man in prison, he can swim up to the surface and enjoy the warmth and light of the sun. As he views the sky, he may decide to reach for it, to expend some energy, make new decisions, and seek a swifter current.

Some people believe that the circumstances of youth set an unchangeable course for their river. But, life is dynamic, and the river stretches and bends as we go. A bad beginning does not inevitably lead to a bad ending. In fact a bad beginning can give us strength to create a good ending. I love the message in this letter:

> I own a drug and alcohol treatment center, and this is a gift I cherish, for it's given me joy beyond words. Six years ago, God led me into sobriety from a life of heroin addiction, homelessness, prostitution, two failed marriages—one husband shot and killed—many close friends dead, and I was abused in all ways as a child. In my sobriety, I've thanked God many times for these experiences. I know the pain of my clients. God gave me the gift to open the door to his love. For 39 years God was preparing me for this. I know this today because I have peace and serenity I did not know was possible.

For 39 years this woman was forced into the mud. Having been "abused in all ways as a child," she got to know the bottom of the river—the seamy, murky side of life that swallows victims whole and never lets them see the light of day. But through unfathomable effort she looked up and found God. With his help she kicked addictions and self-defeating habits out of her life. She fought the undercurrents, disentangled herself, broke the surface of her troubled life and got to a place where pure air and light could provide new energy. She grew strong and rescued others from the depths. Her beginnings then became the basis for a greater good she would do in life. Her wounds became muscles.

29

Her fears became faith. Her mistakes became experience used to benefit mankind. Like her, anyone can choose either to drown in past troubles or to fight to live. The past can always be a springboard and a resource for accomplishment and for the betterment of others.

Each soul will attain a different level of accomplishment here. But whatever the size of the ripples we make, we must learn to be grateful for whatever trials and gifts our Father gives us in the journey. There is magic in gratitude. It frees us from worry and competition in life. It opens our hearts and hands to genuine love, ironically allowing our hearts and hands to be filled again. Let us be grateful for our childhoods, even for the negative ones. Let us recognize that life is what it is, and that we are all doing our best. Let us especially be grateful for whatever love we have received. Love is always a gift. We are to praise God for all things. Feel the praise in the heart of the following writer.

> I am a thirty-two-year-old Native American and was raised by alcoholic parents. I too became an alcoholic. I am sober two and a half years now and am in a program of recovery.
>
> For years I thought I was a victim of circumstances and questioned my existence. A few precious words in your book changed that. When you said, "We all volunteer for our positions and stations in the world," and that "each of us is receiving more help than we know," I was given hope, and my faith in my higher power was intensified.
>
> During those years when I didn't think I could go on, I didn't acknowledge the powerful force that helped me through it all. I see it now. A few times I remember being told I'm not through here. It wasn't time for me to leave. I cry tears of joy at the love I was given, and for what I'm given now. It's powerful. Thank you.

Our Father knew that, in trying to find and follow our life's mission, we would make mistakes. He knew we would hurt ourselves and others, that we would follow false ideas instead of truth. So he prepared a way for us to return—each having learned from our experiences and grown from the things we suffered. When he came he taught us about God's pure love. And his demonstration of that love was when he laid down his life for us. It was part of his mission, part of the entire plan for mankind. We may not understand completely all that he did or why he did it, but I know with certainty that through his example of love, as he demonstrated it, is the way back to light and truth, the way back to Heavenly Father. If you could feel Christ's love for you, his fairness and compassion, you wouldn't want it any other way. Life on earth is our opportunity to learn unconditional love as Jesus taught it, to serve and sacrifice personal welfare in behalf of others. Part of Jesus' mission was to die for us . . . ours is to live as he did.

Abortion

Does God approve or does God not approve of abortions?

In Embraced By The Light, *you have a chapter titled, "Selecting a Body." Does that mean that a baby is not a mortal being until a spirit enters into a body?*

My life, Betty, will never be the same. I chose to have an abortion a few years back following the pressures of family and friends. I know that they meant well and know that they all love me, but I just wasn't thinking about me. About my baby. Oh, my God! Will he ever forgive me? I have another child now, but it does not replace the one I aborted. As a mater of fact, this child is a constant reminder of the one unseen, not wanted, and never held. My arms ache for this child. If I had only known. . . .

One of the greatest souls who has graced the earth is Mother Teresa—a woman who still leaves me in awe of her service and love. She knew that life is precious and once said to a woman considering an abortion: "A child is a gift of God. If you do not want him, give him to me."

Perhaps our Creator says to us at times: "If you do not want the gifts I give to you, I will take them back and give them to

32

another." Choosing to abort a child has consequences in life and in eternity. While on the other side, I was shown spirits who had inhabited the bodies of fetuses, after their mothers had aborted them. These spirits, as full-grown beings, were capable of reasoning and mature emotions. They understood the limited knowledge of their mortal mothers and were filled with compassion for them. Although the opportunity to come to earth at that time had been taken from them, they loved their mothers. But they also sorrowed for the mother who—in ignorance—had destroyed their chance to come to earth.

As spirits before our births, we promised loved ones and God that we would serve them here. We bonded with many others who have similar or related missions. Some of these connections, or bonds, were as teacher and student. We made loving promises and developed plans to help, assist, and guide others, or to be helped, assisted, and guided. Bonds were made to accomplish works of all types on earth. But many of the strongest bonds were those between parent and child. Regardless of whether parents and children planned to spend their entire physical lives together or to separate shortly after childbirth, the bonds were made in heaven. And whether or not we recognize these bonds today is not important; they exist. They brought us into the world. They will bring others into the world through us. Birth, a gift of life, is the beginning of our bonds on earth together.

Many women will never become pregnant. This is not a curse or a punishment. It doesn't imply that bonds were not established in heaven. Bonds of mother and child can be fulfilled in various ways, depending upon needs for the growth of both individuals. Mothers and children are often brought together on earth through adoption, or through other family members or foster care. Whatever path we experience, we can be sure that God has had a hand in it. Why he, or we, chose that particular path may never be revealed to us here.

Since life is a gift, even unexpected pregnancies are gifts from God. What we choose to do with that gift can be a test of our strength and love. We must be willing to sacrifice for the new life, to be responsible and accept when our acts lead to pregnancy. We must even be ready, if necessary, to give that life away, trusting that God will direct the child to the parents it previously bonded with. Sometimes we must be willing to lay down our own happiness and security to ensure that another may live on earth.

There are many factors that determine the fate of an unborn child, many circumstances that lead a mother one way or the other. However, any decision that includes abortion rarely includes God. When a mother's life hangs in balance, God may accept removing the unborn child. In other rare circumstances such as rape or incest he may also give his help in making an eternally lawful decision to end the life of a fetus. But fear, or inexperience, or inconvenience, or lack of preparedness for motherhood are never legitimate reasons in an eternal sense for abortion. This earth was created for our benefit, that we might be born here to experience suffering and joy, to learn from affliction and success, to grow in important but often imperceptible ways. Life can seem cruel, but when we return to our Creator, we will see the wisdom behind our brief moments here. Life on earth is a greater gift from God than we know. A rightful decision to put an end to the gift can only be made with his help.

An unwanted pregnancy can produce enormous fear and anguish, but how we respond to the pregnancy can bring even more serious results. Aborting the fetus can divide the sacred bond between mother and child, resulting in the tearing of spirit as well as of flesh. In the following letter, a young woman shares how she experienced this severing of the spirit after ending an unwanted pregnancy.

> When I was fifteen years old I got pregnant. I was actually happy about it until people began to find out. I was told that I had a lifetime to have kids and was encouraged to have an abortion. I wasn't married at the time, so I ended the pregnancy at the advice of ninety percent of my friends and family. This was many years ago. Then I went into depression. I sought help from a post-abortion syndrome

group in my city, but to no avail. There has not been a day that has passed that I do not cry out in pain for that baby. I have even written letters to it and remember it on what would have been its birthday. And yes, I named him—not that I knew the sex of the fetus, but because I had a dream about him. One night not long after I aborted, I had this dream. It seemed more real, like no other dream I have ever had. You might call it a vision. I was standing in a beautiful garden, like you describe in *Embraced By The Light*; however, this was before you wrote that book.

A young man walked up to me and introduced himself by name. He said that he forgives me for what I did to him. I was puzzled, not knowing what he meant. He handed me a beautiful rose then said, "You were to be my mother." Betty, I was stunned! He kissed me and held me like I have always wanted to hold my child. I asked him to forgive me over and over again. I know that he already has, and it was healing to hear him tell me that he loves me still. But I can't forgive myself. My friends and family are sorry, too. They told me that they should not have encouraged me, except that I was too young to make such an important decision by myself.

But that was years ago, and it is too late now. How do I forgive myself? If I had known then what I know now, I would have worked things out. I would never abort. That life was a part of me then, and is even more, now. I wonder though, did God give me that dream for a purpose? Did he allow me that experience with my aborted son? I didn't want children after I made that mistake, and I was so depressed. After meeting the young man who would have been my son, I am no longer depressed for some reason, even though I still struggle with forgiving myself. I am expecting my first child since that abortion. I learned that it will be a boy, too, but it will never replace the son I lost. I want so badly to be a good mother to it. I want even more children now, and I promised God that I will love them all.

Each day we make decisions that affect us for the rest of our lives and lead us to experiences that develop our understanding. This young woman received counsel from concerned family and friends, people who lacked understanding of the spirit world and the bonds previously established there. In giving into their advice, she made a mistake she will live with her entire life. Her pain has been horrendous and may yet take years to heal entirely—possibly generations. Change can occur, of course, through understanding, love, and forgiveness. But forgiveness of self can be the most difficult thing we do, and it is only accomplished through learning from one's mistakes.

The knowledge gained from a broken spiritual law can be a gift which eventually blesses many people. But for it to change us, the lesson must be internalized and understood. Then that foundation of understanding can help us to avoid further mistakes and violations of spiritual laws.

I might suggest to this expectant mother that in forgiving herself, her aborted son might still enjoy the opportunity of being born to her—this time with her acceptance.

The bonds of eternal love are powerful, and just as breaking these bonds produces consequences, remaining true to them brings rewards. Some children remember their eternal connection to their parents. Memories of the spirit world can remain quite vivid in children under the age of seven or eight, but these memories will often fade as mortal understanding grows and develops. This mother's daughter recalls her choice of parents:

> When my daughter was able to speak, she said: "I'm so glad you are my parents. I always wanted you for my mommy and daddy. I picked you for my parents before leaving heaven.

Such memories are recalled by too many children to discount. How beautiful it is when an eternal connection is recognized and treasured here. When the memory of a spiritual association comes to our awareness, our spirits jump for joy as they remember the former happiness and as they hope for new joys here. The Bible contains a clear example of this is in the Book of Luke. The spirit of the unborn John the Baptist leaps for joy when his mother, Elisabeth, meets Mary, who is pregnant with Jesus.

And Mary arose in those days, and went into the hill country with haste, into a city of Juda; And entered into the house of Zacharias and saluted Elisabeth. And it came to pass, that, when Elisabeth heard the salutation of Mary, the babe leaped in her womb; and Elisabeth was filled with the Holy Ghost: And she spake out with a loud voice, and said, Blessed art thou among women, and blessed is the fruit of thy womb. And whence is this to me, that the mother of my Lord should come to me? For, lo, as soon as the voice of thy salutation sounded in mine ears, the babe leaped in my womb for joy. And blessed is she that believed: for there shall be a performance of those things which were told her from the Lord. (Luke 1:39-45.)

The spirit in John recognized the spirit in Jesus, although neither were yet born. Our spirits remember. They remember why we chose to come to the parents and the homes we came to. They remember that we make decisions in heaven by different standards than we do on earth. Our spirits know that dysfunctional homes and relationships are not ours by bad luck, but by choice, for the challenges that only they can bring. Our spirits remember that we volunteered to come into our present conditions, not only to learn and to help ourselves, but to teach and to help others as well. And our spirits, I was shown, would never ever choose to deny these experiences to another spirit through abortion or other violation of universal law. Our spirits know that our growth depends on fulfilling the promises we made as spirits.

Breaking universal laws inevitably leads to pain and grief. The following letter was sent to me by another young woman who has suffered greatly since ending her pregnancy. These letters have come by the hundreds and thousands from women searching for answers to the pain they feel.

It has been six years since I aborted a fetus, but it still weighs on my mind. I never had any idea it would bother me like this, and for years to come.

I was comforted by reading in your book how the spirit of my child feels compassion for me, and knows that my decision was based on the knowledge I had at the time. I was so afraid back then. I wasn't thinking very clearly. I felt it would have been worse for me if I would have given the baby up for adoption—wondering every day if the child was okay. To me, that would have been harder to get over. Also, I felt this world is too sick to bring a child into it.

I can honestly say if I knew then what I know now, I would have kept the pregnancy and the life inside of me. Now I can only say that I'm sorry I hurt God, that spirit, and myself.

Law exists throughout the universe. It exists, not for our torment, but for our happiness. Spiritual laws are based solely on what will lead us to greater understanding and to being Christ-like. As we keep these laws, we find ourselves walking what Christ called the "straight and narrow path" (Matthew 7:14). On earth, man has created laws to keep order and justice. Some laws are good, others, imperfect. But the universal laws are perfect, and they have a universal force behind them that seeks and demands balance. Breaking those laws brings the reaping effect of that balancing force.

The young women who write of their immense grief for an aborted child recognize, to some extent, the wrong they have committed. They recognize the loss of love and growth that could have been theirs. But as we suffer from the negative effects of our choices, we must not forget the healing of forgiveness. Parents who recognize they have broken a bond must also recognize they can be forgiven for it.

God perfectly understands our lack of knowledge. He knows that most of us do not remember our commitments to him. In his eyes we are like little children: susceptible and even expected to make mistakes. The spirits of the unborn understand this too and forgive us freely for our mistakes, even when our mistakes cost them dearly. But for mothers and fathers to forgive themselves is often another matter. This takes time, but it is essential if we are to continue progressing spiritually. What we do not forgive in ourselves, we continue to condemn in others.

Because I know that God is in control of all things, I believe he can use unwanted pregnancies as a part of our growth. However grievous and painful our lives, God can always use them for his higher plan and for our eternal growth—when we ask him to. Only he knows the perfect picture and the perfect plan for each life. What may seem to us a terrible tragedy may be woven into a plan we know nothing about. The following came from a young woman who many in today's world would judge harshly. She kept her baby out of wedlock, choosing not to abort.

Because of the beliefs of the church that I belong to, I was extremely ashamed when I became pregnant out of marriage. Getting an abortion seemed the only answer for me . . . for all the members of my family. The young man that I was dating left me; he had other plans. He wanted to continue college, so he left it up to me to decide. My parents did not want me to abort, but they too, wanted nothing to do with the child. All through the pregnancy I hated myself for my mistakes, resented my baby for the demands it made on my body. I occasionally broke down and I blamed God for the horrible circumstances he "forced" upon me.

My dilemma led me to your book, *Embraced By The Light.* It took me only a few hours to read. When I finished, I knelt and poured my heart out to Heavenly Father, asking for his forgiveness, his help, and for his spirit to be with my baby and me. Then I prayed for knowledge and peace of mind. As I finished, a warm wave of knowledge exploded through my mind! My heart was filled with love so pure I began to weep. I learned more about God and the importance of our knowledge of the spirits in the spirit world. I knew that aborting the baby was something I could never do. Nor did I want to put it up for adoption.

When my son was born I realized that my baby was not a burden, but a special gift and that we chose each other in the spirit world. I knew that he came to me knowing that I have the emotional strength, intelligence, and courage to be a good single mother, and that I am capable of giving him the love and care that he needs. Having him has changed my life by making me more responsible. Giving into abortion would have been to turn away from that. Most importantly I saw how much my parents have loved me and now have expanded their love by including my son. I saw that people are not judging me as harshly as I believed at first, and that I have many, many friends who have stood by me. And I also know that this was all meant to happen because I had a valuable lesson to learn and I would not have learned any other way.

Whether or not this young woman could have learned lessons in any other way is unknown to me, but I do know that life is full of mysteries and the unexpected. Nevertheless, nothing is without reason or cause and effect. In our very darkest hours, God is at work. "For my thoughts are not your thoughts, neither are your ways, my ways," declares the Lord. "As the heavens are higher than the earth, so are my ways higher than your ways and my thoughts than your thoughts" (Isaiah 55:8-9).

Abortion for most reasons is not a part of the Creator's plan. His plan is life for us here and eternal life for us hereafter. Satan's plan on the other hand is death, pain, separation, and emptiness. When an unwanted pregnancy occurs, it is the Destroyer who whispers in our ears:

Another mouth to feed. One more child to send to school, to clothe, to raise. This was not meant to be your burden. You don't have to sacrifice for this thing. You have choice, so use it. Think of your other children, your husband, you. You have a life of your own. You can work, create and serve without this child. Think of the bills. Think of your figure; you're not getting any younger.

Or, perhaps:

You're too young to be saddled with motherhood. Have fun now, settle down later. Finish school. It's only a fetus; it's not even a baby yet. Babies don't begin until they're born. Do this now and you can still have your family later. In fact, you'll be more careful next time. You'll do it right, with the right man. But you won't find the right man if you don't have this abortion now. Who'd want you with all the baggage? This isn't the 1800s! You have the right and duty to make this choice, to free yourself, to be responsible!

And so the Destroyer of souls gently, carefully, leads us down to the hell of guilt, lost opportunities, broken lives and despair. When we listen to his words, our lives parallel his darkness.

One of the great debates of our time revolves around the question: When does life begin? Does it begin at the moment of conception, at birth, or somewhere in between? I was shown that a spirit may enter the body any time after conception. But this issue is unresolved in many minds, in homes, churches, and in public institutions. Legislation can grant us permission to do many things which by law are legal but which nevertheless grieve the Spirit. Because of freedom by law, certain decisions can be made in haste or under the cloud of emotion and can become permanent and devastating to all involved. In some states it is legal for young girls to have an abortion without parental consent or knowledge. In my opinion, this breaks a higher spiritual law and can tear into and destroy the closeness of families. Freedom of choice is precious, and our individual agency may be the most precious gift we have from God next to life itself. Revolutions have been fought and millions have died for freedom's cause. But, however sacred our laws hold individual liberty to be, a girl below the age of consent should act under the guidance and direction of parents who love her and who are responsible for her in the eyes of God.

But what of abortions by those who are legally adults? Am I pro-choice or pro-life? I am often asked this question, and my response is that I am pro-education. People should be educated about all the effects of abortion on mind, body and spirit. I believe that if people understood all the consequences, they would freely and quickly choose life. They would recognize that life on earth is not about ease or convenience, but about trial and growth. I was brought to make that choice myself. I know how difficult it can be. Doctors told me to abort my sixth pregnancy. As my story in *Embraced By The Light* illustrates, we must make God a partner in all decisions, but especially in those involving life and death. Today my son, Tom, is not only a delightful child but also one of my closest friends and working companions.

In answer to those who would enforce their beliefs on this issue upon others, I would say that our free will to choose is respected by God. He will not enforce his will on us. Likewise we must be cautious when imposing our will on others. No matter how strongly we disagree with what others do to themselves, we should refrain from exercising force against them. But how should we define "themselves" when it concerns an unborn child? Is the child part of the mother's body or is it an entity all its own? Does a mother abort a piece of herself, or a separate being? In heaven I was shown that a new mortal life begins at conception. Whether the spirit enters the fetus at that time or not, the body is meant for that individual spirit. Abortion may not be equivalent to murder by mortal standards, but it does end a life. It breaks bonds of promise and love, and it terminates certain heavenly opportunities.

As serious as this spiritual offense is, we must not use force to end its practice. Human nature being what it is, force only creates further force as war causes further war. More effective than force is persuasion and enticement. People committed to living the will of God should use reason and logic to convince others of the truth as they see it. Force will only hurt their argument and damage their own souls. Anger and fear destroy and impose wrongful control. Picket lines and insults can turn to uncontrollable rage, which in turn leads to murder and violence. I know there is a better way. We can find answers by looking to God for clarity, understanding, and for good sound logic.

We are qualified to judge no one eternally. Only God can judge the hearts of individuals. We can concentrate on helping and serving his children. We can teach the truth as we understand it, but we should do so humbly. God's power is found in meekness, patience, tolerance and love. And the followers of God teach these virtues by example. Most important of all virtues is love. Jesus didn't say to love those who think as we do, or to love those we trust, or to love those who love us. He said to love one another even as he has loved us. His love is the most honest, pure, and unconditional love we can know. He loves the murderer, the rapist, the thief, the liar and yes, the abortionist, the same as he loves you or me. He loves the sick, the weak, the lost, and the ignorant as he does the healthy, the strong, the saved, and the learned. Remember, in everything we do—including righting an injustice or preventing a wrong—we are to love. It is our purpose on earth to learn to love as Jesus loves. And so more of us should pray with true concern for women facing abortions. More should pray for the abortionist. More should pray for both after the act is done. But with hearts filled with anger or fear, how can we pray for them? How can we love them? And if we did love them, how could we hurt them? We may hate the deed but never those who participate in it.

In heaven, free will was gifted to all who would come here, and we willingly accepted it for ourselves and granted it to others. We desired it as a responsibility and a challenge for our lives on earth. We asked God for the right to make mistakes, even to sin or to break spiritual laws so that we might learn. We desired to live with the consequences of our mistakes so that we could be driven from within to revise our lives. And we promised to extend these privileges to everyone who respected the rights of others. We asked God for some distance from our higher selves in coming here that we might learn through adversity how far we had truly grown. He graciously gave us that space, but he is not far away. God is looking over us. He is available and is waiting for our requests for help when we want it.

The love of God is powerful enough to ripple into the lives of those who choose abortions, who perform abortions, and who defend abortions. His love and truth are the only things that permanently change hearts. Anger and insults do not. Pickets do not. Bullets and bombs do not. We are his creation and must stand in line like dominoes—close to each other, filled with love, showing by example and encouragement that the path to happiness lies not in the taking of life but in the embracing of it. Then, when God compels us and offers opportunities for teaching his love and truth, we must teach as Christ taught: meekly, lovingly, and by laying down our convenience and temporal security. Then, like so many dominoes set up by his hand, we touch our neighbor, we unite as one, and God's love and truth ripple out into all the world.

Childhood Abuse

Before I read your book, I had been struggling with the relationship I have with my mother. Even though I knew it was wrong, I felt so much resentment and hate towards her. It was destroying me inside. I couldn't understand why God chose her to be my mother, knowing how much pain and suffering she would bring to my life, and how I would have to struggle to overcome all that she did to me. As I went through the pages of your book, I became aware of what his reason was, and I began to pray for the troubled spirit inside my mother. And now I understand why she had to be such a big part of my life.

My father was a distant person to us. We were not allowed to disturb him because he worked hard. We were not a normal family. Our family gatherings consisted of the children keeping out of sight and the adults just drinking heavily. I really don't remember any times of just talking or laughing or family fun. There was little affection shown, especially by my father. Looking back, I realize that he didn't know how to relate to us. As he grew older he softened, and it was sad to see him try to be gentle and loving.

Perhaps the most heart-breaking tragedy of this world is the abuse of a child. Jesus himself spoke of this crime when he said, "Take heed that ye despise not one of these little ones; for I say unto you, That in heaven their angels do always behold the face of my Father which is in heaven" (Matthew 18:10). And in the same conversation he said, "But whoso shall offend one of these little ones which believe in me, it were better for him that a millstone were hanged about his neck, and that he were drowned in the depth of the sea" (verse 6). Jesus was not promoting the lynch mobbing of child abusers, but he was making a clear point: Abusing children is a sin that the abuser will be gravely accountable for.

Some children become victims of neglect and fear. Some are abused verbally and physically. But most damaging and most concealed is when children are abused sexually. Parents who exercise this angry dominion over their little ones no doubt have suffered greatly themselves. But regardless of their suffering, only they can stop it. Young children are powerless to prevent the horror. Family members, if aware, can plead with the abuser, love, counsel, report to the authorities, but they can never cure the spiritual illness raging in the depths of the troubled one. But with help from God, the abuser and the abused may be changed and healed from the debilitating affliction of this tragedy in all its forms.

Abuse tends to run in families. Most abusers were abused in childhood themselves. In my near-death experience I was shown that some spirits (more powerful than others) are sent to these families as children to break the cycle of abuse, to sacrifice what they might have known in their childhood, should they have gone to another family, in order to prevent future generations from suffering. Breaking the cycle can be extremely difficult, but it can be done. One of the more touching letters I have received comes from a young mother who has abused her children and has been trying to stop. She shows the tragedy through the abuser's eyes and reminds us that troubled parents usually hate what they are doing as much as their children do.

I've been separated from my second husband for over a year now. I have four children, their ages are fourteen, thirteen, four, and three. I'll be thirty-three in a week, and the hardship I've lived and am still living has brought a lot of pain and sadness into all of our lives.

I feel afraid mostly because in the past year I've been working so hard to change a lot of things about myself, and even though I feel a tremendous desire to be a more loving person—to my own children first and foremost, and then also to others—I'm having a difficult time. It is very much easier said than done.

I do pray, although it's probably not enough or maybe not with enough desperation. But even though I notice some improvement, little by little, I'm not happy with the very slow progress.

I know my children are suffering dearly for it. That's why I'm trying so hard.

I have progressed to the point where there is no more physical abuse at all, mainly because of getting therapy, attending parenting classes, being involved with Children and Youth Services, and having my two oldest children in foster care. I just don't feel that I'm able to give enough love to all of my children, and it frightens me because I want so badly for their emotional scars to be healed.

I will not give up trying to work more of the negativity and stress out of my life, and to love my children the way they need to be loved by their mother, but is there anything at all that you could tell me of something I might be doing wrong? Anything that you've learned from your experience that could help me? Is there a special way that I should pray, any particular thing I need to say, or anything like that?

I want to be an even more loving and giving person than I've become so far, and I'm afraid that I may never be the kind of person that I'm striving to become. I don't know if I'm expecting more than I am capable of or not, but I do believe that there just has to be something more that I can become, and I'm just looking for some answers to my dilemma.

I know you can't solve the world's problems, and I know that you may not be able to help me at all, but I just felt a strong need to at least ask. And if this is a problem for you or an inconvenience, I'm truly sorry. I didn't mean for it to be at all. But thank you for at least taking the time to read my letter. God bless you.

Oh, the anguish in this woman's soul. My heart goes out to her and to every parent in her situation. Breaking the cycle of abuse is an unselfish act. It can be enormously difficult and painful, but it's less painful than continuing the cycle. Interestingly, cycles can go two ways. As this woman begins to love her family members more willingly, changes will occur in their hearts. Their love will return to her, strengthening her. Her sacrifice for love will create a self-generating ripple effect and will bless her and her children. But she must not fear the change. Fear of newness and fear of failure are powerful tools in Satan's hands. He will bombard her daily with them. So she must resist fear and continue in faith, loving even when her mind tells her she can't. If she does this, the cycle will quicken. It will strengthen her and heal her wounded broken heart.

Every individual, including an abusive parent, has personal agency. We have the ability to determine our own actions. To give in to pride, fear and anger, or to humbly submit to the will of the spirit, determining to love even when the flesh rebels against it. We have the God-given right and the ability to create waves of positive emotion rather than of terror and abuse. We can send our children on to their own children with backgrounds of love and kindness and patience, or we can deliver them over to the same hells we may have received from our own parents. We face the choice everyday. In every difficulty we can choose to create something new and healthy or to recycle the poison of generations past.

Our tender children are precious to God. They come to us straight from him—innocent, trusting, and forgiving. They bring the light and love of God with them and willingly place their untouched hearts into our hands to be molded as we choose. We can nurture and expand the love that is already in them, or we can crush it.

Here is a letter reminiscent of hundreds I have received. In it, a young woman expresses her feelings during the years after her spirit was crushed by abuse.

After my abuse I became the kind of child that enjoys being alone. I was lonely much of the time, afraid of people and afraid of being rejected. I liked rebellion, being on the edge, tough and self-sufficient. I worked hard and saved my money and bought a horse. I loved the danger of racing as fast as I could, the wind in my face. I guess I was running away from my feelings, getting lost in the power I had when I rode. Still, it seemed that no matter which way I turned, I couldn't do things right. I was embarrassed that I was me. The end result was that I became a very lonely person, letting few people close to me.

This girl became molded, like fired clay, into a mutated soul that sought isolation for her pain. She created a rigidity that could not be relaxed, a fear that could not be comforted. Now she craves the human touch, but cannot allow it. She will never trust herself in the hands of others until she realizes that the neglect she suffered resulted from the fears and false traditions of a parent, not from some personal flaw of her own. Someday she may meet a truly gentle spirit who loves her and deserves her love in return, but it may take a lifetime of reassurance before she willing abandons her illusions of worthlessness.

Tragically, the legacy of abuse often renders children unable to give or receive love. Thus, without the life-force of love, obstacles appear insurmountable, and loneliness, unquenchable. Relationships are fleeting, troubled, and confusing. Simply learning to identify love is a mighty first step for many. Others run away from love their whole lives.

When children assume their own parents don't love them, they have difficulty counting on anyone, including God. When the abusive parent is religious, the damage done to the vulnerable faith of a child can be crippling.

I just put down your book, *Embraced By The Light*, and felt an urgent need to write to you. My sister has been trying to get me to read it for quite some time, but I didn't dare until I felt ready. She had shared bits and pieces of it with me, and I knew it was something I would need to do in my own time. You see, I have been trying to understand and find faith for so long that it almost seemed senseless to look any longer.

I grew up wondering what I had done to deserve the cards I was dealt. I always felt "wrong" or "ugly" or "unloved." I was depressed and cried a lot. I found happiness in nothing. I only found outlets for my pain and sorrow. Why? Because my father, who was a minister, was also an alcoholic. He abused me and my sister and brother physically and verbally. He was a tyrant to us and a friend to the rest of the world. Everyone gushed over him, and we were taught to play along. But it wasn't play; it was hard work pretending to love and honor him, when all I really did was fear him. And because I associated him with God, I naturally feared God as well.

Since I escaped to college, I was able to feel some freedom of religion, but not much. My father was still my father, and his disease was still destroying our family no matter how far away I ran. I survived my college years thanks to the most wonderful staff counselor I met my freshman year. She helped me through my most difficult times, gave me guidance to strike out as my own person, and led me to believe in counseling as a good thing, rather than something to be ashamed of. When I graduated, I continued in counseling and grew even more than I thought was possible. The good news is, so did my father.

My father has been dry for nine months now, and I have forgiven him, even before I read your book. Our entire family has come so far that the past is just that: the past. It doesn't rule our worlds as it used to, but it is there to remind us of how much we all have changed. I'm so thankful for that. But at the same time, I have been saddened that I missed my childhood, that I was tortured by this evil man as I was growing up. I was angered that God let such a man be a preacher. I was confused.

Now that I have finished your book, I feel lighter. I am excited about life and finding my path. I'm not exactly sure what my path is, but I do know it's there. I know now that it's okay to pray and that I shouldn't fear God. I only hope I can remember the feelings I had while reading your book for the rest of my life. And more importantly, I know now that, "We are where we need to be." I don't need to know why now. I almost don't want to know. I just want to live.

Church leaders, religious role models and family members who sabotage our youth do greater damage than any others. The devastating loss of hope in higher ideals can permanently mar a child. I will not quote here from another letter describing the hell of a young girl whose father—a church leader with a large following—raped her while holding a Bible. His incestuous crimes were committed over many years and always with the scriptures in hand. How many more years, how many more tears will be spent while this woman recovers? A lifetime may pass before she can trust any spiritual advisor—or even God—again. At some level she may always be tempted to blame God for the deeds of his supposed servant.

All forms of abuse damage children, but sexual abuse can devastate their souls. Children are so precious in their innocence, trust and love. Their openness delights us. But sexual molestation warps their tender spirits as they innocently seek love and protection, but receive instead, fear, guilt and shame. These emotions brand innocent victims sometimes for life, causing them to blame themselves for the hideous acts against them.

This young lady shares her feelings after being molested for the first time. She was eight when it happened.

I was so ashamed, so confused, so afraid. My whole body was trembling as I walked briskly into the house, praying my mother wouldn't stop me before I reached the safety of my bedroom. But she did see me and knew instantly that something was dreadfully wrong. I ran towards my room, but she followed, asking what was wrong. What could I tell her? I didn't even know what had happened. Whatever it was, I knew it must be my fault. I wasn't afraid of getting in trouble as much as I was of how terrible she would think I was. How dirty I was. How could I have let something like this happen? I hated myself.

Perhaps no act in human experience generates self-hate more swiftly or powerfully than sexual abuse. In an attempt to understand the unimaginable, to reconcile or perhaps to justify the strange sordid actions of an abuser, the victim is quick to assume his or her own role in those actions and to generate and accept the blame for them. Loathing for the filthiness of the actions becomes a loathing for the filthiness assumed as a part of oneself. This perception can strangely settle in over time and become an accepted explanation for one's failures, one's emptiness, one's dirtiness. The guilt, though falsely assumed, seems justified, and over the years it eats the very soul away.

The following letter confirms the despair and the haunting nature of sexual abuse. With crippling emotions of anger and guilt, this woman spent years in therapy without relief, without hope, without peace. Then a desire to love her abuser filled her heart. This opened the way for Christ to come in, and he changed her life forever.

Because of the abuse during my childhood, I was having a very difficult time in my life. Past feelings would creep up and haunt me. They were holding me captive, and I wanted it to stop but didn't know how. I was supposed to love and honor my father but cringed when he walked into the room. How was I to love a man I considered to be a monster?

Well, I was doing pretty well on the outside, but on the inside it was eating me up. All the hate and anger and shame and guilt I carried were about to explode. Since the feelings were becoming too much for me to deal with, I decided to get counseling. My therapist helped me a lot, but I was still left with a lot of sorrow. I still did not have the love for my dad that I thought I needed.

Then I read *Embraced By The Light*. It confirmed everything I had felt but never believed. I felt Christ's love for me in your book, but I also felt Christ's love for my father. How truly powerful a feeling that was. I wanted, really wanted to love my father the way I should. My heart ached for that. It really hurt. But though I wanted to love him, I still had trouble changing my heart.

Because of your experience, I no longer feared God. I had felt his unwavering love in your book and now knew that I needed his help. I needed his forgiveness for the feelings I carried towards my dad. One night, I began to pray very intensely, and I cried out to him to replace those feelings with love and forgiveness. As I prayed, I cried. The tears streamed down my face. My heart was full of sorrow. All at once I felt the presence of many beings. They just appeared out of nowhere. They encircled me, and the intense brightness I felt on and around me was magnificent. Then they moved in even closer, reaching out to me, reaching into my very soul. Their hands moved vigorously, causing a stirring—a definite swirling motion that was going so fast it felt like a tornado, but not destructive. As they continued, a burning sensation started spreading over and through my entire body. I'm not sure how long this lasted, but the feeling was so tremendous I wanted to hang on to it for as long as possible. The warmth and love I felt was so calming and peaceful. I have never experienced anything like it.

The beings left as quick as they came. I opened my eyes and could hardly grasp what had taken place. As good as it left me feeling, I really was not sure what had actually happened or how it was going to affect my life. I knew how it made me feel, but what had the beings done? I was in awe again of the feeling. I knew God had poured his love on me, and I also knew that the beings were ministering angels. I felt them and it felt wonderful.

The following night as I lay in bed, my thoughts returned to the night before. Soon, my thoughts turned to pitch black and I stood in the midst of the blackness all alone. Then two monsters appeared beside me—one on each side. They were huge and extremely ugly. They towered over me and wanted me. They were hairy, with claws hanging in front of them. As I stood there looking back and forth at them, I said in my thoughts, "You know, you probably scared me as a child, but you don't scare me anymore." Immediately both of them disappeared. I realized that up until then they had held me captive. They were my fear that took away my strength and freedom, which left me full of hate, anger, pain and sorrow.

Because of God's love, I was filled with love, and I was able to go to God in prayer, and my prayer was answered. I felt God's forgiveness for me and his forgiveness for my dad. I marvel at how I didn't know this before. I "know" now what Christ's purpose was and is for us, and what our challenge is while we're here on earth. Do we need him? Do we need his love? Absolutely.

What happened is truly a miracle. It has been a long process, one step at a time, but patience, love and understanding have brought me a long way!

This woman came back to God through fervent prayer and her intense desire to be healed. She had suffered fear and guilt for so long, she was exhausted by it and was willing to pay any price to be relieved of it. Her father's sin against her had taken her down a destructive path, but with God's help in facing her greatest fears, she challenged her "demons," and they dissolved. They had no place next to the purity of God's love in her. Demons prey only on victims, and she was not a victim any longer.

God never uses his love to hurt us. To do so would countermand his own law of judgment. "Do unto others as you would have them do unto you," Christ said in Matthew 7:12. So he will never let us down, will never forsake us. His love is extended to all, and he knows exactly how to reach each person, even if it means behaving as the good shepherd and leaving ninety-nine sheep to seek out one that is lost. He would do that. But, as this woman reminds us, preparing to receive his love can be "a long process, one step at a time."

God knows exactly how much suffering we can endure, and he will not allow us to suffer beyond that unless we exercise our free will and demand more. Regrettably, some people do demand more by their hardness and bitterness and refusal to love and to forgive. But God is always in control, and if his direct assistance is exactly what is needed for our spiritual growth, he gives it, willingly and lovingly.

Here is an experience of a young child spared much of the hell she might otherwise have suffered, if God had not intervened directly. Her experience is wonderful, but I am saddened to read far too many letters like this one:

> When I was about three years old, I had a near-death experience. It occurred as I was being viciously abused to the point of death. I called upon Jesus to save me. I saw him high above me and when he beckoned, I floated up to him. He held me by the hand, and I was released from my pain and fear.
>
> We went into a lovely garden where there were other children about my age and size. They were all playing happily. Jesus assured me I was safe now, and that I could play too. I cannot tell you in appropriate words the peace and joy I felt in that garden, but you, Betty, know the feeling. I didn't have a care in the world. I felt completely loved and accepted. Pain and fear were now non-existent for me. It seemed as though there were about twenty or more children there. They were running around, playing. It was so wonderful! Jesus sat on a big rock watching all of us play and smiling a beautiful smile at us, which filled me with complete peace and a sense of being absolutely carefree. He told us stories, and we climbed on his lap and shoulders, and he laughed and enjoyed being with us.
>
> Later, Jesus took my hand and said it was time for me to go back now. I was so sad. I asked him if I had to go back. He said that I didn't have to, but that he would like me to. I told him that I didn't want to go back. He said he understood that, but that if I chose to return, he had something he wanted me to do. I "knew" that if I went back, Jesus would never leave me, or stop loving me, or abandon me in any way. I asked him what he wanted me to do. He told me it was something for my mother, and showed me my mother and sister crying. I knew if I didn't go back, he would get someone else to do the job, but I wanted to please him, and I could not bear to see my mother so unhappy. I said I would go. I asked him what he wanted me to do for my mother, thinking I would do it as fast as possible and get back to heaven. He told me he would let me know when the time came.
>
> I felt myself going down a long tunnel and being sucked back into my body. I hated being in my body again. As I was

getting into it, I heard a man whimpering, "Oh my God, I've killed her! I'm going to get killed for this!" Then yelling and slapping my face, he said, "Wake up, you little bitch, wake up!" As my eyes slowly opened, he said, "Thank God! She's alive!" I felt intense anger because I knew he wasn't really thanking God, but taking His name in vain, and I thought, "I didn't come back to save you!"

Over the years, I have had many spiritual experiences, all reinforcing that Jesus is with me. And I have never forgotten the joy in the garden.

Christ's love is the ultimate source of healing on earth. He is the Master Physician because he possesses the power to heal wounds to the soul, including those caused by sexual abuse. Many children are saved from their nightmarish experiences by being temporarily removed from their bodies during the pain of abuse. Jesus Christ or angels receive them into their arms of love, reassuring them and healing them. To the adult who may not recall spiritual help of this nature and who may suffer from the trauma of childhood pain: you are one of God's courageous spirits. You have endured perhaps greater hardship for a purpose you may never know here on earth. Jesus would say to you, "I love you. You are more special than you know, because you are a part of the Father and me. But please open your heart to me, and let go of your pain. Let me take it from you, and I will fill you with more love and joy than you ever dreamed was possible."

One survivor of incest wrote: "What amazes me, in retrospect, is what a strong spirit I must have had to survive!" She is correct. It takes a very strong spirit to survive such tragedy. An even stronger spirit is one who understands that surviving is only a first step. Love and forgiveness are also needed to complete our spiritual missions in life. They come to us as we allow Christ's unconditional love to enter our hearts. Then we must learn in every way to love as he loves. And we must forgive as he forgives. Victims of profound injuries must find freedom to love and to forgive by ridding themselves of any feeling of guilt for the crimes against them. They must eventually find the grace and understanding to forgive their abuser.

> Then came Peter to him, and said, Lord, how oft shall my brother sin against me, and I forgive him? till seven times? Jesus saith unto him, I say not unto thee, until seven times: but, until seventy times seven. (Matthew 18:21-2.)

In other words: we must forgive until always and forever. Christ gives us this law, not for our punishment or difficulty, but for our peace and happiness. Without a forgiving heart, we will never open ourselves to the gift of being healed. We cannot do it, because the purest gift of his love is the ability to love completely, without reservation, without hatred, without hesitation. Love is the energy that heals even the deepest pain.

A friend nearly committed suicide at the age of forty because of childhood incest. When she finally understood that her anger was directed at her father and not at herself, she lost the desire to harm herself. She made a decision. "I tried to understand him," she said. "I tried to fathom what kind of pain he must have suffered in his life to cause him to give me that pain in return. And as I felt a portion of his pain, my heart broke, and I wept, not for the pain he had given me, but for the pain he had experienced himself, and I forgave him with all my heart." This kind of forgiveness comes only through the grace of God, a grace he freely gives to all who desire it.

The following letter comes from another victim of incest, which had been the family's dark secret for years. Neither parent was willing to acknowledge it. But everything changed when the mother died. What happened when the daughter confronted her father is proof that good can come from something even as horrendous as sexual abuse, when we allow God in our lives.

> Two years after my mom died, my dad died of cancer. The doctors found it and three days later he died. But before that, I had gone through a lot of counseling and had been working very hard on myself and on what life is really about.

I had confronted my dad, and he had denied the abuse. But when he went into the hospital, we talked more, and he admitted it and asked for my forgiveness. I told him that I forgave him and that, although the abuse was wrong, I loved him, and we held each other with tears of joy.

The last time I saw him in the hospital I took his hand in mine and said this prayer: "The light of God surrounds you. The love of God enfolds you. The power of God protects you. Wherever you are, God is, and all is well." At the end of the prayer he smiled a peace-filled smile and slipped into unconsciousness. He died hours later.

When I tell this story to my husband, he's amazed at how I could forgive my dad. I tell him that forgiveness and love is what God is all about, to look past horrible pain and ask God for guidance to help you forgive someone who had wronged you, and that to be able to forgive fully is one of the most peaceful feelings you can experience. Later, I found out from my uncle that my dad had been abused himself by his grandparents. So now I can stop the cycle. As my mother always used to tell me, "There's a reason for everything. God knows. Maybe we'll never know here on earth, but God's love knows all. Have faith that his love works together for everyone's greatest good."

Perhaps the ability to freely forgive is difficult to gain because it is the virtue that makes us most like God. In cases like this one, it is particularly difficult because the offense is so devastating. But forgiving her father is exactly what this woman needed to do in order to have peace and happiness in her soul. It may appear the abuser is getting off easy, but in reality it is the victim who is setting herself free. Forgiving and releasing everyone involved, unlocks the chains that bind—sometimes for a lifetime. By letting go, we allow God to punish the offender in his own time, should that be necessary.

Abuse is tragic for the victim, but it's more tragic to remain the victim. The abuser is responsible for the misery and pain he inflicts on a child and for damaging the child's ability to love and to trust. But as the child matures, he takes responsibility upon himself as an adult. He can remain captive to childhood calamities, or he can free himself through forgiveness of self and others. We all have this choice.

The challenges are high for this life. They are nothing less than completing our journeys on earth and learning to love as God loves in eternity. Forgiveness is understanding, and to understand is to grow. Each soul is ultimately responsible for his or her own happiness and for the success or failure of his or her earthly mission. All have trials and tribulations to overcome. Some may appear greater than others, but the greater the challenge, the greater the potential of that soul. As unlikely as it may seem, those who have suffered childhood abuse undoubtedly chose its possibility as part of their experience to obtain a higher level of spiritual understanding. This understanding could be either for themselves or for one they chose to help. That knowledge might not be much comfort at the time of suffering, but even trials which seem unfair or impossible to overcome serve divine purposes. We are never alone in any trial of suffering, and we will not be allowed to suffer more than we can bear. This is a promise from God. He and his angels surround us, love us, and help us choose the path of greatest spiritual growth. It is his will that we overcome the world and find joy and happiness in our lives.

When A Child Dies

Our five-year-old grandson was taken from us two weeks ago, and I keep asking, "Why?" He brought his grandfather and me so much joy and happiness. Living without him is difficult.

The death of a loved one always comes too soon. Whether death comes at three or 83—the age my father died—the passing of a family member can be one of the most difficult challenges we face as mortals. The closer the relationship, the greater the pain. Time seems to stop as we face the very meaning of existence. Outside interests, and even the faces and voices of those around us become a blur as emotions swing violently. But no death is more keenly felt or more painfully sharp than the death of a child. Researchers have found that nothing causes greater trauma to one's emotions than the death of a spouse. When a child dies, our earthly understanding screams injustice. We feel the child's time has not come yet. He is too young; she, too innocent to be taken. What of the chance to live and love and create? Death in this instance seems final.

A woman who lost her twenty-one-year-old son put it this way: "Being a mother, your natural instinct is to take care of your children. When you lose a child, it is such an unnatural thing, and it is so out of your power and out of your control."

Parents suddenly feel vulnerable, confused, and frightened. They expect their children to outlive them, and when one of them doesn't, the sense of unfairness can be overwhelming. One mother wrote of the bitterness she felt when she learned that her young son had died in an accident.

My husband held my arm and led me away. I didn't want to leave. I knew if I did, I would never see my son again. My legs just wouldn't move. The doctor was trying to prepare me for the emotions I would feel. I heard him say that I would feel grief, then anger, then guilt, and all these things were normal. What did he know! I had my son for eight years. Guilt, yes, I felt a lot of guilt. I would never have the chance to be a good mom. I would never again tell my son how much I loved him.

As the days went on I became even more bitter. People tried to console me, pray for me. It only made me angrier. If there was a God, I hated him for what he had done. God had heaped one misery upon another in my life. No one could tell me about God! I stayed locked in the house, too embittered to see anyone. Most of the day I sat staring out the window. There seemed to be no hope.

Many blame themselves for the loss of a child. Most go through the "would'ves" and "could'ves" of their life. As responsible parents, most just *know* that they could have done something different to prevent the death. They forget or don't recognize that death is a part of the vast and eternal plan each of us agreed to for progression, and some turn on God in anger. They don't see that God, in his love, watches each of us more closely than we watch ourselves. He watches even the little birds of nature in their cycles of life.

Are not two sparrows sold for a farthing? and one of them shall not fall on the ground without your Father. But the very hairs of your head are all numbered. Fear ye not therefore,

61

ye are of more value than many sparrows. (Matthew 10:
29-31.)

During my near-death experience I watched guardian spirits
hovering over children on earth, and I knew that the welfare of
children inspires a special interest in our Father. He will not
always keep them from harm or suffering, but he will allow that
which leads to their ultimate growth, that which was agreed upon
before coming to earth. God never punishes us by taking the life
of one we love. He never lets a child die because he does not
care. God cares more, and is more aware, than we suspect. In
the previous chapter we were reminded that angels of "these
little ones; . . . do always behold the face of my Father which is in
heaven" (Matthew 18:10). Our children are always before our
Father in heaven, always in his grace, always in his generous care.

No child who dies goes to the spirit world alone. God sends
loving, powerful spirits to bring them through the veil and back
into his presence. Sometimes, he may even bring them through,
himself. As a four-year-old child living at a Catholic "training
school" for Native Americans, I developed double pneumonia.
As related in *Embraced By The Light*, I suddenly awoke to the
doctor's words: "It's too late. We've lost her." Bed covers were
pulled over my face, and I noticed how little my body seemed in
that large bed. Then I found myself out of bed and in the arms of
a most incredible loving man. A sense of safety and comfort filled
me as I rested in his arms. He had a white beard that sparkled
brilliantly with a bright and living light. It fascinated me. I ran
my hands through his beard and laughed and felt perfectly happy,
safe and loved. He cradled me as a loving parent, and I wanted
never to leave him. Then I heard the words: "She's breathing
again!" and I found myself back in my body.

To this day I get a sense of calmness and happiness as I recall
this incident—my first near-death experience. For years I wondered who this man could have been. It wasn't until my second
experience with death that I knew. He was God, my Heavenly
Father. No name was ever given, no name was necessary. I

am confident of who he is and what he means to me. And by this I know that when little children die, they are cared for by Heavenly Father. Transition into the next life is easy for them because they are not influenced by worldly misconceptions. A pediatrician, Melvin Morse, wrote an incredible book, *Closer To The Light*. In it he writes of many near-death experiences of children. I too receive accounts of childhood near-death experiences, and in every case, an angel, a pet, a relative, or the Savior himself, assists in that moment between worlds. When children return to Heavenly Father, they are not left to make the journey alone.

This letter is from a woman whose sister died at age six. Her sister's story is like many others I've received. It offers testimony that heavenly spirits are lovingly present at the passing of a child.

I was doing Christmas shopping, and I was passing by the book department when I saw your book. I bought it and came right home and started reading while my three-year-old son was down for his nap.

The more I read, the more things in my life fell into place. I come from a family of nine children, and one of my sisters died when she was six and I was three. I don't remember a lot about her, but I remember a story my mother told me about the night my sister Becky died.

She had leukemia and had been in and out of the hospital since she was four. She had missed a lot of school, but still Mom said the only books she wanted to read were Golden Bible books, like you would get for small children. Mom says she couldn't understand how Becky could read when she had missed so much school.

My sister went blind towards the end, and the night before she died she was back in the hospital. Mom stayed with her through the night and into the next day. Dad went on to work because the doctors said my sister was stable. Dad doesn't cope well at all when things are wrong with his children. Becky was running a very high fever and they packed her in ice trying to bring it down. Then the doctors told Mom she had better call Dad because they didn't think she was going to make it. While Mom was waiting for Dad to arrive, she was holding my sister's hand when she awoke and started talking. She told Mom it was almost time for her to go home and that Jesus was waiting for her. Mom called the doctors in and they said because of her fever she was delirious and not to pay too much attention to anything she might say.

Mom kept listening and my sister said that Jesus was calling her again and now, he was there to take her home. Mom kept telling her they would go home when she felt better, and Becky very calmly said, "No, my real home." Mom broke down then and my sister told her not to cry because Jesus would take care of her. Then she told Mom to tell each of us kids, and her baby brother good-bye. She called each of us by name, except for the youngest boy. Mom told her she would, but reminded her that her baby brother had a name too, and my sister said, "No, my other brother." Mom really thought her fever had gotten worse, because there was no other baby brother. A short time later Becky told Mom she saw the stairs with angels there to lead her home and that it was a very pretty and bright stairway and it was time to go.

Mom kept praying to God not to take her, but when she looked on my sister's face, she knew she was at peace, and Mom then asked God to just take her out of her pain. At that time my sister looked right at Mom and said, "I love you, Mom. Would you say Jesus' prayer with me?" So Mom said the Lord's Prayer, and half-way through Becky told her it was time to go, that God was there to take her, and would Mom finish the prayer for her. Mom finished and my sister looked at Mom and said, "I love you and I'm tired." Then she closed her eyes, holding Mom's hand, and went to sleep. Mom said my sister's hand relaxed and she had a glow about her when she died. Dad made it to the hospital right after.

Mom was so depressed she went to the doctor for treatment, and she found out she was pregnant. Eight months later, my "other" baby brother was born.

I used to hear how good my sister was and how she never complained about her pain or all the tests they ran on her. I grew up crying all the time and praying to God, asking why he had taken her who was so good, and had left me who was not so good. Every night I would look outside at the sky and stars and pray that prayer and cry. Then, when I was twelve or thirteen, I was looking out my window, crying and thinking of my sister, when I saw a shooting star or something. A thought came into my head—actually, it felt more like someone was in my heart talking to me—and a warm feeling came over me, and Becky said, "Don't cry for me anymore. I'm with God and this is where I want to be, and I'm okay and happy. Don't cry anymore. I am with you."

I felt so good and happy inside. I knew I didn't have to cry anymore. I knew my little sister was okay and that it was not a bad thing for her when she died.

Heaven and earth come together at the time of death. What a precious moment for mother and daughter as the eternity of the next world slipped beautifully into this one, revealing the stairs of angels, "very pretty and bright," and the loving guidance of the Lord himself. Death on earth represents a new birth in heaven and is attended with the excitement and joy of eternal parents and loving brothers and sisters.

This letter also reveals the impact of a child's death on siblings. Children need to feel secure in these times, but parents are often confused themselves, battling personal fears of death and, perhaps, self-blame. They find it difficult to comfort their living children. But this is a time when closeness is so necessary as part of the farewell. When young children abruptly realize that their parents cannot protect them from death, more than ever they need the reassurance that God is there for them and that he watches over them always. This letter beautifully illustrates many of the subjects parents can cover with their children: that God is near, that his angels guide the spirit of the loved one back to our real home, that sickness and death don't exist in heaven, that those who pass to the other side always remember us and love us. We need never shy away from telling children the truth about death, that it is merely a new beginning in another place—a place where families can be together again, forever. Teaching children these basic principles beforehand so that they might be better prepared for the death of a family member is one of the greatest responsibilities of parenthood.

A great help for parents and siblings alike is to remember that a dying child has chosen that course for his own benefit in the previous life. Though painful to consider, it is true that a child's untimely death is no accident. In reality, the child's death is a gift to us, a sacrifice made that we might have a greater opportunity for spiritual growth. Certainly, we do grow during and after the death of a child. One mother put it this way: "His young spirit had to leave us to make our spirits stronger."

Each child has a mission to fulfill before dying. We will always miss our departed children, but we can rejoice in the knowledge that their missions were successfully completed. And we can be comforted with the certainty that the child is free from the pain and troubles of this world and is joyful in the loving arms of God.

I have a letter from the mother of two young sons—the oldest has cerebral palsy, and the youngest may live a shortened life due to a heart transplant. Since both boys' health is precarious, the mother has lived with the knowledge that she may lose them at any time. Even though she has great faith, the stress of the situation is trying. Fortunately, she understands that each soul volunteers to be part of God's plan, and she makes the most of every day with her children. She celebrates each day, refusing to live in anxiety and fear. Thankfully, her two sons are still with her, but this woman's faith sets an example for us all.

> Your book has reassured me that when my youngest son's mission on earth is over, I can rejoice for him, and will be able to let him go with a beautiful peacefulness. I will know that we had already planned for our brief good-bye and that soon we'll be together again. I've known for a long time that my children are only on loan to me. I am only, like you said, their "caretaker" while they are here.

After my little one was born, he spent fifteen months on a ventilator. I saw many suffering babies in those fifteen months and realized that death was most definitely not the worst thing. Reading your book helped me to realize that it's a whole new glorious beginning, and that we should be happy for those who have completed their mission and get to go to heaven.

A friend once said to me: "To know and not to do, is not yet to know." If you know that God has a plan for you, and that your children have their own personal agendas in life; if you know that even the years and days of your children are known to God, and that the very hairs of their heads are all numbered by a loving Creator; if you know all this and yet at the time of losing a child, you are still inconsolable with grief, and you blame yourself or God, then you obviously do not yet "know" the truth of God's plan. And yet, this is just as important: you are very human. You are part of the 99.9% percent of us who fear the loss of a child with every fiber of our beings, who would rather lose our own life than the life of a precious child. Yes, even when we do know that death is a part of God's plan, grief still engulfs us. It engulfs us because, in bringing a child into this life, we have opened the deepest part of our heart to the possibility of this tremendous loss—the most painful loss sacred, parental love can bring.

In some circumstances, a child may appear to be in pain as it nears death, and this is difficult for parents to bear. A doctor wrote to tell me about a young patient of his, and I share this story whenever I have the opportunity. It comforts many who struggle with the thought of a child dying while in apparent pain.

A young boy of ten years was brought to the emergency room of a hospital. He had broken bones, lacerations, concussion, just to name a few of the damages to his body. It was amazing that in his condition, he lived. What he told me, I knew I had to write and ask you about.

It seems he was climbing up a tree to get his cat. He climbed further than he thought, about fifteen feet, lost his footing and began to fall backwards. Under the tree was a picket fence and cement sidewalk. As his body fell, he said, he actually stayed up in the tree, sitting on a branch. He watched as his body fell on back, draping over the fence, then bounced to the concrete below. He thought, wow, that must have hurt! Then, he "knew" that he had to quickly get back into his body again. He was unconscious when he arrived here and claims he never felt any pain while outside his body. Have you ever heard of this happening before?

Many have experienced something similar to this. When I was in an automobile accident, I didn't leave my body, but I experienced everything moving in slow motion. I felt no fear or pain. I seemed to be observing the events without emotion. In more dramatic situations, God often removes us from our bodies during crises. The body may appear to be suffering but is merely responding mechanically. All the while, the spirit looks on like an observer. This is not an unusual experience. In *The Awakening Heart*, I shared a perfect example of God's unlimited powers to exercise his will. It's the story of my friend, George, who died and then returned to his body during his autopsy. He learned firsthand how God's love can anesthetize a person in death so that he or she does not experience the trauma.

Years ago during my first marriage, I was doing my best to raise four children. My personal independence had been tailored by the demands of my children who ranged in ages from three months to four years. Money was tight, and my marriage was shaky. On one occasion I took the children with me to visit my sister, allowing me to distance myself temporarily from my greater problems. Around midnight, three-month-old Cynthia woke up crying. She often awoke for another feeding, so I changed her, got her a bottle, wrapped her in her blanket, and sat down to feed her. The night was chilly and her warm little body felt good next to mine. The glow of street lamps outside filtered through the windows, producing a cozy feeling in the dim room, so I sat rocking the baby in their half light. She finished her bottle and fell asleep, but I rocked her a while longer, feeling the warm sensations of love that come in serene moments like this. After a while, she seemed to be sleeping soundly, so I laid her down and went on to bed myself.

When I checked on Cynthia early the next morning, she was still sleeping. The darkness of the fall morning still shadowed the room, and she appeared peaceful, so I didn't disturb her. Later, my sister checked on her and came to the kitchen where I was having coffee with my mother. "Betty, you should look at Cynthia," she said. "There's something wrong with her face."

I ran to her and saw instantly that Cynthia had not been sleeping, but had died sometime during the night. The color of her face had already changed. The coroner listed crib-death—now called SID'S: Sudden Infant Death Syndrome—as the cause of Cynthia's death. I became hysterical when he told me the estimated hour of her death. It was while I held her in my arms, rocking by the light of the street lamps. All the while I thought she was nestled snugly, safely in my arms sleeping.

Grief does not describe all that I felt. I was only nineteen years old, had three other little ones, a crumbling marriage, and the weight of my child's death on my shoulders. I was crushed with grief and guilt. I kept telling myself I should have known something was wrong! I had held her in my arms, loved her, fed her, rocked her, all without the smallest idea that something more had happened. Every night for years afterward, I checked on my children two and three times at least each night, often waking them up if they slept too deeply just to make sure they were breathing. The older ones would mumble in their sleep, "Momma . . . I'm okay, leave me alone!"

Shortly after Cynthia's death I asked my brother, Billy, where babies go when they die. I needed an answer that would soothe my aching heart and bring me comfort—I missed her so. He comforted me by saying they go into the heavens and become brand new stars added to the sky. I used to gaze at the stars wondering if the smallest, faintest visible star were Cynthia. When clouds blocked the sky, I wept for the loss of contact with her. I was always grateful to my brother for giving me an image to hold onto while my wounded heart began to heal.

I understand how ineffective words can be at a time like that, how inconsolable a broken heart can become. And I wish—oh, how wonderful this would have been—to have known about God's plan for us when that precious one died. How she had a unique purpose in life, a mission blessed and deemed worthy by God. How angels watched over her while she lived, and how her days with me were given according to her mission and God's perfect will. How the loving Father, sparkling white beard and all, waited on the other side to receive her into his arms when she left mine, and to welcome her back to her true home. Perhaps knowing these things might have helped. Perhaps during one of those long and sorrowful nights when fear, guilt, and loneliness gripped me—when I watched over my children from a darkened doorway, or searched for my daughter between passing clouds— my spirit would have remembered these words of truth, of reality, of eternal meaning, allowing my shoulders to relax and my heart to quiet and my soul to hope. Yes. I wish I had known then what I know now.

Positive and Negative Energy

Betty, one of the many topics that struck me was your discussion on negative thinking. Now I am trying to be more aware of my own negative thoughts, trying to change them to positive thinking before they can become harmful to myself or to others.

I have always had fear. Every day has been a struggle for me. At times in my life I have been so afraid and depressed that I could not get out of bed.

Our world's current state is lacking love. Violence, war, hunger, hate crimes, etc.—what could solve all of this? Love. True, uncomplicated and wholehearted love. Full of positive energy, motivated by the desire to be kind and giving—love. What a concept, a truly wonderful solution, so simple yet complex. I have faith that if we work love within our own circles, and those circles reach out and those reach out and so on, we can achieve awesome results.

*M*uch is happening behind the scenes of life. The invisible world is an actual part of our reality. I am referring not only to our heavenly home but also to the spiritual environment that surrounds us and extends inward to our spirits and outward into the universe. We cannot see this world of natural and dynamic energies, and as a result many people discount it. They see only with their eyes and hear only with their ears, and they ignore the subtle suggestions of the heart and spirit which interact with and are affected by these spiritual energies. For example, a young man may fill the space around him with degrading and destructive music and television. What he may not understand is that every spiritual energy clings to its own likeness. This music and these visuals have power to bring all the energies of this young man's life into harmony with them, to transform him into their own spiritual likeness. Other examples are the people who, by the very words they speak, fill the space around them with negativity. "I can't do that." "Oh, my aching back." "Why doesn't anybody like me?" "I hate this or that!" They fill not only their heads but their hearts with these sentiments, never realizing the powerful ripple effect they create.

To understand the power of the "unseen world" we should understand what it is composed of. Everything in the universe is made of energy, including our bodies and spirits. All that exists, materially and spiritually, contains energies which vibrate at various speeds. The energy that makes up plants, for example, vibrates at lower speeds than the energy that makes up human bodies. The energies that make up inanimate objects, such as stone or water or air, vibrate at even lower speeds. Each organism and each particle of matter has a unique level of energy. A key distinction, however, between animate and inanimate energy is that the energy composing life is capable of expanding. It can grow.

Associated with the vibration of energy is the possession of sound. Energy of both living and non-living entities create tones unique to each entity. These spiritual tones are refined and pure, and they vibrate at such high frequencies that most humans cannot hear them. Some animals can, however.

Light is also associated with energy—particularly life-force energy. An aura of light projects from all living things, sometimes static, but often moving and shifting much like the aurora borealis in our polar skies. This light's intensity increases as the energy producing it grows.

Life-force energy can also expand by merging with other energies. In relationships, we refer to this as synergy. Each person is able to share his unique current of energy with others. By doing this, we influence each others' energy, often increasing or decreasing it.

Spiritual beings can inhabit the space around us and share their energy with us. These beings may come from God or Satan, depending on which energy we open ourselves up to. Because like attracts like, a spirit's influence always produces after its kind. Our spirits are aware of spiritual beings near us, but our minds, in the cognitive, material, world make decisions for our souls. The war between these two forces can be intense; the spirit or "emotional" part of us choosing one direction, the flesh or "thinking" part often choosing another. The question of life is always the same: which will win, the spirit or the flesh?

In every moment of our existence we tap into the energies surrounding us. We acquire the energy of plants as we eat them, smell them, feel them, wear them. We acquire the energy of animals in the same ways. We exchange energy with other individuals as we interact with them, touch them, hear them, look at them, draw near to them, even by reading their words. Sometimes we take energy, sometimes we give it, which explains why we feel drained or invigorated after interacting with certain people. Sometimes we give and take simultaneously. But rarely does neither happen. Whenever we are near someone, we are either affecting them or being affected by them, usually both.

All energy exists in two forms: positive and negative. As mortal beings, we have power and agency to choose which of these to draw from and to create in. An important purpose for mortality is to help us learn to recognize and to choose the positive even though the negative more fully surrounds us. We make this choice consciously or unconsciously in every moment of the day, and these millions of tiny choices create the foundation of our identity.

We are what we think. We are what we say, what we do, what we fill our lives with. Ultimately, every being creates himself by these countless, crucial choices.

In heaven I watched a man who, being filled with positive energy, naturally surrounded himself with positive people, creating positive results. I also saw the reverse: how people who unthinkingly repeat negative phrases are changed and twisted by the power of their own words. A woman who habitually says, "Oh, my aching back" whenever something negative occurs, in time may produce her own change of posture—complete with chronic back pain. More tragically, she also creates a disposition of negativity which may grow into true meanness of spirit. Such is the result after years of feeding on a steady diet of misery. Using negative pet phrases is worse than a simple bad habit; it can indicate a growing surrender to negativity. Harsh words can also fill a room with negativity so pervasive that sensitive people will perceive it hours or days later.

Connecting with either form of energy can become habit-forming. People who have suffered major trauma can compound and lengthen their suffering through chronic negativity. Those who suffer depression intensify and extend their anguish through choices that let them taste their pain again and again. This may create unrelated negative experiences, an effect well-illustrated by this letter:

> I wanted to thank you for writing *Embraced By The Light*. I apologize for using such a hackneyed phrase, but it really has changed my life. I'm an unemployed teacher who has been depressed for almost two years now.
>
> Two years ago June, I popped out the groin muscle in my left leg. It was very painful and I needed physical therapy which lasted three months. Two months later, I was moved to a new classroom where the assistants did not like me, my ideas, or philosophy, and I was fired after eight months.
>
> That summer I took a job cleaning, but after three weeks, I severely injured my back. It's been a year now and I am still in pain. Six months after that, I sprained my right ankle.

Then I re-stressed my groin and back injuries. Six months after that, I sprained my left ankle.

Needless to say, I have been very depressed and I feel like I'm a bad person. I still don't have a job and my part-time minimum wage job is in jeopardy because the company is going on strike. I have bills that I haven't been able to pay. I have less than one-hundred dollars in my bank account.

Last night I read your book and it made me realize how much negative energy I was using. As I read, I realized that my back pain was suddenly gone. When I finished the book, I decided to write and tell you how helpful your book is. It was a relief to know why these things were happening and how I can change. This morning, when I woke up, my back pain was still gone. I hope it stays that way, but if it doesn't, I've decided to think of positive things to be thankful for.

I'm thankful for my parents who have let me continue to live at home. I'm thankful I have a home and bed to sleep in. I'm thankful for my friends who have listened to me gripe and tried to help and encourage me to feel good about myself. I'm thankful my feelings of hatred and revenge against those people who caused me to be fired are going away. I'm thankful your book made me feel better. And I'm thankful you wrote it.

Breaking the cycle of negativity begins with awareness. We must understand where our energy comes from and whether it is positive or negative. When we feel fearful or discouraged, we need to honestly look at what is happening. Are we adding negativity to an already negative situation, or are we experiencing an opportunity for spiritual growth? For example, those who mourn the loss of a loved one may feel grief, confusion, and anger. This negativity is normal and understandable. After a point, however, this negativity becomes damaging. It feeds on itself and supports other contrary influences. The original negativity is natural, but we may make it unnatural by choosing to sustain it. By recognizing this mistake, we may break the cycle much more easily, as did this writer:

I have been suffering from depression for a couple of years now, and since I've read your book, it's changed my attitude, because you've shown me the best way to cope. It's true that positive energy attracts more positive energy, and little by little, day by day, I feel my attitude slowly changing back to the person I used to be, before all the rotten things happened to me.

Besides awareness, gratitude also helps ward off negativity. Being grateful for the good things in life invites their continued influence. But remaining positive in difficult times requires a maturity that comes from experience. One lady wrote: "I'm so worn out trying to 'self-help'—talk positive to myself, etc.—but I'm still defeated! It's almost impossible to have 'positive thoughts' when you try your very best and don't succeed! Over and over and over."

A very wise Native American teacher, Speaking Wind, answered this dilemma by saying: "Then, quit trying . . . do it instead!"

Being positive doesn't mean forcing ourselves to overlook negative ordeals. Failing at something "over and over and over" happens even to positive people. It can break our hearts and bring temporary despair, but it can also increase our endurance and strengthen our character. Looking for the positive effects of negative experiences helps us to develop higher wisdom. Being positive means opening ourselves to insights, solutions, and even miracles. A simple way to do this is to ask God to surround us with positive energy and then to consciously absorb it. I do this by visualizing a dazzling shaft of pure white light around me which represents God's energy. As I see it in my mind, I *feel* his love surround me. I invite the light to fill me with love and knowledge. This light banishes all my fears and personal darkness. Basking in it is like taking a vacation from the world. When I come back, I'm rejuvenated. My faith in God is strengthened and my hope in his plan, restored. I'm ready to learn from my trials, ready to accomplish good things.

Wherever we go in the universe, whether in the spirit or in the flesh, we are influenced by positive or negative energies, and these will always take us in one of two directions: toward love or toward fear. In my visit to heaven I saw how the power of fear can cripple and diminish an entire family by extinguishing hope and happiness. I also saw the enormous power of love to nurture and unite families and friends.

One of mortality's greater purposes is to teach us the results of love and fear. We are to learn to love, to fill ourselves with its energy, and to share it with others in ways which expand and multiply goodness within us. But in doing this, we come against the opposing forces of evil in the world, and this often translates into fear in our lives. Fear is the greatest of Satan's tools. Through it, he prevents people from giving of themselves and from discovering the love residing in them. Even after death, some spirits actually fear the light of God and refuse to enter its presence. This fear comes from the negativity encouraged upon us by Satan—the only force which can keep us from the light. Fear binds us by chains of our own making, and only the love of God and the acceptance of his truth can free us. In the spirit world we literally remain in darkness until our fear loses its power to keep us from God. As I entered the spirit world, I was bathed in God's love until I was compelled to move toward the light. It was my own desire and freedom from fear that released me to do that. I knew that others would linger in the darkness until they were likewise free of fear. Sadly, many of us exist in this same state in the flesh—held back by fears of failure, of the unknown, or of change. Such fear can become a cancer, arresting our development. But, as the woman in this next letter learned, it's never too late to start overcoming our fears.

I have never before written to an author. In this case, I feel extremely moved to write to you because you have touched my life so deeply.

Mrs. Eadie, I'm a member of Alcoholics Anonymous, and until I read your book I felt tainted. I am a happy, recovered, and grateful member of AA.

Every word that I read in your wonderful book told me that I have a particular reason for being. Since receiving this knowledge from you, I can talk to God and to his spirits with joy in my heart. I am aware now of negative feelings that may make the spirits sad, so now I concentrate on positive feelings.

At last night's meeting I spoke of your book and passed along the title, and suggested that it be made a regular part of the inspirational readings that AA finds so helpful, uplifting and essential to healing. A change of lifestyle and thinking is so very important to conquering our devastating disease.

Thank you for all you have given by sharing your experience. I can now live unafraid and prepared for the promises. I am fifty-eight years old now, and had many unhappy experiences. I regretted them before, but now I know I can live expecting the best if I live by the laws you mentioned. I know now that all was not in vain.

Actually, *nothing* is in vain if we learn from it. Every negative experience can be turned to our benefit when we humbly learn from our mistakes. We can always change and move on. For many, though, anxiety saps life from their souls. One reader wrote: "I realized I had never really feared death . . . what I have most feared is life!"

Constant worrying is fear of living. Jesus said, "Can any of you by worrying add a single hour to your span of life? If then you are not able to do so small a thing as that, why do you worry about the rest?" (Luke 12:25-6.) Having faith in God and in his plan for us implies that we don't weaken ourselves or others through chronic anxiety. We must trust that he is aware of our situations, trust that if we have made mistakes, he is able to bless us to do better now and in the future. The anxiety produced by doubting his will or his judgment can literally drive us crazy. We live and thrive by doing things, by testing our limits, by opening ourselves up to new experiences and challenges, by seeking joy and even happiness as we step out—not in fear or anxiety, but in faith. Faith opens us to new and sometimes wonderfully crazy ideas. Why? Because in faith, we believe that God—in his strength and good grace—will show us when we go too far, and that if we get hurt, he will help us to learn from the experience. God sends blessings that will amaze us when we trust in his power to bless. I discovered this personally.

When I returned from the spirit world, I felt shocked, even traumatized, by the loss of God's presence and love. I became depressed and began to fear mortality. I became afraid to venture outside the house, to speak with people on the phone. Never before had I experienced such a mutation of my soul. Cycles of highs and lows without apparent causes drained me daily. In desperation I tried everything I could think of to overcome my depression, only to fail and then to fear trying again. Then one day, I noticed myself claiming my disease, calling it "mine." It was *my* pain, *my* fear, *my* depression, as though it were my closest friend. I was nurturing it, holding it close to my heart, and all the while this "friend" maliciously sucked life from my soul. From then on I no longer claimed it as mine. It wasn't my friend, wasn't my enemy, wasn't *my* anything anymore. Once I dropped the illusion of fear, going out of the house was just going outside again, and I had conquered the depression.

Depression is a natural home for negative energy and can be as crippling as any physical illness—as the following letter and hundreds like it attest.

I want to know the reason I was born on this earth. I have not had a pleasant existence so far. I have a lot of health problems, but none so great as my broken heart. I have wished for death, but I won't commit suicide.

This is the bottom line. I'm twenty-nine years old. I have nothing. Yes, I have food to eat, a place to sleep, roof over my head, etc. I am grateful. Yet, I had to move back home a couple of years ago, since my wedding failed two weeks before it was to take place. Moving back home was not easy. It is such a negative atmosphere.

I work for a local chiropractor. It is also a negative atmosphere. It is about to get the best of me. My boyfriend, my friends at work, and a few other things are all I have. I don't have any children; I have no animals; I am not very close to anyone at my church; I feel like I have no positives coming in.

I hope you understand what I am trying to say. I want answers. I want you to know that I love God with all my heart. He is my life, but most days I don't feel well enough to run for him.

"I don't feel well enough to run for him." This dilemma is real. People suffering from depression cannot escape without real effort, but they have lost the energy required to give that effort. The cycle of depression is seductive, even if we believe in God and look to him for support. So we must be watchful, and we must evaluate the little things in life that either sustain or defeat depression. The music we listen to, the shows we watch, the words we use, the thoughts we allow into our minds: we must carefully select these in order to diminish the negative and to expand the positive. These energies are real and they do affect our spiritual health. If we accept this, we will more easily make positive choices for ourselves. And, as one positive choice leads to another, we begin a new and a healthier cycle.

True and lasting happiness does not come from circumstance, but from within. Problems may surround us, but we have the power to transform them into teachers. It is never the situation but how we choose to react to it that really matters. We have the power to exercise faith in God and in his plan for us. We have the power to grow in confidence of our ability to meet problems head on. And in doing these things we develop power to transform our fears of life into love of life. In some cases, we may need help identifying our fears, and wise counsel is valuable. But the greatest Counselor of all is our Creator, and we can bring ourselves before him at any time, in any moment, to seek his help. When we do, we open ourselves instantly to the powers of heaven and to the fullness of life, complete with the growth and happiness our Heavenly Father intended for us from the beginning.

The Problem of Evil

My mind cannot conceive how evil can exist in a world that is God's. How is this possible? Why is this possible?

Since we are spirits created by God before the creation of the earth, and some of us chose to come to this earth, why then do people commit the horrendous crimes against their fellow man, such as child abuse, serial killings, rape, etc.?

The question of evil has puzzled us since the beginning of time. Through the ages many have tried to place it in a framework of logic to give it meaning and purpose. Some philosophers have used the fact of evil to argue that God does not exist. Most of us, I believe, ignore the larger question and simply deal with what evil comes into our lives as best we can. But the question does have answers. One reader wrote, "You say God has absolute power over all energies. Why, then, would there be a devil who has power over our spirits?"

Ultimately, the devil—or Satan—will not have power over our spirits. His eventual fate is eternal banishment. God does have absolute power, and there is no room for Satan in the Kingdom of God. In this sense we might regard the master of evil as an illusion, because he is already defeated by the power of Christ.

But why does evil exist at all? The answer is that our spirits grow faster and stronger through adversity. The pain of experiencing wrong-doing and loss burns into our souls and encodes itself into our cells and our energy. The lessons we learn from our troubles become part of our very essence. Negative experiences also grant us the power of empathy, to see others as we see ourselves, to comprehend joys and sorrows and all the human impulses. As our eyes are opened and we grow in empathy, our ability to love unconditionally increases. To develop our highest potential, to become like God, we need to gain that love which only opposition allows us to gain. Without an opposing energy, our power to love would never be strengthened sufficiently to allow us to progress in the eternities.

Satan is the spiritual personification of opposition, as he stands in opposition to the Kingdom of God—to all that is good. His evil, opposing nature is real, and his plan is to defeat the purposes of God. Without him, there would be no battle, no victory, no gain.

Satan is the master of illusion. He mirrors life, creating false images that deceive even the most astute. He cleverly counterfeits true principles and holds false ones up for admiration. For example, he convinces many that the riches of the world are a means of freedom. Riches, however, weigh us down with the responsibility to properly manage them. They do offer means to bless others if we diligently learn how to use them in wisdom. But wealth in the hands of the unprepared and unwise becomes a millstone, dragging the rich by the neck into greed, confusion, dissipation, and eventual misery. Once people have riches, they rarely let them go willingly, and in their fight to keep their "wealth" they usually impoverish their souls. But this is only one way in which Satan provides a testing ground. There are many ways he cleverly and carefully leads people away from the truth.

Satan can disguise himself as an angel of light, appearing to be the answer when in fact he is the problem. Fortunately, a false spirit posing as an angel of light casts a long, dark shadow. That is the nature of evil. It is a tree that bears bitter fruit that can always be detected over time. Evil will take on any form necessary to tempt us, to test us, to claim us, hoping we don't look too closely at its real composition. Remember, like cleaves to like. A darkened soul is more apt to receive a shadowy visitor.

Readers have asked, "What do you mean, 'Satan would have us'? Does not God 'have us' already?" God's love for us never wavers, but it is in our power to turn our backs on his love. Various doors stand before us each day, and we choose which ones to enter. Satan uses negative energies to deceive us into choosing doors which lead into his world. Many people choose those doors and entice us with their voices to investigate. They often appear to be happy. They pique our curiosity and whet our appetites. They attract us, even thrill us. And so, damning the consequences, we enter the world of consensual darkness where Satan blinds us with ever greater deception, drawing us in deeper and convincing us to remain. Thus he cleverly holds us captive—not with his talons, but with our own. Once enslaved, we turn our backs on God until our pain is so great that we frantically look for relief. Hopefully, we will look to God again, believe his words and keep them—not just because we are supposed to, but because we desire to. Yes, Satan would have us, as he has many. But we hold the keys to the doors leading in and out of his realm.

It is important to recognize that Satan, the Deceiver, masterfully uses our own fears to hold us captive. Fear is the opposite of love. It warps and destroys love's power to heal and to expand us. Some of us in this life and in the world to come are afraid to go to the Light and accept Christ's love. And Christ will not force us; rather, he gently and ever so patiently guides us along. During my near-death experience, my transformation by his healing love began in the darkness before I ever saw him. This love grew in me until my fears departed and I believed I was accepted of him. Then I couldn't be held from him and I went to his light. While in darkness, each of us has the right to feel God's love. But we must accept it. Light and darkness cannot occupy the same space; it is an impossibility.

A man recently wrote to me who didn't accept God. During his near-death experience he passed through the portals of death only to be met by a large animal covered with soft fur. It held him closely, lovingly, until he recognized that it wasn't an animal after all, but Jesus. The man understood he would have been held as long as needed for him to make that discovery. When he returned to life, the man knew he must accept God. He knew also that God always teaches us at our own level. Some may be ready to meet him and embrace him in all his glory. Others may not be ready for some time. Regardless, his love for everyone is the same. It is without conditions or limits. And it is the only anecdote against fear and the Evil One.

The tauntings, whisperings, and temptations of the Prince of Darkness are everywhere. Since many people choose to listen, the ripple effect of evil shadows everyone's lives whether we choose darkness or not. Secret crimes, lies, lust and carnality tempt every soul alive and are encouraged by the soft malicious voice of evil. Native Americans call Satan the Trickster, and it is true that he tricks us into thinking his thoughts are ours. The following letter reveals one way the Trickster tries to reach us.

> For many years I have been plagued with intermittently blasphemous thoughts about our Lord and Savior. They are not continuous, but they occur just the same. For quite a time, I took some comfort in the idea that, because these thoughts did not come from my heart but were only in my head, they were not "genuinely" generated by me. I figured these thoughts were the devil's attempt to try and win me away from God. But now I am not so sure.
>
> I am unable to share this with anyone because I am so ashamed. I know that with prayer anything can happen, but I have been praying about this for years. If this is instigated by the devil, then I know God will forgive me these thoughts because they would be a test by the devil to try and turn me from God. If, however, they are self-generated and willful,

and I am unable to rid myself of them because I am inherently evil, then how can I expect forgiveness?

Oh, the sick marvels of this Trickster. Not only does he get us thinking negative thoughts, he also gets us doubting their source, and ourselves, and God's power to forgive! This writer fears he is not acceptable to God, that he's not forgivable, and that therefore he will be cast off into eternal fire. To a certain extent, he's already there. How long has he been casting about in circles, looking for answers, hiding his shame, seeking his own elusive identity?

To dwell upon a thought is to give it energy. To act upon a thought is to give it life. The Lord discusses this principle in Mark 7:15. "There is nothing from without a man, that entering into him can defile him: but the things which come out of him, those are they that defile the man." When we give something place within our nature, it manifests itself physically and spiritually. Giving place to negative thoughts by repeating them, pondering them, gnawing on them, gives them energy and thus the power to transform us into their image.

In his letter, the man shares his love for God, and this can become his opportunity for further growth. When a negative thought comes, he should remind himself of this love and know absolutely that God loves him even in that moment. Then he must look for the cause of the negativity and cast it out, again replacing it with his love for God. In time, the negativity will die for lack of support. Also, it is crucial to know that no one's spirit is inherently evil. Bits of darkness may creep into us because mortality is a test that teaches and strengthens us, but we are children of God and like him are beings of truth and beauty and light. Ugliness in all its forms is foreign to our true nature.

Often we can recognize something evil inside as it is mirrored back by people around us. In this way we can learn and grow. One man, disturbed by the behavior of some, wrote this:

Your book stated that we should love everybody, just like Jesus said in the Bible, but some people are just downright rotten, and not only would it be hard to even attempt to like them, but it's very difficult not to loathe them for what they do. If a spirit chose to come to this earth for a growing process, how did that particular person turn out to be so evil?

Other readers voiced the same concern.

It's so sad that the spirits who came to earth come so excited and full of hope, ready to bring love and receive it, but end up bitter and mean. I know only God can judge, but there are so many fallen spirits, it seems.

Yes, evil exists in the world, but what we see as evil is a matter of perception. What is quite normal and understandable to one person may be the height of immorality to another. As a child, I was taught I was evil by nature and that my Indian heritage proved God's displeasure with me and my sinful tendencies. I was born a heathen and would die a heathen, I was told, unless the church reached into my life and saved me. I was only a girl of four and living in a church-run school, so I accepted this completely. I saw God as mean and vengeful and myself as wholly unworthy of his notice, unless it was to punish me as a "sinner." Eventually I saw the error of these teachings, and I worked hard over many years to develop a belief in myself and in my people. But despite the false teachings I received, I harbor no ill will toward my Christian instructors. I am not to judge them. They gave me life when others abandoned me. They taught me to read and write. They even shared love with me when they had a chance. God will judge their characters and lives, and I will be grateful for the good they brought to my life. After all, they could only give me what they themselves believed to be right.

This statement may appear contradictory, but in an important respect I no longer view evil as evil. I view it as opposition with a purpose. People choose the wrong, not because they want to hurt themselves, but because they have not yet learned to choose the good. Through false traditions of those who teach them or through the enticements of Satan, people are led to believe that negativity will solve their problems. Negativity seems to have the instant ability to serve without effort and so is usually the first route taken. As people choose a path not intended by God for them, they will eventually learn, but through a harder, longer process than necessary. Regardless of the process, though, whether in this life or in the next, it will yet turn them to God. "For it is written, . . . saith the Lord, every knee shall bow to me, and every tongue shall confess to God" (Romans 14:11). Every knee shall bow and every tongue confess. God will use any means at his command to reclaim his lost children—even if it is through the things which they suffer. Hell is a tool at God's command both here and in the hereafter and is a state of being that individuals place themselves into. It claims its own: those who refuse to turn from negativity. But since all will eventually confess that God is God, we know he will eventually reclaim all his sheep, even the one who leaves the ninety and nine for a time.

I know the endless love of God, and I know that if there is a way to reach any soul, he will find it and use it—for eternity if need be. Every spirit has the seed of God in it, a seed that only he knows the greatness of, and we cannot judge.

Evil exists for a divine purpose. Because of it, we become aware of our weaknesses. As we gain control of appetites and desires, we begin to see how the influence of evil has strengthened us. The force of opposition can actually propel us forward. When we see it for what it is, we become less susceptible to its negative influence, more able to let our spirits take command of our bodies. We become free from ignorance and fear and therefore more wise in choosing our course down the river of life. Moreover, we are awakened to the multifaceted nature of God's love for his children.

While accepting that God's mercy claims all his children, some wonder if the wicked will ever get punished for their deeds. One man asked, "What happens to those who murder and hurt people? When they die, do their spirits go to heaven, and all of a sudden they are loving spirits and have no punishment for their rotten deeds here on earth?"

All who commit heinous sins against others must one day come to know what they have done and to understand their reasons for doing it. They must also come to know what their victims felt because of the pain inflicted upon them. Some choose to delay this awareness, refusing to take responsibility and-refusing to learn. But one day they will awaken to a full knowledge of what they have done, and this knowledge can be punishment in itself. It can be hell.

When I died and witnessed my life review, I experienced every nuance and meaning of my past actions. I understood exactly how my actions on earth had affected other people and what those people had done to others as a result of my actions. By this I came to fully understand in what ways each action had been either positive or negative. I also clearly understood my reasons behind each action and discovered motives that Freud never dreamed of! But because I now perfectly understood my motives, I had the power to forgive myself for the wrongs I had done. I understood my own ignorance in life, that the reason behind many wrong-doings was that I had simply not learned internally to do the right things yet. I had been blind to the affects of my deeds and habits. To know but not to do, is not to know. And on earth I had not known. Now I understood why others had done negative things to me. Seeing events from their perspectives, I could forgive them freely because I perceived their ignorance, too. We can only give what we have to give, and there are many on earth who are raised in negativity, who have adopted negative words and actions as their response to every stimulus. I could not blame them for responding to their own negativity in negative ways. Nor could I blame myself.

God weighs not only the actions of a person but the intents of the heart as well. Because of his perfect knowledge and love, we could never receive a more thorough or merciful judgment by any other means. I had sinned and had broken spiritual laws that I never knew existed. I had hurt people, doubted God, acted ignorantly in countless ways. Yet standing before Christ, I marveled that he did not judge me at all. He knew the tiniest remotest thing about me and yet accepted me just as I was. He even delighted in me. I was no saint, yet he claimed me as his own and held me in what seemed an eternal embrace.

In discussing matters of evil, many people ask if there is a literal place called hell. I learned that God has many mansions, and that there are many kingdoms and levels in heaven. Where we end up will be the perfect place for us. But I can say that I did not see "hell," and also that I find it hard to conceive of such a place, given what I experienced. I felt greater mercy and understanding from God than I had ever imagined. To say that the fires of hell will claim anyone forever is to deny the extent of God's love, of his understanding, and of his willingness to forgive. We doubt his judgment in the first place if we believe he would send us here, block us from heaven, and then expect us to return to him unblemished. We must not think in black and white, but more like God thinks, without limiting any possibility for love and redemption. We should try everyday to see the good in people as he sees it. Not that we should blindly trust all people, but we can temper our judgment with the recognition that a piece of God dwells in each person, which is always redeemable.

For 25 years I have thought about this judgment and forgiveness and about the worth of each soul to God. My experience was just my personal experience, not the collective experience of all, but in pondering these things I have come to the conclusion that no soul, once remembering his or her true nature and previous life with God, would behave in ways God would not approve of. To do so would damage their own happiness. But in life we don't remember. We cannot hear, see, or physically feel God. We act blindly and perhaps our true colors or our true ignorance comes out. These revelations about ourselves teach us what we need to work on to become more like God, and he kindly gives us the time and space to work on them. No purpose of life is given to force us from God. Every purpose brings us nearer to him and prepares us to become more like him.

But there is more to our lives than individual progression. We have billions of spirit brothers and sisters with whom we share this life, and we are collectively responsible for this world we live on. We all lend our energy to it. Our thoughts, words, actions, talents, and light blend to form a collective environment and experience. Our combined energy helps create or destroy the well being of each person. Therefore, each action of each individual blesses or lessens the welfare of every other. This interdependence of all things living and non-living is perhaps best understood by our native peoples—in America and elsewhere. By listening to their teachings and weaving them into our own ways, we may bring a simple and priceless harmony into our lives that is missing. Each soul is unique, but the principles of life are eternal.

Often connected to the question of evil is the question of calamity and natural disaster. In witnessing the terrible suffering on earth, some wonder just how constant God's love is. One reader wrote, "You said the Lord is all loving. Why, then, do some people suffer so from disease and acts of nature such as earthquakes and flood, etc.?"

Natural afflictions of the world come for many reasons, but we must put them all under the general heading of "Blessings." Some afflictions come as a result of personal choice. Gluttony, for example, brings natural health problems. Fear and anxiety produce their own forms of ailment. Some physical conditions occur as a result of our spiritual health. But every opposition is a gift from God and can be used to refine spiritual awareness and increase love if we choose to use them that way. The same is true for earthquakes, famine, pestilence, and other natural disasters even though they appear to be random and not brought on by choice. We knew before coming here that some trials would be very traumatic and that we might not understand them or learn all we could from them. But we volunteered for them anyway, seeking all things that might refine us, humble us, and empower us to use our divine gifts to overcome and grow beyond these adversities. We hoped and we covenanted that by enduring these trials we would return to God stronger and more like him.

However, knowing that we chose to endure tragedy, and knowing that God allows it, does not make tragedy any less painful. The pain is part of the growth process, with the greater pain often triggering the greater growth. At times the pain or the calamity can be so severe that we need the love and prayers of others to enable us to endure it. The increase of love and prayer leading to greater faith among people may be the purpose behind some disasters. Or this may be one purpose among many as multiple truths are taught to all involved. A loving God allows tragedies to occur because he loves us and knows exactly what we need and what we can endure in order to grow.

We live in troubling times. Evil seems to be reaching new depths and broader acceptance in the lives of many. But truth is also expanding in the world, surging with new light and new ideas and generating exciting opportunities and challenges. For many this is a frightening time as old orders change and new values seep in. Time is speeding up. "What is the world coming to?" is a question as old as the world but perhaps more applicable today than ever. But regardless of its condition, this crazy, mind-boggling world is ours. We chose to come to it, and we chose this period of time in which to come. Many of us were among the strong ones, ready and determined to come and bless this world in these chaotic times. Now's our chance.

Our action or lack of action will have an impact. Planet Earth possesses a spirit, a life-force all its own. In a very real way it is a living entity. Currently the earth suffers from evil and abuse heaped upon it. It suffers from the misuse of its energy by man, and this abuse has taken its toll. Mankind has now changed the nature of the energy within and surrounding the earth. Like a magnetic force, this energy is beginning to pull and distort the earth's harmony, throwing natural forces off balance. If we do not return to the truths of God, seasons will continue to be altered, earthquakes will split the earth, floods will rage, disaster will follow disaster, and all this will be a direct result of our collective disregard for universal laws. Our actions magnified by billions of souls will literally change our environment, first spiritually, then physically.

As dire and unavoidable as this sounds, we must not become fatalistic. We have the power to reverse this process. As I came back from death, I was shown many catastrophes that await the earth if mankind collectively continues to break universal laws. These catastrophes are not for our punishment; they come as natural results of our choices. We determine our own destiny and will face the evil or good that we create. I was told that denying our Creator, who is God himself, would be the foremost cause of these consequences. So I was given to know that calamities need never occur if we will bring ourselves into harmony with God and the universe. We can restore the spiritual balance of our creation if we choose to.

And many are choosing to. Our world stands on the brink of a spiritual renaissance, a revival of spirituality that will sweep the earth and change it in significant ways. To effect these changes, the great Awakening has already begun. Light and knowledge have begun to flow from heaven in greater intensity. Those sensitive to it will respond and fill their lives with this light and knowledge. Evil, by its opposing nature, is rising up to challenge this Awakening. But the harder the opposition, the harder the angels and good people will work to create it. If not for evil and its polarizing effects, the Awakening in fact could not happen as quickly as it will. God has set this in motion, and it will not be stopped. Once he begins a work, his energy quickly fills it and expands until the work is finished. The world will suffer greatly through this process of rebirth, but its outcome is sure—not just because God has ordained it, but because millions of good people will exercise their free will to embrace this gift from heaven. We can fail individually, but we will not fail collectively.

Those who understand the message of God's love must share it with courage and confidence. People not yet sure in spiritual truth will be supported and guided by those who are sure until they come into their own understanding. We can and will see our world cleansed of all evil and blanketed with a greater glory, even the glory and love of God. But we must each believe and act in that belief. "For God so loved the world, that he gave his only begotten Son, that whosoever believeth in him should not perish but have everlasting life" (John 3:16).

The Power of Prayer

Your passage about prayer was particularly helpful since I always find myself repeating prayers of begging and wondering if Jesus hears me, or if what I am asking is appropriate. Now I understand that my prayers have been demonstrations of doubt, also. I need to practice faith and patience.

Can the Lord really hear us when we talk to Him? How do we know? Or do we have to pray a certain prayer?

God so loves his children that he bound this new world of ours to our heavenly home in an unbreakable covenant. Contained in his covenant is the promise to watch over us and to hear and answer our prayers. He promises not to intervene in our lives every time we get into trouble, but to let us work through our problems and stretch our spiritual muscles. And while he lets us act freely, he also prepares the way with experiences perfectly suited for each person's mission and growth. He is constantly involved with us, yearning for us to make the right choices and waiting for us to communicate with him through prayer.

While in the spirit world, I could look in on the earth, just as I might look into another room. Conversations on earth are heard in heaven and understood regardless of language. The Spirit speaks a universal language, deeper and more powerful than voice. It communicates accurately and clearly, piercing through mankind's ignorance or false understandings and recognizing each person's true desires. And I discovered that it is our desires, not the wording or form we use, that provides the energy that makes our prayers effective. Without a desire to connect with God, our prayers become hollow and meaningless. But with true desire, our prayers not only ascend to heaven, but they nurture us as well. They take form as an energy that if visible would be seen to add light to our presence or the aura around us. Our souls glow brighter in prayer as our spirits communicate with the Divine, because we are made more divine by the act of honest communication with Deity.

Through prayer we bring life to our souls. Not only do we open ourselves to an increased endowment of God's love and light, but we also call down the powers of heaven to overcome trials. In sending up a desperate cry for help, we call angels down to our sides to fight for our cause by adding their energy to ours. By sincerely seeking wisdom, we open ourselves to impressions which can come immediately or at odd moments and provide keys of knowledge which unlock doors of opportunity. By offering heartfelt gratitude and praise to God for his many mercies, we bring down blessings without number because of the ripple effect. As we pour out appreciation to God, we open up space in our lives for new blessings.

Any form of prayer is a personal moment in the presence of God. Verbal prayer is often the most powerful, but prayer can be silent, too. It can be a formal offering at preset times, or it can evolve into a constant state of being, continual meditation that communicates with God at all hours. Christ encouraged his followers to pray without ceasing, meaning our hearts should always be in communication with God. Our thoughts can be prayers, too. There are times when, whatever the attitude of the body, the soul can be on its knees. As prayer warriors, those times would be continuous.

Through prayer we are reminded of who we are, where we are going, and what God would have us do. By listening to God's answers to our prayers, we learn the language of the Spirit, which is so important for us to learn. But before we can listen, we must invite. Satan provides many arguments against praying—he tests our spirits—telling us that we lack the necessary faith or desire or experience. A common roadblock to prayer is a feeling of unworthiness. One reader wrote, "I often feel I don't have the right to trouble Jesus with my problems when there are always other people worse off than me."

Not troubling Jesus or Heavenly Father may trouble them even more. As an omniscient, all-powerful, and loving Creator, God has the power to listen to and answer all prayers at all times. To pray to him sincerely is not to trouble him, but to trust him, and he will respond to our trust. All people need his help, from the strongest to the weakest, from the most perfectly in-tune to the most jaded. Nobody need consider themselves above or below the power of prayer. Abraham Lincoln, certainly one of the strongest among us, became stronger by placing his burdens before the alter of God. As President, he said: "I have been driven many times to my knees by the overwhelming conviction that I had nowhere else to go. My own wisdom, and that of all about me, seemed insufficient for the day."

God already knows that our wisdom is often "insufficient for the day," but before violating our personal agency, he will often wait to help until we ask him to. If we recognize him as our father and ourselves as his children, our prayers will occur naturally. We will understand that we don't need to change his mind, we only need to open ourselves to the blessings he already wishes to give us. Prayer isn't the act of "overcoming God's reluctance," says Richard Trench, an English theologian, "it is laying hold on his highest willingness."

Think of prayer as calling home. Quite often, Joe and I have anxiously waited to hear from our children. However, knowing each child, we can usually guess why we have not heard from the "silent" one. Children seeking independence rarely ask for advice when they've made choices they fear parents will reject. On the other hand, Mom and Dad are usually the first to hear when a wrong choice was made and a mop-up crew is needed. Then Joe and I have often stated, "If you had asked, we would have given you some advice that could have prevented this!" Just the response they didn't want to hear. But unlike a phone call to Mom and Dad, a call to our Heavenly Father comes without limits, without price, without busy signals, caller ID, or call waiting, and without scolding, anger, or premature judgment.

The daughter of an alcoholic mother wrote:

> I have been so frustrated. God has never answered my prayers, and I have always believed in him, but was so out of touch. I couldn't reach him for my own anger and self-pity and most of all, self-hatred. After reading *Embraced By The Light* last night, I prayed the *right way* for the first time, and I finally feel I had an audience.

The "right way," of course, was simply praying in faith that God heard and accepted her prayer. I was shown that prayers go to heaven as beams of light and spiritual energy that reach God when offered sincerely. Even if we don't have faith in him, our desire for faith and expressions of willingness to find him reach him.

God knows beforehand what we need, but he wants us to grow by exercising our spiritual strength and constantly seeking his help in the face of opposition. The world may tell us to rely on our own egos and talents. Satan may tell us there is no God. Our own consciences weaken us with accusations of unworthiness. If we are going to pray effectively we must exercise faith sufficient to blast through these doubts and speak to our Father who is waiting patiently and lovingly for us to reach out. Sometimes it takes extraordinary circumstances to impel us to call on Father. One woman shared some of these circumstances in her own life.

> Betty, thank you for not quitting! I am writing you from jail. My poor decisions about drugs and choice of "friends"

landed me right here! I thought that my world was going to
end. Little did I know that God was actually helping me by
saving my future, my life and most of all my spirit. Thank
God! I can honestly say that.

When I first arrived here I had a cell-mate that had been
in here for some time. She had a good attitude and was
friendly but I didn't care; all I wanted to do was to sleep off
my "high." She immediately informed me that everyday she
read aloud to some of the girls and that she hoped that it
would not bother me. She rattled off the name of the book
and told me that this was her third time reading it to them.
She asked me if I cared to read it. I didn't care to because I
hadn't picked up a book in years. I just was not the least bit
interested.

On the third day of her reading to the others while I slept,
I awoke and began sobbing. I vaguely remember her reading
aloud, but is was obvious to me that something she had read
had touched me deeply, although we never discussed it.

A few days later, my roomie was transferred to another
program and was told to "roll up," which means pack your
things, you are leaving. She left me quite a mess to clean up,
including all the books that she had borrowed from the
library cart. When I looked at her selection and read the title,
Embraced By The Light, my heart skipped a beat, and my body
felt just warm all over! That night when there were no distrac-
tions, I began reading your book.

The next day, I asked my closest friend if she had read
"Embraced." She replied excitedly, "Yes, in fact I have read
her second book. I ordered it through the mail! . . . ."

Betty, I am still here. It's been one month later since
starting this letter, and I am so thankful to you! I am grateful
to God that he allowed someone to share such a spiritual
experience that I can relate to. After I read "Embraced," I
became more active in every way. I started going outside
and playing basketball and I went to church, but most of all,
I STARTED PRAYING AGAIN! I actually have more of a "life"
in jail than I did outside. My mother says that her daughter
has returned . . . she can see it in my eyes, my face, and hear
it in my voice. With your help and God's, I am back!! I feel so
spiritually "tuned-up" that I can't wait to share it. Of course,

I have shared your book with twelve other inmates and anyone new is handed your book after meeting me.

I have now read both "Embraced" and *The Awakening Heart*. I feel that it was intended that I should read them both. You see, I have had experiences in my life that might be rough, but I have always known that I was directed to become a leader of women somehow.

I understand that not everyone gets as emotional as me from reading "Embraced," and that surprised me at first. But after reading "Awakening," I can see that one must be open to spiritual growth, ready to receive and ready to give and to love one another.

Prayer has helped me tremendously. Last week I had to go to court but had not been able to talk to my attorney. I was nervous about that, so I prayed to God and told him what I felt my lawyer should know about me and my change, so he should express it to the judge. When I appeared in court, I wasn't at all surprised when my lawyer conveyed to the judge the things I had prayed about. He even shocked himself.

With my new ability to pray, I wanted to help others too. I looked around the courtroom and saw another girl sitting there waiting to see the judge. She looked so alone and frightened. I forgot all about me and my problems and began to pray for her. When it was her turn to come before the judge, I began praying for the judge. I prayed that he would make the best decision for her. When the judge called for a ten minute break and asked her attorney to conference with him, the girl turned to me and looked me right in the eyes, as if asking me for help. I calmly nodded my head and mouthed to her, "It will be all right." When the judge came out, he told her that he felt that she was worthwhile and had a lot to offer society, but because she had been driving while under the influence, she had to go to jail. She is in here with me now, and we have become the best of friends. She is also surprised at her "new" attitude. Of course, she has by now read your book.

I am leaving tomorrow, I just wanted to finish this and let you know that my change of spirit has made a difference in here. I know that I have made a positive effect here in jail and I can also see the "ripples."

Thanks for helping me find myself again and for reminding me of God's love for us all. I will miss my sisters in here, but we are going to keep in touch. And, we have all read *Embraced By The Light*. I know the positive changes that we have made, and the closeness that we feel and share, are all a part of your "Ripple Effect!" We love you!

This young woman continues to teach the love of God to all who listen. Her purpose and role seem obvious to me as God uses her as a light for others to see.

Heavenly Father uses the tool of circumstances to lead us to him. Some believe in him instinctively and seek him out early in life. Some find him only in dire straits. But knowing that he lives is only a first step to finding him. Even when we find him we can lose him. Some people lose faith in God because their prayers seem to go unanswered. They don't recognize God's helping hand in giving them what was best instead of what was wanted. The dilemma of unanswered prayers is as old as mankind. Job, in his afflictions, sought God day and night, wondering if the Almighty had forsaken him. He had lost his children, his wealth, his reputation, and his health. Painful boils covered his body. His wife and friends told him to repent of imaginary sins, then finally to curse God and die. In desperation, Job sought God even more urgently. His constant efforts kept him focused on God.

Oh that I knew where I might find him! that I might even come to his seat! . . . Behold, I go forward, but he is not there; and backward, but I cannot perceive him: On the left hand, where he doth work, but I cannot behold him; he hideth himself on the right hand, that I cannot see him. But he knoweth the way that I take: when he hath tried me, I shall come forth as gold. (Job 23: 3-10.)

Job's faith never failed. After losing all he had cherished, after even losing his ability to "find" God, he still prayed, knowing that God was testing him, trying him, even as a refiner tries gold. What can we do when our prayers seem to bounce off the ceiling? This woman asked for help in learning how to pray for her daughter:

> I am writing to ask you to explain in a little more detail, if you would, the phrase in the chapter on prayer that says, "insincere prayers of repetition have little, if any, light, and having no power, many of them are not heard."
>
> My reason for desiring clarification is that my prayers of long-standing for peace and reconciliation with my daughter have not been answered. It is a painful existence being separated from a child and grandchildren. I want to approach prayer in the most acceptable way. I hear conflicting instruction. Some people say to ask the Lord for your needs and then leave the outcome with him, while others say we should pray about it repeatedly, make novenas, ask Mary's intercession, etc. As I said, it's confusing to know which approach is most pleasing to God. As a Catholic, I say the rosary, which is repetitious prayer, and my mind does wander. Is this insincere prayer? Please, can you help me to get a proper direction in my prayer life?

No doubt this mother's prayers were heard. Although she may have prayed in a "repetitious" way, her desires were sincere. Learning to call upon our Father, though, in a more natural way, honestly sharing her concerns and feelings, may not only help her prayers to expand and grow in intensity, they may also help her think through her problems and find new answers. Sometimes, we almost seem to stumble onto answers while praying, both because God is helping us and because we are helping ourselves by being specific. But in the case of this mother's prayers, another factor may have prevented her from receiving the answers she desired.

Prayers of intercession for others must be balanced against the needs and desires of the one being prayed for. God honors each individual's agency. The daughter's desire, in this case, may not be the same as the mother's. But God, perfectly recognizing the mother's love and anxiety, blesses the mother with the spirit of reconciliation. "Blessed are the peacemakers: for they shall be called the children of God" (Matthew 5:9). As this woman continues praying and working for peace within her family, the spirit of peace will bless her soul, making her an instrument to bless others. The spirit of peace may also rest upon her daughter as a result of the mother's prayers, but the daughter—acting for herself—may reject these enticements entirely. That is her right. God will not force peace upon her, but he will allow her to live with her choices until her own understanding and pain produce the growth that is necessary for her. This growth will lead to a desire for peace and reconciliation and love with all the people in her life.

Sometimes we need to pray for discernment to know what to pray for. If we pray for a gift that continues to elude us, we may be missing the lesson we are supposed to learn. Perhaps we are to work more on our own to earn the gift, or perhaps we are to learn to live without the gift, or possibly we are to continue praying for it, which stretches faith and teaches patience. The whisperings of the Spirit will let us know. The Spirit may even help us feel whether the thing we pray for is rightful to ask of God. Jesus encouraged us to pray without giving up when he shared the parable of the widow who refused to take "no" for an answer:

> ... There was in a city a judge, which feared not God, neither regarded man. And there was a widow in that city; and she came unto him, saying, Avenge me of mine adversary. And he would not for a while: but afterward he said within himself, Though I fear not God, nor regard man, yet because this widow troubleth me, I will avenge her, lest by her continual coming she weary me. (Luke 18:2-5.)

Our Father, unlike the unjust judge, will not grow weary of us. Job, in his afflictions, prayed for relief without ceasing. David, once fallen from grace for the murder of Uriah, prayed until the end of his days that his soul might not be left in hell. Eventually he received a promise that he would be released from its grasp. We are not to pray without feeling or doubt, but if in the energy of our souls we feel to *pursue* God for a specific answer, we may safely follow the example of the widow and pray repeatedly until an answer comes.

Some are given a gift for prayer. Our Creator gave each of us strengths and abilities, and the gift to pray with faith is one of the most powerful. Not all gifts come at birth, however. Many are developed over years if we seek them diligently, asking God to bless us with them. The gift to pray is a gift we might all seek. This letter from a woman who has also seen heaven reveals her own gift of prayer:

There are similarities in our death experiences, such as the incredible, wonderful, unconditional love, the total acceptance of who we are (our spirits), the communication without words . . . like just "knowing," and the free will given us. When I returned I knew I had an urgent mission although I now have no idea what this is. One of the first things that I was taught while there, was not to judge people but to accept them with God's love. A special gift that was given me when I returned was the gift of prayer. I go through life now praying about everything! When I pray I feel an "energy" leaving me. I have been accused of having a direct line to God, and many people ask me to pray for them, and their requests have been answered by God. Once I heard over the radio that a young boy had been in an accident. I "knew" that he was seriously injured. I immediately started to pray for this boy; however, another "knowing" told me that he had died. I continued to pray and I felt an enormous surge of energy leave me straight from my heart. I prayed all that afternoon and continued into the night. I told no one. Around midnight, I "knew" that my prayers had been answered. The next day, I was told by a friend that another friend's son had been in a horrible automobile accident, it was the accident that I had heard on the radio. She told me that for eight minutes the boy had no signs of life. An incredible feeling of humility came over me. God had used me in a special way, he used the gift that he had given me. I don't know who benefitted more from this experience, the boy or me. *Embraced By The Light* showed me where my prayers had gone, and I smile when I think of the angels running to answer my prayers.

By prayer the dead have been raised and the sick have been healed. More importantly, broken spirits have been lifted and healed. As one prays and listens, the life-giving words of the Creator enter the soul. It is one thing to pray, it is another to listen to the answer. A gentleman once told me, "If you pray, people say you are holy. But if you say God spoke back, people say you are crazy." But listening to God's response is what makes prayer truly alive.

We each have an inner voice, that deep part of our soul that recognizes pure truth. It speaks to us, confirming and teaching truth. It perfectly understands the language of the Spirit of God. It acts as our conscience, intuitively warning us from danger, both spiritual and physical. This inner voice has full access to our subconscious memories of the pre-mortal life, and this voice resonates in our beings when a hidden truth from that time is made known to us.

Many people experience this voice while reading scriptures or other inspired works. Some experience it when encountering a truth that can't be known except by a confirmation of the Spirit. Some have written to say that they experienced it while reading *Embraced By The Light* or *The Awakening Heart*. "What I found in your book was an innate truth," said one reader, "and as I read I felt that I was only being reminded of things that I already knew to be true." Just as I remembered things from the pre-mortal life when I went to heaven, this reader recalled the truth of these things as he read about them. Another reader said, "As I read your book, a special warmth came into my heart, the warmth one receives from the Spirit when a Universal Truth is present." And another reader summed up the miracle of divine communication by saying, "I believe we are all connected to the Lord by a piece of him in our souls."

This inner voice is a link to our true identity and home. Unfortunately, many of us become so caught up in the things of this world that we ignore and finally squelch that quiet, delicate voice. Recognizing it requires time, patience and faith. We must believe, or at least want to believe, that this voice exists before we can truly become sensitive to it. Notice, I haven't used the word "hear." Rarely do we hear this voice with our natural ears. Rather, we experience it as feelings and thoughts. Many people feel it as a warmth in their chests; they know something in their "hearts." Some experience it as pure truth flowing into their minds, rapidly revealing new knowledge. On occasion, both sensations will come, allowing us to know spiritual truth with perfect clarity and conviction. This communication—whether from the spirit within us or from the Spirit of God—is the fruit of sincere and faithful prayer. It brings tears to our eyes, an excitement to our souls, and always a humble sense of gratitude for what has been given.

Preparation to receive the word of the spirit can be helpful. Going to a quiet, secluded place can remove us from the cares and pressures of life and open our hearts and minds to divine promptings. A quiet place can be in nature or in an empty room. Jesus told his followers to pray in their closets, meaning that they should pray in private and from the innermost part of their hearts. Listening to beautiful music or reading inspirational literature can also help create the proper mood. Jesus said, "seek and you will find" (Matthew 7:7). Part of seeking is preparing. This reader describes the importance of developing sensitivity for spiritual communication:

> I believe that if we just allow ourselves to be sensitive enough, this communication of which you speak—where the thoughts and feelings of other spirits and God just appear in one's spirit's mind—can be obtained here on earth, too. Because many times in prayer it is as if my thoughts are guided to the right answer, and deep down I know what needs to be done.

As a child I found special prayer places in the Black Hills of South Dakota near my home. I will never forget the sweetness of the wild flowers and the natural incense of sage. More recently I found a beautiful wooded area near a beach not far from my Seattle home. Powerful, massive trees there, arching over a small brook, create a natural refuge. I have named this place Tipi Wakan, which in the Lakota language means Holy Temple. For years I have felt God's spirit there as I pour out my heart and receive his sacred gentle answers. Now, as my schedule takes me to other states or countries, I seek out a Tipi Wakan wherever I can—a simple, quiet place of solitude where I can experience the sweetness of God in my heart. A quiet room serves just as well. Anyplace becomes sacred when prayerful words are spoken, and God, in answer, fills the heart and mind with holy love and light.

When I pray, I envision the energy and love of Christ surrounding me. I allow myself to bask in his glow, even if the glow is at first only created in my mind. Our thoughts have great power to create results, and visualizing God is one way to exercise faith in him. I have received letters from others who also visualize our Father or Jesus as they pray.

> *Embraced By The Light* touched me so much that I just sobbed through the book. A friend of mine, a Roman Catholic priest, also read the book and said that he would have to re-read it because he was crying so hard during his first attempt that the words just swam off the page. What touched me most was your encounter with Jesus. That's how I imagine him in prayer. Your description was so vivid that I felt that one could just reach out and touch him.

Christ can feel so near to us in prayer, that sometimes we can almost touch him. At these times, the act of praying becomes almost a revelation in itself. Visualizing may even turn to vision.

After I visualize this power surrounding me, I call upon the Father's name, similar to the way Jesus did in the Lord's Prayer. Next I offer all my gratitude to him, my thanks for the good in my life and even for life itself. Then I ask for the things I desire. God already knows what I desire and what I need, but verbalizing my desires and needs creates strength and opens me in greater honesty before God. As I ask for his will, I invite it to be done, because only he knows what is best for me. I trust him so much that I welcome whatever his will is into my life. Next, I thank him again, declaring my love for him. Then to finish my prayer, I close in the name of his son, Jesus Christ, and say amen.

Sincere prayers have power to produce miracles. I have seen many in my life. And I am convinced that countless more occur each day in the lives of those who reach out to God. He answers prayer in his divine voice, in his divine way. If we wait patiently and faithfully, answers will ultimately come.

We will never know all the effects of our prayers in this life. We won't know all the good we do, the hearts we touch, the lives we bless. We will not even know what good we have brought into our own lives through prayer. And we cannot know—until we get there—what joy we give heaven by the power of our prayers. Prayer is the soul's sincere desire. It is also heaven's desire. Angels rejoice over the soul who lays his doubts aside and offers his requests to God. The heavens are literally moved by the faith of a mother praying for her children, or a father's plea for wisdom and strength. God himself hears the muffled cry in a pillow at night, the lonely whimper of a frightened child, the groan on the bed of death, the troubled prayers of the homeless. A single word, "Help," can reach his ears and bring forth his angelic forces. His covenant with his children is binding: he will hear our prayers, he will bless us and encourage us to fulfill our missions on earth. And when the time is right, his soft, perfect voice will pierce our hearts, enlighten our minds, and confirm to our souls that the most loving being in creation is only a moment, a desire, a prayer away.

Many Religions, One Truth

I was fascinated by your book, Embraced By The Light, *but I have a disturbing concern I'd love for you to address. I'm Muslim. What do you think would happen to me if I died? Would I come to the Light of God or would I have to meet Christ? This information could affect a lot of religions.*

Religion is a personal matter. One's religion, one's faith and beliefs may be influenced by, or even dictated by, a church or other individuals. But deep down in a person's heart of hearts, he cannot be dictated to. Each individual spirit claims the freedom to believe for himself. If we were to analyze each person's deepest beliefs—including assumptions, guesses and hopes—we would never find two people who believe exactly the same thing, even within the same religion. In all the affairs of humankind, matters of faith are intensely subjective and are colored by individual interpretation and desire. Therefore it is safe to say that no two of us believe in exactly the same religion.

God understands this. He is perfectly aware of our diversity of belief. After all, he is the one who drew the veil over our knowledge of him and of the pre-mortal world. By this he ensured mortality as the perfect place for each of us to discover our own natural level of light, knowledge, and spirituality and then to progress beyond that level if we so choose. Without his powerful presence to sway us, we exercise agency to either follow his Spirit or forsake it, to heed the enticing of our own spirit or to ignore it, to seek greater light or to cleave to shadows. Nobody is forced to become faithful or to believe in God.

Each of us makes natural decisions about who and what we are and who and what we will place our faith in. Along the way, we seek out others of similar dispositions, and churches spring up in response. They serve our collective beliefs and needs for fellowship and worship. Throughout history and all across the globe, people of like-minded faith have congregated to unitedly offer thanks and praise to God. They study and share truths as they understand them and rejoice in the portion of the Spirit they receive.

When I entered the spirit world I basked in the love and light of Christ, and at that moment two burning questions arose in my mind. Since I now knew God as a being of unconditional love, I wondered why some religious leaders made him out to be angry and vengeful. And I wanted to know why there were so many different religions. Jesus kindly answered both questions with the same answer.

Each religion on earth, he explained, exists at its own level of truth. Religions mingle truth with man's beliefs. But each religion is important because it unites and nurtures people at a distinct level of spiritual growth. As people explore truths at one level, a desire awakens in them for the next level. And that level— whatever it may be—is the next step in that person's individual growth. I understood that everything which awakens us to truth is good. And that even the simplest of truths are better than no truth at all. I was told that all truth eventually leads to Christ—even if we have to find him in the next life. Each person returning to the spirit world will come to know that Jesus Christ is the Son of God and that he was sent by our Father to restore His truth. Jesus is known by many names around the world, but what we call him is not as important as what he represents, especially in the sacrifice he made to bring us home to our Father. Christ came to earth to take superstition out of religion. Then by dying on the cross, he opened the gateway to heaven, showing that *love* will ultimately take us all back to the Father.

Many faiths on earth do not include Christ but are loved and used by God nevertheless. Our Father never turns away a person who searches for him. He created our mortal conditions and knows perfectly what we face in sometimes godless circumstances. A person born to a home that does not recognize God is not cursed, but rather blessed with the needed opportunities for growth uniquely available in that home. Any person searching for any degree of light, in any religion or system of belief, is graced by God with opportunities for greater light. To accomplish that, God uses many means. Sometimes he prompts a person toward one religion or another. Sometimes he places teachers of greater knowledge into a religion to raise its level of awareness and growth. His goal is to bring us all to a knowledge of the pure and perfect truth.

Spiritual progression is not a race. We proceed at our own pace. But we should never put it off. By opening ourselves to new truths and greater faith, we increase in light. By becoming more Christ-like in love, we naturally perform purer service for others and thus develop greater peace and confidence within.

Usually God allows our growth to progress naturally. But he knows what's right for us and on occasion quickens our advancement. The surprises at these times can provide lessons for life. One man wrote of such an occasion.

> In the eighties I suffered from a massive heart attack, during which I had a near-death experience. It changed my life. I traveled through a very brightly lit tunnel and when I reached the end of it, Jesus was there. He placed his hands on my shoulders and said, "Go back, my son; your work is not done."
>
> This would not seem important to you, Betty, in that your experience was so much more intense than mine. But what

is different is that I didn't believe in Christ. I am of the Jewish Faith.

It was then that my spiritual journey to him began. At first it was a step by step by step experience. Then I started praying to God, thanking him for each day. This was something I had never done before. I wanted to go back to church, but my new understanding held me back. Later, almost ten years, when my father-in-law died, I read *Embraced By The Light*, and oh how I was moved! I could not pray enough or show God enough how much I loved him and missed him in my life! Now, this year, I will be baptized and confirmed into the Catholic Church, as a believer in Jesus Christ. I want you to know that your book played an important part in this wonderful time of my life, as did my experience with Christ.

This man's sudden knowledge of Christ changed his life, and now he is entering a new belief system with a portion of truth more comfortable to him because of what he knows. I have received thousands of letters and have met many people who have visited the spirit world and met Christ there as I have. At first I feel great excitement and joy for these people because Christ's love has come into their lives. But as I look deeper, I see that some of them suffer greatly for the changes to their core beliefs. Some churches excommunicate them for their new beliefs—even for their beliefs in Christ. Husbands and wives divorce. Children turn their backs on changed parents. Distrust and suspicion run deep. But do these people turn from their knowledge of Jesus? In all my journeys I have not found a single one—in any religion—who has denied Christ after meeting him on the other side.

Sometimes, as the following letter indicates, the prospect of a new belief system can be frightening, even if the new belief system includes Christ.

My son died suddenly a year ago and I am trying to find something, some belief to comfort me. You speak of Jesus as welcoming you after your death. Where does this leave a person who is Jewish? We do not believe that Jesus is the son of God, but, rather, a man who lived and did good for others. I want so desperately to believe I will be reunited with my son, and I believe your story, but what happens to a person of a different faith from yours?

We need not fear meeting Jesus Christ. Our spirits already know him, and when we meet him again, we will regain that knowledge. Even today our inner voice will speak of him if we open ourselves and listen. Although I had some knowledge of Jesus before my death, I never dreamed he would meet me when I died. But I recognized him at first glance, knowing with a perfect knowledge who he was. All will have that experience at some point. Even while living on earth, we can gain a knowledge of Christ if we desire it. By finding him here, we raise our level of spirituality and power to do good.

God is pouring out knowledge of his Son upon the earth. The Awakening is for all people of all faiths. While in New York recently I met an Iranian Muslim. During the war between Iran and Iraq he was fatally injured. What he experienced on the other side changed him forever. He had believed all his life that Allah, or God, was divine but that Jesus was simply a good man, perhaps a prophet, who had begun a new religion. Now, as he entered the spirit world, he met Jesus and learned that he was more than a prophet; he was the literal Son of God. In amazement he learned from Christ that his lack of understanding did not require forgiveness, that all will yet have the opportunity to learn of him and his teachings. The man was filled with joy and was given a message to bring back to his family and friends, that Jesus Christ awaits us with love and that we will find greater joy in turning to him than in any other way. But they were not receptive. Their families had been Muslim for countless generations, and they were not about to accept the word of a wounded soldier that Christ was the Son of God. His friends and community first turned against him, and then his wife and family left him. But the man knows what he knows, and today in the strength of his unbreakable convictions he shares his knowledge with all who will listen.

Not everyone will meet Christ at the moment of their deaths. In his wisdom he chooses the appropriate messenger to greet us. It may be a family member or an angel, or even a beloved pet—as a few have written to tell me. It may be a departed religious leader or a magnificent light filled with love. But I have spoken with many who have been there and returned, and most were met by Jesus Christ. Those who had not believed in him before, often came back to find their worlds turned upside down.

One man went through a tunnel with a bright light at the end. Standing in the light was a spirit being. As he drew nearer, the man recognized the being as Jesus Christ. He ran to Him and fell at his feet, repeating over and over how sorry he was that he had forgotten him on earth. Jesus helped him up, took him into his arms and held him like a baby. Christ told him that he loved him and that He was his brother who had died for him. As the man shared this story with me, he wept tears of grief that he could not be with his brother, Jesus Christ, at this time. He retains the memory of Christ's love, and he yearns to be with him again.

I, too, yearn to be with him again, and I often weep for the lack of his love in this world. However disturbing it is to some Christians who reject my story, the light I entered after dying was the light of my brother and Savior and God, Jesus Christ. He is my religion, the one eternal truth that defines all others. In this life or in the next, he will come to each person, and each will know what I know.

> Today I completed *The Awakening Heart.* I think my three greatest joys in the book were learning of Holly, of David Stone, and especially of Tom Eadie's awakening to God. My adult road has not always been smooth, and there are times when I know I have not listened to God or worshipped him in the "conventional way" as some church groups stereotypically say we must. Reading your books has helped to show me more positively that, indeed, how we choose to worship is an individual expression, and that we are not to criticize others for their beliefs or lack of them. For those who do not believe in Jesus, I have always prayed

that somehow their eyes will be opened. I drew such joy from learning in your books that "non-believers" can dwell in the valley until they come to know God's love.

God granted us a miracle a month before my future father-in-law passed away. The night he was taken to the hospital we feared he would die before we could get there to be with him. I was invited into the room to see him, and though he was peaceful, he could barely whisper when he spoke. I told him that I loved him and that I would take care of his son. He responded with, "I love you. Now, go home." That night, thinking we would not see him again, we all grieved. The next morning our miracle came. He rallied overnight and even talked to his wife on the phone. He said, "I'm gonna live!" When we visited him at the hospital, he was glowing and said, "I love everyone! I even like that guy on the wall!" That guy on the wall was a crucifix of Jesus.

I had just completed reading your first book, Betty, when I felt in my heart that during the night my soon to be father-in-law had met our Lord, and that his statement was his way of letting us know that he was one Jewish person who had seen the Savior. I find much comfort in that. Thank you for sharing with us . . . that all will come to love Jesus, if not here, then in the Valley in his time.

People of all faiths are awakening to Christ. He will never shock people out of their belief systems in a way that will hurt them, but as the world's spiritual Awakening continues, he will deliver his message to more and more people directly. I have discovered that many members of the Jewish and Muslim faiths, especially, are now awakening to him at a greater pace than most. This is evidenced by the many letters I continue to receive from them. In the following story, a man who had not known Christ met him after death, then returned to share this knowledge with his son. The son graciously shared the experience with me.

My wonderful dad went to the Lord after battling liver cancer. He was, in this life, Jewish, a soft-spoken, generous man. I asked him to come back to me after he was gone, if he could. I never expected it would happen, but it did. It was not a dream, not a ghost, he was as three-dimensional as you and I. This Jewish man told me about the light. He also told me about Jesus Christ—imagine that—and said that he was happy. I was in awe of all this. I hugged him and he was gone as quickly as he'd come. Never have I seen his face again.

At a Jewish funeral there is no wake, no viewing. I never saw my dad dead. After this baffling experience, I immediately called my mom. I told her what he was wearing: a charcoal-gray pinstriped suit with a light pinstriped shirt and a printed tie. She paused. She told me this is what she buried Dad in. . . .

All people will eventually know Christ as their Savior; "every knee shall bend and every tongue confess," but they shall come to him in love, just as he comes to them. He is kind and merciful, and when he reveals himself in his divine role to anybody, he does so that they might live more fully, that they might grow in love and spiritually, which is the purpose of mortality. However, when I say that we are here to learn and grow spiritually, I do not mean that we have to earn our way back home. None of us can do that. We would have to become perfect in every aspect, and perfection of that nature will not occur here, but later. We can only attempt to become Christ-like here, to become beings of love.

Jesus established the way to return to God. He said, "I am the way, the truth, and the life: no man cometh unto the Father, but by me" (John 14:6). He opened the gate through his sacrifice and showed the way both through his example and his teachings. He reminds us of our true nature—which is divine—and of our reason for living on earth—which is to mature in our capacity to love.

As our spiritual awareness grows, we must not condemn others who worship differently. The Bible tells a story of Jesus and his disciples traveling among the people, teaching. One day they notice a man using Jesus' name to cast out devils. The disciples stop the man, telling him that he is not a member of their group and therefore should not use their Lord's name. Jesus' response is: "Forbid him not, for there is no man which shall do a miracle in my name, that can lightly speak evil of me. For he that is not against us is on our side. And whosoever shall give you a cup of water to drink in my name because you belong to Christ, verily I say unto you, he shall not lose his reward" (Mark 9:38-41). Doctrinal differences should not prevent followers of Christ from loving all people, accepting the good they do, and encouraging more open and helpful fellowship. After all, most of us will experience several religions in our search for truth. At each stop we may discover new truths, new opportunities. Then, if we have grown sufficiently, we may become restless again and open ourselves to yet greater truths. Some will even reach the fullness of truth that is available in life. But, remember, progression is eternal for all souls.

> Over the years I've been to the Christian Fellowship, Baptist, Presbyterian, Catholic, Non-denominational, and Unitarian-Universalist churches. Each left me feeling that it wasn't quite right. I had so many questions about God, the meaning of life, the afterlife, reincarnation, the soul, etc. But the answers that were given to me just weren't quite right. I had no true peace. I began studying Taoism and Buddhism, Zen, but those too, just weren't quite right.

In my own past, I too explored various religions that did not satisfy my spiritual needs. I have learned that if we look to religion as the sole House of God, we will find disappointment. Religion can point us to God, but religion does not keep him. Even if we are active in a church and a congregation, we must find our Heavenly Father individually, each for ourselves. And Christ does not love us by the group, but by the individual. He loves us equally, and if we wish to show our love for him, we must learn to love each other equally as well—regardless of religious belief.

Christ said, "If ye love me, keep my commandments" (John 14:15). However, learning which commandments are his and which are of men can be difficult. For this, we need his Spirit. A twenty-five-year-old woman wrote:

> I was raised in a very loving Christian home and learned and studied scripture, yet I have always struggled with my own faith and relationship with God. It was drilled into my head that the slightest sin would send me straight to hell and, like you, I feared God, and I rebelled against religion. Yet during my years of rebellion I felt an emptiness and a void in my life.

This is a recurring theme in letters sent to me. One woman described her experience growing up in what she calls a "full gospel church."

> As I grew older I heard more and more about God's wrath and how everything, it seemed, was a sin. It was so stifling spiritually—I was always scared that I had done something wrong and God was going to punish me or strike me dead, and the devil would torment me in hell for eternity. I grew up and drifted away from God, although I still feared I would be hit by a car, and before I could beg for forgiveness, I would be cast into the "lake of fire" I had been told about.

This woman goes on to write about the death of her grandfather when she was eight. She had been close to her beloved "Papaw" and was tormented by doubts about his eternal destiny. "I wondered if he had asked Jesus to forgive him, and if he was in heaven. I became consumed with the thought of my Papaw in hell. But he was such a good, loving and wonderful man. I begged God to take him to Heaven." For three days she couldn't sleep. She refused to eat, and her parents became concerned for her health. It wasn't until her grandfather's spirit appeared to her and reassured her that he was happy and that he loved her, that she could continue on with life. But, indoctrinated with such fear of God, she remained tormented by guilt for her own marginal or even imaginary sins. Any feelings of joy in life were quickly drowned by torrents of fear coursing through her. Finally, while reading *Embraced By The Light*, she felt God's Spirit touch her as she read about his unconditional love for her. Relief swept into her, washing away all fear. Now, a lightness of being she couldn't have imagined before rests upon her, and she takes joy in life, has many happy moments, and finds meaning through serving others in love. She listens to the gentle spirit voice within her instead of to the harsh voice of condemnation so prevalent in the "full gospel church" of her childhood.

Each religion that leads us to God has its place in the world, though some focus on the negative as a motivating force toward obedience. These religions reserve God's love for the righteous few and preach hell as the awful reward for the sinful majority. This kind of preaching may itself be sinful. If so, those who preach such distorted doctrines will certainly be grateful that God will extend his hand to them with as much energy and love as they suppose he reserves only for the righteous.

Some of these distorted views have worked their way into the native peoples of America. In the past century and a half, Native Americans have been grouped onto reservations and told to rely upon the whites for truth and sustenance. Many native children were rounded up and placed in boarding schools that forbade the practice of native languages or customs. The children were forced to conform not only to the dominant culture's language but to its religion as well. These training schools taught the children that God is found in buildings reared to his name, not in the life that surrounds us, that his words come only from men and the printed page and not from the Spirit that breathes life into every soul. These schools did some good, but the spiritual fear and negativity they engendered still haunts the lives of many former students. One Native American man shares his experience this way:

> Like you, I too was brought up scared of God. I didn't know or understand why I had to go to a church to find or speak to God, and the times I did, I was very uncomfortable and afraid to move or even look around. I could never hear what the

preacher was saying. I learned to be ashamed there, too, because when they brought the offering plate around I didn't have any money to give. It seemed that everyone watched each other place money into it. I remember asking my mother for some money to put into the plate and she usually didn't have anything but pennies. So I would be embarrassed by only having pennies to put in that plate. After a while I quit going because I figured I was too poor and shamed by it.

Another Native American tells how he was driven from God by the intolerance and harshness of well-meaning people.

I recently bought *Embraced By The Light* to quench my curiosity. Needless to say, I was enthralled by it. I read it from cover to cover in less than a day. I should add that I am an Ojibwa. I, too, went to a Residential School where I was taught being an Indian was bad. We were segregated from our sisters. Prayer was forced down our throats. When I left, I swore I'd never return to Jesus Christ for anything. I hated everything and anything to do with Christianity. I have felt so very alone all these years.

Last night, for the first time, I laid in bed and had a good cry. I have not shed a tear for so long it felt good. I gave myself up to the Creator and asked for his love. I have not felt this close in his love for so long. I cried and asked my mother who had died many years ago, before I was five, to wait for me. I wanted to see and touch her.

Your book has given me hope that I will see my loved ones, my mother and my Creator. I now ask my angels to care for me and guide me through as I learn to love both myself and others. But most of all, to love my Creator and to make peace and friends with him.

Gitchi Meegwetch!!! (A big thank you in Ojibwa)

The suffering which people experience through misguided religious teachings can last a lifetime. In some cases only a powerful experience with the Spirit of God can undo the chasms left in the soul. Fortunately, God is always extending his hand to those who have faith in him. The sins or wounds of the past can always be healed through truth and forgiveness.

Gratefully, God's love fills many religions and many houses of worship. The example of Christ in loving and helping one another is followed in countless congregations and lived in millions of lives. This young woman's family never went to church until the kindness of a local congregation changed all that:

> The summer after I graduated, our air conditioner over-heated, and our house burned to the ground. The little Baptist church in this very small community did everything they could for us. They took up a love offering, donated clothes and other items, volunteered their time to help clean up the mess, and opened their homes when we needed a place to stay. We then became members of this loving church family. We were faithfully there every time the doors opened.

This loving congregation taught the Lord's message by practicing it, and there is no greater way to teach it. God always provides the means for us to approach him. Whether through a person, a church, or a stranger, he will seek to bring us closer to him. A religion therefore can become a life jacket, holding a person's head above roiling waters. We must never deprecate this life jacket by ridiculing or attacking another's faith. This offends the same Spirit that seeks to lift others to new truths. Love, meekness, and patience are the tools of the Spirit—and are the Spirit's messengers.

But what of those who turn from the Spirit in their lives? Do they consign themselves to hell? Our preachers who teach hell so eloquently don't preach without reference; the Bible itself refers often to hell. Jesus said, "Woe unto you, scribes and Pharisees, hypocrites! for ye compass sea and land to make one proselyte, and when he is made, ye make him twofold more the child of hell than yourselves. . . . Ye, serpents, ye generation of vipers, how can ye escape the damnation of hell?" (Matthew 23:15, 33). Jesus did not mince words with the misguided spiritual leaders of his time. In calling them the children of hell, he knew far better than they what this means.

Hell is a translation of the Hebrew word Sheol, or the Greek word Hades, meaning underworld. The term hellfire most likely comes from atrocities committed in the valley of Hinnom, near Jerusalem where a sect of idolatrous Jews burned children as religious offerings. The children's suffering left indelible impressions on those who watched. Afterwards the site became a garbage dump which burned, seemingly, without ceasing. The terms "eternal fire" and "hellfire" may come from this. But in speaking of hell, Christ did not refer to an actual pit of fire on the other side of death, but rather to a state of being. Hell is the absence of God, a void of light and truth. Spirits who find themselves in this void have placed themselves there by choosing separation from God. Most of us experience periods in life when we feel as though God has abandoned us. During such times our thoughts become dark and confused, and we feel spiritual and even physical pain. But these feelings result from our own thoughts, imaginations and misunderstandings. God does not abandon us. When we feel this way, we must take responsibility ourselves. Our hell ends when we return to God.

Many people have experienced a portion of hell after death and have returned to describe it. Interestingly, no two experiences seem to be alike. In one letter, a woman writes about her turbulent and fear-filled life and then describes her death. Upon dying, she entered into the initial black void where peace and love filled her and convinced her that heaven actually existed. As the beauty and power of heaven became certain, she suddenly feared it, feeling unworthy of its pureness and incredible light. Within moments she plummeted into a dark and bottomless pit—a place which matched her own feelings of self-worth. Then her sufferings began.

> My whole body felt the pain of burning. There was no flame, no light, just the horrible pain of burning! I heard the anguished screams of others combined with my own. I

couldn't see anything in the darkness . . . just falling, burning and screaming in torment. I was in hell!

I felt that even God didn't enter into this damned place, and that he didn't even know I was there. I had a lifetime to prepare for this day—God had already given me every opportunity to believe—but I had chosen the way of unbelief. Mostly I had relied on myself in life and done things my way, making myself god over my life. I knew that God had not sent me to hell, but that I had sent myself. Terror consumed me as I realized there was no way out, no way to stop the anguish, pain, and horror of hell. This was for eternity. I couldn't even commit suicide. No one could help me. I would fall and burn forever and ever and ever!

Then my thoughts went to God, and I realized that I did believe in him and that I was terribly sorry, not just for the torment of hell, but because I no longer was able to be close to him. The peace, the love, the joy I had experienced just moments before would never be there again. At this point I wanted nothing but to be with God.

Then it stopped. I felt the peace of God again. And then, shortly after that, I felt life returning.

Because this woman had removed herself from God during her life, in death she judged herself undeserving of heaven's love and beauty. She determined that God's love did not extend to her, and she plunged into the hell she felt worthy of. But God's love did extend to her, even in that dark pit, and the moment she realized she needed him, he rescued her from agony.

Jesus taught that "with what judgment ye judge, ye shall be judged: and with what measure ye mete, it shall be measured to you again" (Matthew 7:2). This is frightening to consider. How many of us offer the same compassion to others as we might one day, or one eternity, wish for ourselves? During a television interview I had, a woman in the audience became angry with me because my version of hell did not go far enough to suit her tastes. She demanded that a hell of fire and eternal suffering exist to consume all who fall short of God's grace. Perhaps she should be careful what she wishes for—and how she judges those who fall short, in her eyes, of God's grace.

Here's another letter indicating the negativity we can create for ourselves on the other side.

In my life, much of the teaching I received about the Lord was done through fear, such as "If you don't go to church you'll go to hell."

I got involved with drugs in my teens, and at seventeen ended up getting in a near-fatal auto accident. My body lay in a field for some time before I was found, and it was then that I had my experience.

I found myself above the earth, suspended in the universe. I sensed a oneness with all Creation, and during this sense of awe, a kind voice spoke to me calling me by name and said, "Are you willing to receive me?" I asked who he was, and he said, "This is Jesus who is speaking to you." Then thoughts rushed through my mind of what my friends thought. They thought that anyone who believed in Jesus or God were Jesus-freaks. After just thinking these thoughts, though not saying a word, I found I was slammed into this tunnel.

It began with marvelous lights shooting around me and then I was literally dumped, like falling out of a laundry shoot, into a cavern that was very ancient. It wasn't very long before I realized where I was. There were all forms of ghoulish creatures there, demonic. I couldn't stand still, for there were worms and snakes everywhere. Then the torturers began to chase me, screaming my name as I ran from them. I pleaded for the Lord, Jesus, to deliver me, and he heard me.

"And he heard me." What glorious words. Our thoughts and words and actions may place us in hell, but Christ is always aware of us, extending his arms, waiting for us to call upon him, to be converted to him and his truths. In every negative near-death experience I know about, it is the person's own fear and guilt that defined and created the suffering. Hell is a tool. It is real. In God's hand, it can provide a crucial, if painful, learning experience. The length and intensity of the experience is determined by us—by our accepting God's love or rejecting it. In my opinion, the sooner the better!

Let us not judge others or wish punishment upon them. If we follow Christ's example—as it says in Matthew 5:44—we will love our enemies, bless them that curse us, do good to them that hate us, and pray for them which despitefully use us and persecute us. In my experience I saw that God allows his children to bathe in a realm of loving darkness for as long as they want to before returning to him. I bathed in this love until a beam of light reached me, and when I went toward that light, I went because I wanted to. I saw that some could not or would not move toward the light. Perhaps murderers, rapists, and others who refuse to accept God's truth and love are among the lost sheep that Christ will yet rescue and hold close until they heal. A transformation of soul must occur before they will feel comfortable among beings of light. God's tenacious love can cause this transformation, but the person must be willing to accept it. And only when he truly accepts it will his desire naturally draw him toward the light.

The truth will set us free when we are ready to accept it.

We hold the keys to prison's door and heaven's gate. When will we choose to learn within the perfect love and light of God? As soon as we do, we throw off our shackles of fear and guilt. By turning the key to heaven, by desiring to enter therein, we allow our Savior to reach us, to save us, to teach us how to become more like him.

I am grateful for his love and understanding, for his tolerance and patience. His perfection is no longer the source of my despair, but of my hopes—because he knows me and loves me just as I am. As I feel his invitation to draw near him, I recognize that all the love and joy I once felt in his presence can be mine again. I don't need to be perfect to be helped—I only need to want the help. He is ready to claim me from any trouble, from any despair, from any hell if I will turn and move toward his light.

This is my religion: that Jesus Christ lives, that he died to open the way for us all to live with God again, and that doing his will in mortality will bring us closer to him both here and in eternity. I willingly open my heart to accept his love, and I expect to receive it, in all its fullness, when I meet him again.

Unseen Forces, Dreams, & Premonitions

Five years ago my grandfather was going into surgery for what was a very dangerous operation. We have always been close, and I had a restless night for worry. Suddenly in my sleep I saw his face in front of me saying, "Don't worry. I'll be all right, no matter what the outcome."

I have dreams of things to come. Once I dreamed of the building where I was to work long before I got the job. I try to keep track of my dreams. Are these from God? I feel that they are. I seem to know the difference when they are just dreams and dreams I'm to pay attention to.

One of the grandest mysteries of God is his foreknowledge. Truth is knowledge of things as they were, as they are, and as they are to come. God, possessing all truth, has the ability to know all things in advance. This being the case, we can trust him to give us only that which will be good for us in completing our life's mission successfully. Sometimes God foresees circumstances in our lives that will need to be changed for our good, and he intervenes in one way or another. When he does, however, he always honors our freedom and agency to do whatever we choose. To intervene, he may place

125

certain persons into our lives to guide or persuade us in a new direction. Or he may give us meaningful dreams or place influential thoughts into our heads. He may send divine beings to inform us or protect us. In Chapter One I mentioned an example of God's unseen forces in protecting a woman during a car crash. Here is a similar story from a young mother:

> I, too, like your son in *The Awakening Heart* was in a terrible accident in my car. I had just dropped off my precious son at the sitter's house and was rushing to pick up my husband to do some shopping for Christmas. I was only blocks away from my house when another car ran a red light, slamming into my car with great force. Betty, it happened so fast that all I could say was, "God, I do not want to get hurt!" By then, my car was spinning out of control. I felt a strong, very strong hand or arms holding me so that I would not move. After the accident and at the sight of my car, people couldn't believe that I was all right. The paramedics arrived and asked if anyone was with me.
>
> I looked in the back seat where I usually strapped my son in, and it was totally smashed. If he had been in the car with me he would not have survived the collision. I immediately began thanking God. After X-rays showed that I was fine, the technician asked me if I had on my seat belt, which I did. However she said, "Why is your right shoulder so red when it should have been only your left side?" I knew then that God sent down one of his wonderful, STRONG angels to save me.

I receive many letters confirming God's active role in preventing accidents or injuries that in his divine wisdom would not be for our good. In these cases, perhaps our knowing about his intervention creates the very growth of which we stand in need. Although we have forgotten that we chose our path beforehand, God has not forgotten. He is an active partner in helping us stay on the path which holds the experiences we need for growth.

I am reminded of God's loving intervention when I think of an experience involving my youngest daughter, little Betty.

Before leaving on an extended trip, I prayed for the protection of my family while I was away. In my prayer, my thoughts were drawn to little Betty—whom we now call BJ, for Betty Jean. As a rather serious and cautious young lady, BJ had decided of her own accord not to drive until she was eighteen. Now, at eighteen, she had had her license for only a few months, but she had been trained well to drive defensively. I was confident of her driving, but this day, I prayed for my daughter's special protection. Before leaving the house, I hesitated—still feeling the tugging within—then kissed her good-bye and left. Driving away, I silently censured myself for being overly-protective, but my uneasiness persisted.

The phone call came the next morning. Soon after my leaving, BJ and two friends had gone to the store. Rain had lifted old oils from the road, and BJ's Jeep hit a slick spot on an S-curve. The Jeep rolled and landed upside down in a ditch. To this day, the pictures of the accident chill me. The Jeep was totaled. But remarkably, BJ and her two friends were unhurt. Stoically BJ told me on the phone all she could remember, trying to be brave. But sudden sobs filled her voice when she told of feeling strong hands come from behind and hold her against the seat as the jeep rolled then flipped end over end. "Mom," she cried, "I know it was an angel!"

God spared BJ and her friends, he sent his protective forces to aid them, I believe he also affected the traffic for those few moments, as the road, usually busy at that time of day, was empty. More vehicles could have easily been involved, but their unusual absence kept other drivers from injury or worse. God in his all-knowing ways had allowed the accident to bring minimal harm to human life but maximum learning to those involved. After the phone call I prayed in humble gratitude.

A few weeks later I received another call which gave even clearer perspective to my precious daughter's delivery from harm.

I cannot possibly accept all the calls that come for me. Since *Embraced By The Light*, thousands of calls have come. My son, Tom, who manages my business, visits with the callers and kindly explains why I can't speak with them. At the end of the day he faxes me a list of the calls in case I find time to return any of them. One day he called me, sounding very concerned. "Mom," he said, "you have got to call this woman. Her son, who just graduated from high school, was killed." The tone in his voice said everything, and I took the number and called.

I gave my name and asked for the woman. As she came to the phone, I heard a gut-wrenching cry, then her voice: "Oh, Betty, Betty, thank God you called! You are my only hope." Her cries and her sobbing voice tore into my heart. In all my life I have never heard cries that wracked my soul with such grief. She told me how her eighteen-year-old son—the same age as my BJ—had been killed in an auto accident. "Why did this happened?" she pleaded, as the odds against it had been astounding. The road it happened on was remote and normally desolate at that time of night. But the other driver had been drunk. And the difficult thing was that he had lived, while her son—the innocent victim—had died. Why?

Images of BJ's Jeep seared my mind. She had been spared by God's intervention. Why?

Then I imagined this boy's car, mangled, twisted, totaled like BJ's, and the boy remaining lifeless, never to walk away. Instead of remaining strong for the two of us, I cried tears enough for us both—sobbing as she sobbed and experiencing pain I didn't know existed. BJ's survival had not been her own doing, but God's—just as the boy's death had not been his own doing, but God's. What enormous pain. What enormous vulnerability. What enormous gratitude.

We each have a time to go. And when that time comes, no earthly power will prevent it. But until then, no earthly power beyond that of our own agency can cause it. God is with us, masterfully preparing the way. He is in control. He giveth and he taketh, and by each he blesses us more fully than we can comprehend.

Later, when Tom and I discussed this experience, we recognized that the Spirit had caused him to respond powerfully enough to this woman to persuade me to call her. The same Spirit had persuaded me too. This is one more reminder of how God orchestrates his forces—which often include you and me—to bless his children in need.

Sometimes God reveals his presence and we may not understand why. I recall the story of a boy of ten who lived on a farm. He made a commitment to pray to God and to read from the Bible every day. Even in his tender years he knew God lived and could help him if needed. One morning on the way to the barn to get some tools, the boy felt a distinct impression: "Don't go in the barn." He turned around and attended to other chores instead. Years later he was asked by others why God had warned him not to go into the barn that day. "I don't know," he said. "I never went in."

Whether we know it or not, God is always watching over us and sending perfect aid for our journey. Here's the story of a woman who received a message from beyond that restored a lost sense of purpose and vitality to her life.

I lost my father four months ago and his death is a great loss in my life. He was seventy-one years old and died of heart failure. My husband and I had just arrived at my parents home, when my mother came running out and said that something was wrong with my father. We felt for his pulse and found none, so my husband and I started CPR. We brought him back to life for about fifteen minutes, but by the time the paramedics came I remember hearing his last puff escape from my Dad's lips, just as you mentioned in your book that your Dad had done, and I whispered in his ear to go to the light.

After he died, I wasn't the same. My family worried about me and wondered when I would come back to them. They tried getting me out for walks, but I would only spend time in my room. I just blanked everyone out of my life. My heart had turned to hurt, denial, and all my mistakes. I pulled away from everything and everyone who meant so very much to me. Then three months later, I received a message from my Daddy. He wanted me to go to the library to look for a book about angels. That is when I found your book, *The Awakening Heart*. Looking back, I can see now that my Dad had sent me to check out this book so that I could understand that he was safe and would always be our angel and that it was time for me to go back to my life and be loving and caring again.

This woman received a direct message from her father, spirit to spirit, but another way God intervenes is to give counsel by the Spirit in dreams or premonitions. Anciently, people listened to their dreams and looked to them for guidance in life. But today, many discount the remedial and spiritual influence of dreams. We have come to believe that dreams simply provide a playing field for the tired mind, providing a way for the brain to rid itself of daily emotions or to amuse itself while the conscious mind shuts down for the night. While this is partly true, dreams can also provide important lessons as our spirits reconnect with God while we are asleep.

The following experience is from a young man in Texas. It illustrates how dreams are able to function on several levels: providing emotional healing, answering questions, and guiding our steps into the future. This particular dream illustrates four truths. First, that God's blessings are on their way to us even before we are aware we need them. Second, that our earthly connection with family members continues beyond the grave. Third, that dreaming is an excellent vehicle for communicating with those departed family members. And fourth, that messengers from the spirit world can offer assistance and often do offer support and help, but that it is our choice to accept or reject that help. This young man chose to accept the help which he received.

I can't tell you how many times I ran across your book, *Embraced By The Light* before I actually acquired a copy. The book would almost beckon to me to pick it up whether it was in a store or on some friend's coffee table. Finally, I asked a friend if I could borrow and read her copy. She gave it to me instead and I started reading that night, but a phone call came and someone visited, so by the time I got back to the book, I was too tired to concentrate. This same thing happened to me for weeks after, and I never got far into the book. I'm not kidding! Soon the book ended up under my bed just collecting dust.

Then one night I dreamt about my wonderful grandmother visiting me. The room we visited in was colored the most beautiful shades of blue. The colors moved, flowing in and out of each other and it created an effect that glowed in the center of that room. My grandmother, whom I called Memaw, had died when I was in the eighth grade. We were very close and I loved her very much. I was not allowed to see her for two years prior to her death because my family was trying to hide the fact that my parents had divorced and they thought that if she knew, that it would break her heart. I come from a very dysfunctional family, where I faced a lot of trauma due to physical and emotional abuse by my father. I don't think that Memaw ever knew that was going on. She was my greatest champion and had a loving, genuine spirit. I had always loved music and singing, but my father was against it. He forbad me to participate in any school activities that involved the arts, because he wanted me to stay focused on things he considered masculine. There was no way that he could have possibly understood that the love of God and music burned in me. Music was the savior of my life, and it helped take away the pain and reality I faced through my childhood.

I began secretly competing in singing contests, and during my lunch break I would take my lunch into the choir room and teach myself how to play the piano. Memaw would encourage me from the side lines, sending me money and telling me to always pursue my dreams. Then she had a heart attack and was moved into a nursing situation. I no longer had contact with her, except for an occasional visit before my parents divorced. I remember the last time I saw her, I was leaving her hospice room and a voice inside me told me to turn around for one last look. She thought I had already left and never noticed when I ran back into the room to look at her from behind the white cotton partition that hung from the ceiling. "Good-bye," I whispered. "I love you Memaw. I'll see you in heaven. Thank you for loving me so much." And that was the last time I saw her on this planet. Until the dream.

I was struggling with deep depression and anxiety. My life was a mess and I had massive energy problems and developed agoraphobia. I couldn't even leave the house for groceries. Then it happened, my Memaw, my precious grandmother came to me in this dream. She told me to concentrate on the color in the blue room when I was depressed. She also told me that everything would work out fine. She went on to say that God had a reason for me to go through this. We sat on a bench in the middle of the blue room and she held my hand until she got up to go. When she rose to leave, she said, "Grandmother has to go now, I will see you again soon." Then before she faded out of sight, she said one more thing. She asked me why I had not finished "that book." I asked her, "What book?" She replied, "The one underneath your bed." Memaw told me to get up and read it now. It was three AM, but I got out of bed as if I had been awake all that time and looked under the bed and saw "the book." It was your book, Betty. *Embraced By The Light*!

Well, I dusted off the book and ran a bath for myself and began your book from the beginning. Betty, I felt like a child again. Now, you have to picture this, I'm a 200-lb., tall, blonde Texan male and I was scooting around in the bath tub like I was a five-year-old who had just found the best bath tub toy in the world! After every chapter that I read, I would close the book with my thumb still inside, sit straight up in the tub and shriek with delight! I felt like the home I had been searching for was right there inside my hands. I had come home! That was the beginning of my spiritual awakening. You handed me "The Light" and I am forever grateful.

Thank God for allowing Memaw to visit her grandson in his dream. Her comforting appearance, love, and devotion to him was all he needed to follow where his heart was leading him in the first place. And Memaw's love, added to her reminder, was what he needed most.

We spend about a third of our lives sleeping, but most of us are literally in the dark as to what really goes on then. Everybody dreams, whether we recall dreaming or not. Most dreams occur just before waking or shortly after falling asleep. When people are deprived of dream-state sleep they suffer mental and emotional trauma. This eventually leads to breakdowns. Dreams help heal our minds and our souls. The dreamer himself is the star of most dreams, regardless of identity or gender. When several characters are involved, the dreamer can find bits of himself represented in each character, with lessons to learn from each. Most dreams proceed in symbolic imagery, often causing difficulty in interpretation, but often leaving a sense of knowledge having been conveyed. As several events in the Bible indicate, interpreting dreams cannot be done confidently or accurately without the Spirit's guiding power. If we want to know what our dreams are telling us, we must open ourselves to the power of God.

I have been humbled to learn that God has directed people in dreams to seek out *Embraced By The Light* or *The Awakening Heart*. In the spirit of humility, I share these only to evidence again that God will use any tool at his disposal to reach his children. The ripples of our lives are often created in heaven.

My wife was very ill and not expected to live. I tended to her at her bedside and tried to help her overcome her fear of death. One morning she told me that she had been visited by an angel during the night, in a dream. The angel showed her the cover of a book and told her to get it and read it. My wife could not recall the title, but she did remember, somewhat, its author's name. She described the book as being blue, with rays of light on it and that the author's name was Betty Eady, or something like it. She was so anxious to get the book that she wanted me to go immediately to the bookstore for her. I went not expecting to find it, but wanting to calm her down. When I got there and described the book, I was shocked when the woman waiting on me reached right to the book and handed me *Embraced By The Light*. I took it home to my wife still in shock! She held it to her like it was truly a gift to her from God. I will never forget that experience. I read it to my wife and what a lovely experience! She lost all fear of death, and so did I.

Another letter came shortly before *The Awakening Heart* was published. I believe that this dream was meant for me more than for the one who received it.

I was very ill and prayed that God would either heal me or help me find some way to learn to live with my pain. My prayers were answered in a peculiar way, and I thought that I should write you and see if you understand what I experienced.

During a dream, two people came to me dressed in Native American attire. Without speaking, they showed me a book written by you. The strange and unusual part of it was, the book cover was wrapped in white buckskin and had fringe and other things on it, but there was no title. I "knew" that this was a very spiritual book and that it had some importance. I have tried to find it, but no one knows what I am talking about. Do you?

I didn't know what she was talking about, but I guessed the book might have been *The Awakening Heart* because its cover, although not wrapped in buckskin, has a picture of me wearing a doeskin dress with fringe. But the book had not been released, so while I wondered at this dream, I didn't give it more attention—until I began my book tour.

The tour would take me away from my family for three weeks. So they gathered to wish me well and to say good-bye. My daughter, Donna, brought me a farewell gift she had made. She had wrapped it in red cloth and carefully tied it. It smelled of South Dakota sage. My heart almost stopped when I unwrapped it. On the red cloth lay the most beautiful book, a book covered and fringed with white doeskin. A pocket sewn onto the cover contained a traditional "medicine" pouch in which each of my children had placed something that would remind me of them while I was away. From my son Joe I found an Indian-head nickel, reminding me of the time years ago when he had dropped a quarter into a machine, only to get back a wooden nickel. He had cried for days over his loss. From Cheryl came a teddy bear charm which reminded me of her collection and adoration of teddy bears. And so on, until I had a part of each of my children with me. I looked further and discovered, under this lovely cover of doeskin, my new book, *The Awakening Heart*. None of my children had heard about the letter of the dream with the buckskin book. I could only sit and cry tears of joy, not only for the beauty of the gift and of the givers, but for the message of affirmation that was sent to me through a dream that was not my own. My new venture and especially each family member were noticed by God, and he was behind us all.

God works in mysterious ways, and those ways come to us as quickly as we accept them. In these days of awakening and transformation, he will deliver his truths to the world through whomever he chooses and through whatever means please him.

> And it shall come to pass afterward [in the last days] that I will pour out my spirit upon all flesh; and your sons and your daughters shall prophesy, your old men shall dream dreams, your young men shall see visions: And also upon the servants and upon the handmaids in those days will I pour out my spirit. (Joel 2:28-9.)

Not all dreams are pleasant. Some come with images of darkness, as though they came directly from hell. These dreams, too, are dreams to understand and to learn from. They bring to the surface what is normally hidden in the recesses of the subconscious.

A 38-year-old woman suffered from nightmares. Night after night she was attacked by horrifying demons in her dreams. She sought help from a sleep clinic, where she learned the practice of "lucid dreaming," which she describes as "being aware that you are dreaming while you are dreaming, and then taking control of the dream." When the nightmares came again, she was ready. "I stopped suddenly, turned around and faced the creature and screamed at him, 'Who are you and why are you doing this to me?' He (the devil) looked at me incredulously, as if to say, 'What are you doing here?' He then began to shrink, getting smaller and smaller until he disappeared completely, never to return! I couldn't believe what had just transpired, and my joy was overwhelming! I knew I was rid of him! I felt free for the first time in what was now thirty-eight years!"

What a wonderful dream of stark symbolism. She had come face to face with her greatest fear. When she faced her demon, he gave her an important message by asking, "What are you doing?" When she woke up she wondered just exactly what she was doing in her life. With this awareness, she was able to begin making necessary changes in herself.

Another woman who had been sexually abused as a child was shown in a dream how to deal with the scars and the lessons of her life.

> Betty, I believe your mission is to help people like me. I was so confused and scared before I read your book. Now I feel complete and not afraid. I prayed to the Lord halfway through the book, asking him to show me my mission in life. That night, in my dream, he sure showed me! I am somehow supposed to share with the world my pain and survival of the molestation I experienced from my stepfather. I just now have come out and told my mother. But now I am supposed to share and help, and give strength to others like me. To teach them how to tell someone about it, and to realize it's not their fault.

> Thank you, Betty. I truly believe that I am to love everyone and spread hope and love and joy. I feel I have a purpose now, a goal.

It could be said of these dreams that the women were simply tapping into their subconscious minds to heal themselves. In part, this is true. They connected with their spirits, that part which is closest to God, and received answers to the problems they faced. Regardless of what we choose to call the process, the healing occurs. And when we are prepared to recognize God's hand in this, our entire beings can truly be transformed into purer, healthier souls.

Another category of dreams, however, involve more than tapping into our own spirits. Dreams of prophecy draw directly upon the foreknowledge of God. They serve a number of purposes, preparing us for events to come, offering hope, and giving direction. Many of the ancient prophets took great hope in their dreams and visions of Christ, both of his mortal ministry and of his advent in the last days. Today, many prophetic dreams and premonitions tell of trials to come and warn us to prepare ourselves temporally and spiritually for the future.

This letter comes from a woman who had several prophetic dreams after having her own near-death experience:

> I dreamed of my grandmother in a dark room. All that you could see was her lying in a bed covered with white sheets, and Jesus dressed in white, standing at the end of her bed. A few months later she was diagnosed with cancer, and she died soon after. Her minister said to my mother after he left my grandmother's room, "I have never in my life felt the presence of God as I did in that room." My mother said he was visibly shaken.

This prophetic dream not only prepared the woman and her family for the change to come but also offered the hope of a glorious afterlife—for the grandmother and for all who live as she lived. When the grandmother's time came, Jesus was there to receive her, prompting the minister's sense that He indeed was present.

This hopeful and prophetic dream came to a woman, raised by foster parents, who now desired a family of her own:

> Our first child was born one day, then died the very next day. He died due to a blood clot in the brain. Betty, I went through a terrible time. I was only nineteen years old and I got so angry at God. I would kneel at my baby's grave

and cry and ask God, "Why did you do this to me?" I had no family and we had looked forward to the birth of this baby so much.

I must have cried buckets of tears and blamed God and told him how much I hated him. But one night I dreamed I was standing outside, looking up at the sky, and the form of Jesus appeared. And in this beautiful deep voice I heard him say, "At the age of twenty-one you will bear another son."

I woke up from that dream with the most wonderful feeling of peace.

And yes, two years later, at the age of twenty-one, I gave birth to a son.

This dream carried a very clear, beautiful meaning, but some prophetic dreams require more time to understand. Most are not understood until the events prophesied in the dream actually transpire. I had a dream before writing *The Awakening Heart* which I didn't understand, except that it was significant. I reprint it here exactly as I recorded it in my journal the morning after.

I was entering a large airplane with some people that I knew, but most were unfamiliar to me. The pilot explained to me that this was a maiden voyage for the plane but not to worry: the plane was being carefully monitored. I sat next to two friends and companions—Nancy and Georgia—who have traveled with me separately when on tour with *Embraced By The Light*. My deceased father was with me as well. He sat in his wheelchair next to me in the middle of the isle. After the plane lifted with tremendous thrust and traveled for some miles, my father motioned to me with a nod of his head to pay attention to the view outside the window. When I looked out, I saw that the plane was descending and that the tops of the trees were clearly visible. I mentioned this to the pilot, but he assured me that all was well. Looking back at my father, he motioned to me to put my head down and to prepare to land. I warned everyone and we got into position for a sudden landing. My father motioned me to look again. When I did, it looked as though a giant mower had mowed down a path of trees, making a runway on which our plane could land. The runway seemed to go on forever. Our plane landed safely with no one hurt, and the pilot received a message that new transportation was on its way.

Nancy, came to me and said laughingly, "Honey I have a good book that you can read while we are waiting." She handed me a beautiful book.

I could not see it's cover because brilliant rays of light shown so brightly from it that my vision was blocked. As I held the book I could feel great love from within it, and I did not want to let it go.

"What book is this?" I asked her.

"Your new book," she scolded and laughed.

Then Georgia handed me some Snickers bars—my favorite candy bar which I like to eat when I miss dinner on tour.

A year and a half later, as I wrote the final chapters to *The Awakening Heart,* I remembered the dream and reread it in my journal. It was still not completely clear to me. However, the coming months would prove to me that this was a dream of true premonition. The new plane represented my new publisher. The flight was the launching of my book, which was a grand take off. The book flew rapidly into bookstores and within two weeks onto the national bestseller lists. When the plane descended, it landed safely on a path that had been paved by my first book, *Embraced By The Light.* And the Snickers bars? Well, I ate many of them while touring, just as I had with *Embraced By The Light.*

There exists a spiritual veil which blocks us from God and his mysteries. While we dream, the veil thins and partially lifts. It is wise to pay attention to dreams, to record their images and our impressions of them, and to review our notes from time to time. God communicates with us through dreams—and through waking premonitions and unseen forces—in order to send messages and reminders meant to further us in our life's missions. These communications are to be accepted and under-stood by the individual who receives them. We can never predict when they will come, but if we believe and are open to them, they *will* come. And when they do, we should explore their meanings. God will help us interpret them if we remain willing to accept his interpretation regardless of what it holds. If meanings do not come at first, patience and wisdom will allow truths to manifest themselves naturally in our lives. God will not think less of us if we do not understand the meaning of a dream or a vision. He purposefully keeps from the conscious mind all things which are meant to be known at a later time when meanings will make a greater impact. Having some advance knowledge—by way of prophetic dreams, for example—helps us prepare for the moment of understanding and for the purpose such a moment may serve. God's ways are only mysterious because we don't understand them. He uses what already exists in our lives for his purposes. Hence the use of symbols from our waking lives to send important messages to us as we dream.

Before sending this chapter on for its final editing, I went over it one last time to make sure it was right. Everything seemed good to me until I got to the final paragraph. Here my thoughts became fuzzy, and what I had written made little sense. I worked and reworked the ending, pushing to complete it so I could move on. Frustrated, I finally gave up and went on to bed. The next morning I recalled a portion of a dream that had come. The dream was not clear to me, but I felt it was important, so I prayed and asked for understanding and direction. I was prompted to read some new mail on my desk which I had avoided, not wanting to be distracted from my book. The prompting persisted until I sat down and pulled out a letter. As I read, the Spirit told me it had guided me to this letter, which was from a Native American man serving time in a correctional center. I read with excitement of his incredible dream.

> I saw your book on the shelf in the library here, and when I pulled it from the shelf, I saw you. But what really amazed me, is this wasn't the first time that I have seen you! I was with you in a dream!
> We were standing by a river and I was greeting some people with you by my side. You kept repeating one word to me the entire time, "Ta'ton'ka." I know you don't know me

personally as in this world I am a 29 year old man, and live far from you. But in my dream we had a beautiful little son and our lodge was made of white buffalo hide—as white as snow! The sun was always shining. The river was alive with fish, and we could soar over it in flight as though we were the south wind. We went on to have many daughters and sons who grew up to be strong and made us proud. We were sitting on a rug of bearskin and you were milling corn with two of our eldest daughters when you said to me, "Tatonka, our son, take him," meaning, take our son, Tatonka. You were heavy with child, I touched your belly and, correcting me, you said, "Tatonka, this one," meaning, not this child, that one. Then you pointed to another of our sons. When I woke up, the son you had pointed to was standing there right before my eyes! It was a wild experience!! Our union of souls runs deep. We shared a vision and we will meet in this world—I can feel it!

The dream or vision was so strong to this man that he closed his letter with, "What did you mean by 'Tatonka?' As I understand this word, it doesn't make any sense when used alone."

I laughed aloud as I read this. He was so convinced that his experience was real and meaningful—even as he wrote, his spirit could feel the reality of it—that he was searching for meaning from me, as if I had truly been there. But the meaning of his dream does seem clear to me. Perhaps by sharing my feelings about it, you will feel encouraged to open yourself to your dreams, your visions, and their meanings for you in your life.

The setting of his dream is very meaningful. All of its symbols are spiritual. The river, the lodge, and the natural beauty that surrounds it are reminders of the higher nature of self. The river and the people at the river could mean the river of life as we experience it here on earth. Greeting the people could mean his relationship in heaven to a higher plan which could include guardianship from those who return back to God. He will have many acquaintances, among whom perhaps are those he is meant to help here. Me beside him as his wife could represent a marriage to greater and higher knowledge and understanding—as might be found in my books. With higher understanding at his side and being married to it, he has internalized what knowledge he needed to empower him.

The lodge of white indicates purity in his dwelling place, comfort, light, and love—not in his habitations but in himself, his body, the dwelling place of his spirit. The ever-shining sun indicates happiness, peace, tranquillity. The river filled with fish could represent abundance, no worries. Soaring with the south winds gives the sense of freedom, ease in venture, joy, serenity. Many children means continued life, creativity, God-like qualities. His wife milling corn with daughters signals family unity, contentment. A wife heavy with child is the creation of new life or a new beginning. Pointing to an older son indicates a child who already exists or one who is already prepared for the journey. Waking up to the vision of the older son, or seeing him in reality, is as though looking into a mirror, the man is the son, the son is the man. What he sees is himself.

The word repeated by me in his dream, "Tatonka," has deep meaning. This man is of the Ojibwa Nation, but the Spirit chose a word from the Lakota Sioux tongue which has deep meaning and purpose. It means buffalo and has other significance springing from the mystical story of the White Buffalo Calf Woman. In this case I believe the buffalo represents something about the growth of the dreamer, and I look for the meaning and energy such a name might symbolize to the Native People. To us the buffalo represents the carrier of healing medicine. When buffalo were plentiful, everything was plentiful in our lives, and so we believed the spirit of the buffalo brought abundance. The buffalo is sacred, powerful, and is a gift of life from the Creator. When a buffalo is killed for food, all its parts must be used to avoid offending the Creator, who gave it. To dream of this animal is, to me, a sign that the dreamer has the gift of healing—to heal himself and to heal others. His dream calls him to move forward out of bondage in a strong and powerful way for all those who will be sent to his path to receive the healing powers of God. He has the knowledge of God and the abundant blessings he needs to move ahead, to use his healing gifts through the power and strength of the buffalo.

God can use us to awaken each other. Perhaps this dreamer has been searching for years for his path, his mission. Maybe his vision was clouded by self-doubt or a sense of unworthiness. By presenting the truth to him in a dream—using me as a mile marker or connecting point by leading the dreamer to my book and my picture—God is helping his awakening to begin.

Time and greater insight educate us concerning the symbolism in our dreams. The Creator uses time to bring forth truth in a season when the meaning may carry more significance for us. Experiencing truth in dreams and visions leads to greater acknowledgment of them and therefore greater acceptance. This openness, in turn, allows for other similar experiences which can then lead us to total enlightenment.

As we grow in spirit and in our ability to recognize God, our dreams will have fewer and fewer symbols to weed through. We will have a more complete and direct line of communication with God. Yes, dreams serve more purposes than as nocturnal escapes from the daily grind. Dreams and visions are often brief partings of the veil which allow our souls a peek into heaven. By them we discover there is more to life than what our everyday senses tell us. Dreams and visions help us to see our actions in all their facets: in the beauty of harmony and abundance, or in the nightmarish details of things we ought to change within ourselves or in our circumstances.

How empowering it is to know that we are so blessed, so directed by our Creator, to know that even in our weaknesses he never gives up on us. He encourages us in unending and marvelous ways to find and use our natural strengths for higher purposes, for a higher plan.

A Need To Love

I wish to express the deepest gratitude to you, Betty, for your message of love. Nothing is more important, and I live every day focused on the beauty, reward and essential need for us all to share it.

I believe love is given and received in many forms: via friendships, family, the love between spouses, and so forth. I'll go one step further and say the love of oneself is also part of it. If we can begin to love ourselves, then that will be expressed in our dealings with others.

s I stood in the presence of Christ he spoke these words: "Above all else, love one another." He was firm, emphatic. This was the most important truth I would learn in my experience with him, and he wanted me to understand it, to feel its full impact. It is the most important thing we can know. To love is the reason we exist. To learn to love more fully is the reason we have come to earth. Love is the energy which holds the universe in place. It is the gateway through which we return to our Creator. It can conquer any problem, ease any suffering, heal any disease. Love creates and magnifies the joys of life. And, at the moment of death, love turns all earthly pain into indescribable bliss.

We were conceived in love spiritually, and love is the center of our beings. It is the energy of our souls, the spark of our divine nature. Being made of love, we cleave to it and seek it in all that we do. When we do not have it, or when we have lost it, we grieve. Its presence or absence colors our every action. It is life. It is happiness. It is salvation itself. "God is love; and he that dwelleth in love dwelleth in God, and God in him" (1 John 4:16).

On earth our spirits miss the electrifying power of God's love. Our minds are veiled, but our spirits remember his love, and silently we cry for its comfort and soothing warmth. Some of us spend our lives weaving in and out of relationships, searching for the essence of this divine emotion, hunting it, craving it, but never finding it in this world. Some of us cry to God for this love, expecting him to send it to us through another person. But it first must come from ourselves. One woman cries out in a letter, "I miss love—being loved—so much! I want to break out and run—escape!" This sad, tearful quote is the soul's recognition of suppressed love that already exists within her. Her love cries out to be released and expressed, to be free, to run—even to escape—from the barriers of this world of flesh. It yearns to expand and blend with another. For some of us the search seems never ending.

> I hope that God loves me—but I fear he doesn't. He seems as indifferent as everyone else in my life. I feel like I've been living out a life sentence of solitary confinement as far as love is concerned.
>
> As an only child of busy parents, I prayed for companionship, but never got more than a morsel here and there. I was still a child when my father died. My mother and I were never close, and that relationship got even worse. I married to get away from my unhappy home. Less than a week after marrying my husband, he basically told me that he owned me and he could gamble, drink and do whatever he wanted. And he did. Alone and scared I remained. Time passed, we had children, my husband became ill. I prayed for God to spare his life. I said I would love him as he was and not complain about the indifference. But he still died.

Later on I prayed that God would send me a man who would love me and my family. Seven years later I met someone and grew to love him with all my heart, but I was afraid to thank God for his blessing, as my prayers all seemed to backfire before. It took time, about two years, but I eventually found the courage to thank God. I thought God saw that I had suffered enough and after a lifetime of loneliness and despair he had answered my prayers. Only two weeks after my prayer of thanks, I got dumped! How could a God that loved me give me hope only to take it away? That awful day my very soul withered and died. I wish for just once in my life I could know the love of someone or something. I wish my terrible pain mattered to someone.

The terrible pain this woman suffers will subside when she forgives those who have given it to her. But because so much of the pain and loss is so rooted in her infancy and childhood, it may take the rest of her life to overcome it. Understanding her loss, however, can release her from the fear of it and help her to love and to accept love from others. Then her open heart will attract other open hearts, and she will experience greater love, real love, in her life.

When our souls are unsettled, subconsciously we draw to our lives the kinds of experiences and relationships we have had in the past. We do this in order to relive them, to make sense of them, to attempt to make them work for us—this time. It happens again and again, and until we understand the truth behind our circumstances, the cycle of failure continues. To recognize love, one must know it from the start. In order for this woman to see clearly the love her children and possibly her husband have for her, she must recognize the love that exists within herself. She must understand that her own feelings of being loved are not contingent upon actually being loved by others. She can love others first, because she came here—as all of us came here—capable of creating love. The divine spark of love exists within us all, and it is the key to this woman's earthly and eternal happiness. By releasing love to friends and enemies, to those who help and those who hurt—including her parents—she will discover the meaning of her experiences: that they are meant to help her learn to love, not to feel loved. She does not need to wait for love to come to her. Sadly, until she learns that she does not need to wait for love to come to her, she will pass her unloved feelings and perspectives along to her children. They will be given the same burden to work through in their lives.

When we turn to others for the parental love we crave—or for any other love we lack—we pressure them into filling a void they cannot possibly fill. As spirit children of God we were filled with his love as we basked in his presence. No mortal being can fulfill the emptiness created by our distance from him. However, the love of parents for their children comes closest. God expects parents—especially mothers, who are co-creators with God—to validate their children through a close and tender love. Like our Heavenly Creator, mothers and fathers mirror great feelings of love to their children. They show them they are lovable and worthy of continued love, and their children rightly look to them for this. With this love in place, children proceed in life, maturing in love by sharing it and accepting it as freely as it was given from their parents. Without this love, children proceed into adulthood in ignorance and try to capture parental love—God's love—with counterfeit and deceptive emotions. Attempts to replace lost parental love by demanding it from somebody else inevitably bring feelings of inadequacy, fear, and eventual rejection. This substitute love may feel satisfying for a time, but in forcing someone else to fill our needs, we only mask deeper desires which are based on the false fear that we are unlovable. This fear creates the need to control other people, to possess them rather than to bless them. Moving from relationship to relationship we hurt and get hurt, and we suffer pangs of loneliness until we finally learn that the only love we can ever possess is our own.

God knows how desperately lonely we are. He knows how difficult it is to develop true love in a world of heartache and mistrust. To help us he has given sources and examples of love. Many of us have been nurtured by loving parents. Some have loving brothers and sisters. Some receive joyful self-sufficient love from friends or religious leaders—love which demands nothing but gives freely. Some find it in a baby's face. Some in the arms of a spouse. Some even in the eyes of a stranger. And many of us find love in the words and spirit of our Lord. When we are ready to start emulating this kind of love in our own beings, we will find sources of it in others.

All of us have chosen trials to overcome in this life, some of them severe. Perhaps the most difficult trial to completely over-come is the lack of affection in early life. When the foundations of our lives are poured without the precious ingredient of love, the structure of our entire lives may grow unstable. If we do not fill that foundation with our own love and forgiveness, we may suffer instability for a lifetime. In the following letter I include the woman's religion because it has given my spirit peace in helping me understand some of my own pain.

> My purpose for writing you at this time is because I have such a longing for Heaven. I am in my seventies and am a Roman Catholic Sister, a nun. My mother died when I was a baby, and I grew up feeling that she never loved me. I suffered much from a stepmother, but not one time did she ever comfort me. My father was a good man; however, I never received love from other members of my family. I grew to become a very sensitive person and I hurt deeply from other's behavior towards me. I have prayed to forget about the hurts I have received, but they do not go away, they just keep coming back.
>
> So, I am asking you to please pray for me that I can continue to do what God wants me to do. How can I get in touch with the Spirit?

I understand this Sister's pain. A mother's love is the mirror to our souls. Without it, suffering can last a lifetime. The word "Momma" is often the last word whispered as the departing one slips from this realm. "Momma" may be waiting on the other side, or her long-lost, or long-deprived, love may simply be the last wish of the departing one. A mother's love comes closest to the pure love of God. Without it, our foundations in life are altered, but we must remember that as developing spiritual beings, we chose the possibility of emptiness for a reason. I wonder how many people have been blessed by the caring actions of this Sister? Have her tender hands, her sensitive words touched people she might not have helped had she had a more loving childhood? Did she sacrifice love in her youth that she might serve in a special way throughout her life? This, my spirit feels, is the reason. A perfect experience for the perfect person for the perfect outcome. I trust and believe that with all my heart.

But still, she suffers. And she still reaches out for love. I pray for her, asking that she finds the power to forgive those who hurt her, to see her life's experiences as God-given, and to allow her own heart the joy it richly deserves by continuing to fill it with love for others—then giving it to them. I also pray that she recognizes the Spirit—one with whom she already is in touch and through whom is transmitted the love of God to our souls.

As we continue our quest for love, we often find it in all the wrong places. Especially when sex is mistaken for love. No greater attraction brings two people together more quickly than the physical desire of the flesh. Some people who are not willing or perhaps do not know how to become more emotionally involved are willing to pay for sex. The only personal investment they can give to a relationship is their money. In a society seeking instant gratification, sex is often a means to an end, a connection where love doesn't exist at all. God has given us the power to consummate our love through the powers of sexual intimacy. However, when we confuse physical attraction or emotional need with love and then engage in sex, we actually consummate the counterfeit. To consummate means to finish or complete. Is it any wonder then that a society that promotes sexual expression in casual relationships suffers from cynicism, mistrust, and broken lives? The sex act without love and oneness is self-based, self-indulgent and self-destructive. Too many people do not know the consequences, or do not yet believe in the consequences, and seek to find love through the giving of this sacred part of themselves.

> I am a very loving man, but it is easy for me to fall in and out of love quickly. Let me explain. There is a big part of my heart that wishes and hopes for love in a marriage, but that would be a big adjustment for me because I am not ready to commit to that. I have had many relationships up to this point, but I feel fear and shame, too, which can have a "wet blanket" effect on a relationship, because I feel in my heart that these relationships somehow are not right.
>
> Betty, how does Jesus feel about one very obvious thing—premarital sexual love? Unfortunately, I never had your luck with having a loving, caring, relationship between a man and woman. Unfortunately, yes, waiting for marriage is ideal, but, especially at my age, there comes a point when things just happen naturally when you are in love. Does Jesus forgive us? I mean, when there are not real feelings of love? I'm in a real conflict spiritually and emotionally over this. It is not ideal, it is very human. Am I supposed to live a "non-loving" existence for moral reasons?

The best vantage point in a letter like this is being the reader and not the writer. Powerful feelings of attraction and physical desire can masquerade as love. This man has come to believe that love is linked to physical and sexual attraction. Therefore his "love" lasts only as long as his attraction. Then he is on to his next temporary passion. This, of course, is not real love but is one of love's counterfeits, which is base by nature. It is a learned behavior that, if not overcome, weakens and sickens the souls of men and women.

In the Bible, Hosea speaks poetically of the confusion between love and lust. After chastising unbelievers for fornication and adultery, he states: ". . . and their abominations were *as* they loved." Love is not an abomination, misplaced sexual intimacy is. In confusing lust for love, Hosea's people were destroying themselves and their nation. Jesus spoke of the need for purity when he said, "For out of the heart proceed evil thoughts, murders, adulteries, fornications, thefts, false witness, blasphemies: These are the things which defile a man. . . ." (Matthew 15:19-20). How does Jesus feel about fornication? I think the Bible makes his feelings quite clear.

Another writer asks, "Does God punish us through love?" No, he does not. However, our distortions and misunderstandings of love can often lead to pain. God allows this pain because he wants us to learn what real love is and what it is not. He wants us to learn that true love, pure love, is giving and sharing without ego. That it is constant, eternal, and unconditional. Through the struggle and pain of broken relationships we learn that, in order to love as God loves, we must first find love within ourselves. One of the most painful yet best teaching experiences we can go through is divorce. Divorce runs rampant in our society as marriage continues to lose its value. Many people discover that life after the honeymoon is not worth sharing. Often, they find that the love they knew was not really love after all, but feelings of emotional and physical attraction. Perhaps a glimpse into some private experiences will help us find answers to this heart-wrenching dilemma.

> I have been divorced twice. I don't know what I'm doing wrong. Is it that I don't know how to love and what love is? When you mention how wonderful and complete you felt when Jesus held you, I long so much for that feeling. Perhaps I don't love myself, thereby not being able to love others. I get so confused.
>
> I have had so many bad love relationships, though not violent or physically abusive or anything like that. They have just always ended badly. I'm always left feeling hurt and empty and not understanding what went wrong.
>
> I feel very selfish asking God for his help with this. There are so many people who have such terrible things happen to them. I'm grateful for so much, but love has always eluded me. It feels as though I am being punished for something I have done. I don't understand this. What is my purpose here? To suffer this life without love? Am I being selfish and shallow for wanting this in my life? Do you have suggestions

on how to feel worthy of love and to love yourself? I have enormous problems of feeling unworthy of most things, such as love, happiness, peace, respect, etc.

I have always wanted to feel the love back that I gave to others. Now I realize it was not so much that I was not getting it, but that some of the time it may have been that I could not accept it because I felt unworthy.

The inability to love oneself indicates that one's love is not strong enough to share with others. We can only give what exists within us. Low self-esteem and low self-worth make ready door-mats for those searching for love outside themselves. Because of the mutation in their own love, many are willing to scrape their feet on the wounded as they enter their lives and pass through. Those who grovel for love see themselves as the problem. They suppose they are not subservient or fawning enough. They lower themselves as far as necessary for love and as a result lose even more self-respect. The resulting anger and pain is bewildering if not crippling. When we place our happiness solely in the hands of others, disappointment is the only possible result.

I have suffered emotionally at the hands of so many people in my life that I cannot tell you all of them. This has left me utterly, ultimately, truly alone. I am very much a loner. Every time I reach out, it seems I get slapped down. My heart has been pretty hardened, but I do seem to have developed some compassion for the underdog. On the other hand, I feel like a snail. I have tried for so many times to love, to give, to care, and I have been turned away.

My parents rejected me as a child, and my first love raped me and abused me. I have had many boyfriends in my life, but the good ones passed me by or I stupidly passed them by. My family and friends have dumped me too. Obviously, I got off to a bad start in life, and the kind, compassionate, sensitive soul I really am inside has become very angry and selfish in order to protect myself. The hurt goes on and on, but I still believe in God and I am trying to struggle for a new life.

I have recently met a truly wonderful man but because of some of his major character flaws, I have not become involved. If I did I would be a darn fool. But he awakened in me the desire to love, to want to be close again, and my heart kind of spilled over with feelings of happiness, just by feeling that loving warmth. It's sad. Seems to be the story of my life. Perhaps, there will be the right man, someday, maybe.

God feels the pain of this woman as exquisitely as she does. But he allows her to suffer, knowing that her struggles will teach her the only sure way to love. And that is to first find love in herself, then to give it to others, expecting nothing in return. As she puts away any thought of *getting* a man for herself and becomes involved in *giving* herself through loving service to people around her, soon she will see the miracle of like cleaving to like. When her heart is filled with healthy, honest love, others possessing a similar love will naturally be attracted to her. She will learn the truth of the irony: the only way to receive love is to give it away.

But how do we gain this healthy and honest love? Some of us were raised in families without love, or in families filled with love's counterfeits. Parents usually mirror the experiences of their own childhoods and perpetuate false traditions. Their children simply reflect what was reflected to them. How do we break this cycle?

In heaven I was taught that complete love exists on three important levels: love for God, love for self, and love for others. On earth Jesus taught this principle when asked what the greatest commandment was. "Jesus said unto him, Thou shalt love the Lord thy God with all thy heart, and with all thy soul, and with all thy mind. This is the first and great commandment. And the second is like unto it, Thou shalt love thy neighbor as thyself." Because of his love for us, Jesus revealed the keys by which we may unlock the love which exists within us. If we truly love God with all our hearts and souls, we will pattern our lives after his words. As we live the universal laws he has taught us, we will grow in light and strength. Then we will be able to discern Satan's counterfeits and walk away from them. If we love God enough to follow his teachings, we will be able to differentiate between love and false love in others. We will love all people with a Christ-like love, the kind that helps others without being seduced by them. This pure, tough love is kind and patient, but it is also protective and honest. It does not allow us to grovel. If we have love for self, we will do things which lead to happiness, which give us light, and which bring peace into our lives.

Loving ourselves does not mean to grow in ego. Rather it means to find greater humility as we recognize our weaknesses and our absolute dependence upon our Creator. Self-love is allowing God to flow through us. It is respect for our own divinity. It is learning to accept who we are with all our perfections and imperfections. As we do this we become open to changing ourselves—not to impress others, but because we are true to our spirits, to who we really are. On the other hand, by not accepting ourselves, we fear change. We become rebellious and develop a self-defeating stubbornness. This inability to accept oneself, this fear of self, gradually makes acceptance from others difficult if not impossible.

Fear of self opposes love of self. They are opposites. Fear of self usually stems from debilitating experiences suffered in childhood. Parents and other trusted adults can damage tender feelings of self-worth through critical words or violent actions. Abandonment and abuse can devastate a child's feelings of worth. The child quickly adopts the belief that he is unworthy of love and so expects love neither from others nor from himself. Feelings of unworthiness lead to anger, emptiness, and a haunting inability to love others. This void creates an emptiness of soul.

> I have been experiencing a spiritual hunger for quite some time and I have asked the Lord to please bring me closer to him, to guide me in my life and to show me how to love again.
> I am a victim of child sexual abuse and was abused all my life and by family members. My mother was an alcoholic,

paranoid schizophrenic, which seemed to run in her family. The abuse also included verbal, emotional and physical abuse by my own father. I have felt so unworthy of God's love, of anyone's love, even that of my husband's. My body felt dirty and my soul lost and empty.

I have known that love is "all important" and I desire it with all of my heart; however, now as an adult, I cannot trust love. I am filled with confusion, anger, depression, and drug abuse. I had thought of taking my own life but did not have the courage to do so.

Your two books were an essential part of the change in me and my journey to self discovery. After reading *The Awakening Heart*, I got with the "right" psychotherapist who guided me, without judgment, on a journey into the depth of my soul. I met the "real" me there, and I also met Jesus. I wanted you to know that I now have found peace and I am finding joy.

And this letter sends joy rippling into my own soul! I have sought out many of my childhood friends and have learned that more than half of them went to early graves, having experienced similar troubles to what this woman shares. Emptiness, abuse, crushing blows of unworthiness: these kill and destroy. We are God's children and are worthy of love. No matter what has been done in the past or who we are today, we are worthy not only of God's unconditional love, but of self-love as well. Criticism may have shrunk our spirits, abuse may have damaged us, violence may have wounded us, but we are worthy of love. We may make mistakes each day, each minute, but we are worthy of love. God knows this and gives it to us boundlessly. When we begin to give it to ourselves by accepting who we are, then by blessing ourselves with small victories, we will gradually gain the power to offer true and honest love to others. Nothing is so great that it cannot be overcome with help from our Creator.

We deserve our best efforts, regardless of past failures. We deserve to forgive ourselves, even as we forgive those who may have damaged us. Too many of us punish ourselves and others for mistakes that God has already forgiven. Consciously or subconsciously we pile the pains of our past on tables before us and feed on them daily, guarding them protectively, hating and caring for them in the same moment. We are part of God. We are made from his love. The purity within us is striving to get out, and will get out if we will stop fearing our weaknesses, hating our enemies, and feasting on negativity. We can accept who we are—the good and the bad—and we can forgive all who hurt us.

Jesus said to love our neighbors as ourselves. Who are our neighbors? When asked this question, Jesus responded with the story of the Good Samaritan. The moral of the story is that everyone is our neighbor, even those different from us. As we give our love to others in acts of service and charity, a whole new world begins to open up.

> I love doing things for others, feeling their joy and love from one little thing that I have done! Bringing supper over, or a pie, or cookies, or watching their little kids for a while or whatever. It makes me feel good about myself to know that I'm capable of making someone feel good! I feel like I'm actually doing something right, and I'm excited to know that I am living a part of my life as God wants us all to! I love life!

Expressing our love freely and expecting nothing in return is the purest form of love. Acts of kindness have more power than we realize. Serving others regenerates the soul and lifts tired minds and hearts. No matter how small, each act of kindness adds energy to the entire world.

A friend recently shared a story about a time when he was helped greatly by a generous woman. He was grateful for the help but felt uncomfortable because he knew he could never repay her kindness. When he finally found the courage to share this with the woman, she responded, "You can pay me back by passing it on to others who need your help." Her reward therefore became never-ending, as did his by following her example. The two now share an uncommon bond of love founded in kindness, honesty, and service. The ripple effect of a single act can last forever.

A Need to Love

Love and gratitude exist together. I've learned this personally as people who don't know me write to express their love. One woman wrote, "I don't know why I'm telling you this, but I want you to know that if there is any way I can help you, and I have no idea how, I am volunteering." I was humbled by her offer, and by many like it. People filled with love want to share with others. In this letter, a young boy is taught a beautiful lesson about love. His story reminds me of the pure love of Christ.

When I was a boy around the age of twelve, one of my chores was to fill the coal bin in the back of the house. I hated the job because it was so dirty. This particular winter evening the light in the shed was out again. While shoveling, I thought I heard a noise in the back of the shed. At the same time, I heard a pop and saw a beautiful glowing light off to my right. The most important thing for me at the time was not to move the shovel or make any unnecessary movements to scare it away. I wasn't afraid, because it was beautiful and seemed to convey a sense of peace and tranquillity at the same time it seemed to say, "Look at me." I saw that it illuminated the floor where it was and it was at least a foot off the ground. While giving me time to examine it, I was surprised to see that it extended outside the wall of the shed. I can remember trying to see the snow it also illuminated. There was a presence that seemed to say, "You will always remember what has happened here." Then, there was a form of energy that started in my feet and ran up my legs. The most important part of this was that the energy ran up both my legs at the same rate and time. It was very prominent when passing my ankles. When the energy passed completely through my body I felt an utter explosion of Love! It must have been very similar to the love you felt when meeting Jesus. Because it was so unconditional, I didn't have to think twice what to do next. I immediately filled up the coal buckets with so much joy in my heart that the bin and buckets were never as full again. I even remember picking up a piece of coal and topping off a bucket and said to myself, no one picks up coal with their hands to top off a bucket! It was all for the love of being able to do something special for my mother, who looked after the coal stove.

The burst of energy described here sounds like the most powerful energy that is produced in heaven. I experienced something similar when I entered the arms of Jesus. It was the explosion of pure unconditional love which lacks all motives that do not include God. There are no words to express the beauty or wonder of it. And there is no experience on earth that even vaguely compares. Love is the source of all joy. As we release it to others, we will find the most soul-satisfying emotion available to us.

Here, a young student attempts to describe the love for Christ that suddenly grew and erupted in him. His expression of love is classic, pure and beautiful, just as in the letter above.

I am a college student and my grandfather died quite suddenly. Not only did I lose a friend, family member, and a man who loved me very much, but I also had to experience the pain and grief of those around me: My grandmother, mother, brothers and sisters, and his friends whom he left behind.

I just wanted you to know that your book, *Embraced By The Light,* has helped me with the closure process. While I still must endure the grief of my family members, I know that my grandfather is in good hands.

While I was reading your book, something amazing happened to me. I started reading and kept going, knowing that at some point I was going to start crying. I felt a tugging sensation in my body, like there was something inside me attached to a string from the outside world and someone was tugging on the string. Tears came to my eyes and I knew that something dramatic was about to happen, but I didn't know what. Being a Christian, I closed my eyes and prayed to God for him to get my roommate out of the room as quickly as possible so I could stop fighting this tugging in myself. I desperately needed some time alone to do whatever it was that was trying to happen to me.

My prayers were answered in about one minute. My roommate left the room; a friend came and got him to go smoke. Once he was out of the room, I continued to read a little more. I got to the part where you were traveling through the tunnel and seeing the light at the end that was in the shape of a man. Then, coming out, you encountered the loving light. All of a sudden, it hit me like a ton of bricks— my eyes shut tight, I gritted my teeth, and every muscle contracted in my body. It felt like someone had taken that invisible string, attached it to the back of a pickup truck, and hit the gas. I couldn't move, speak, hardly breathe. I was filled with such joy and love for Jesus Christ that I was actually PURGING this love in energy from myself. I felt like I was using all my strength to send this love to heaven. Knowing that my grandfather is up there with God and thinking about this during the experience made it even more dramatic. It was the MOST INTENSE thing I have ever felt in my life, but it was not painful or saddening. The only way I know how to put it into words was that I was "shooting my love for Jesus to heaven." I still do not know if it was me sending my love to heaven, or some other spirit interacting with me, and I was wondering if you could help me understand this a little better because you are so experienced with this. Anything you can tell me, anything at all, about this "thing" that happened to me will be helpful.

What a beautiful experience of unbridled love. This young man could search forever and not find the right word to describe his experience. But to call it God applies the highest energy to it, and in my opinion, clearly defines the love he describes. Love is an emotion of energy that unless expressed, remains unseen. It has power to change the universe. It is endless, it never dies. It cannot hurt, it cannot possess, it cannot withhold. God is Love. He created us in his image. And we have the power in the flesh to express love for God, love for self, and love for all humankind. The Apostle John, so loved of Christ, tried to lead us to this understanding. "Beloved, let us love one another: for love is of God; and every one that loveth is born of God, and knoweth God" (1 John 4:7).

Near-Death Experiences

I don't tell very many people about my near-death experience because some people's eyes glaze over, or they look at me like I need to check my marble collection. And I don't want anyone to make light of the experience; it is too serious and important.

It took me several years to talk about my experience to anyone because I didn't think they would believe me and would think I was crazy.

I have told bits and pieces of my experience to friends. On one hand, I feel like they think I'm nuts. On the other hand, I feel a little guilty if I don't tell them, because I think I should share my knowledge so that others may know that Jesus is real. I have not come to terms with this.

In reading the Bible, have you ever wondered what Lazarus experienced? Lazarus lay dead for four days before Jesus came to the tomb and restored him to life. His story is in John, chapters 11 and 12. Lazarus' spirit left his body and went—where? Millions who have experienced what we now call "near-death experiences" know the answer. Lazarus went home. With God, he again experienced the beauties, powers, and love of his former home. He undoubtedly met family and friends and delighted in the glory of eternal peace. But when the Son of God called him to mortality again, he came. Lazarus left the supernatural beauty of his true home to return to the wilderness of this world.

For years I called my near-death experience "my death experience." The term "near-death experience" had not been coined yet. And besides, I had not *nearly* died; I had died. My spirit went to Jesus who confirmed that I had died before telling me that I must return to earth. Death, I realized, was not as final as I thought it was.

Unfortunately for those who leave their bodies, either through death or spiritual experience, and come back, life changes. In the Bible we are not told what Lazarus experienced after coming back except that the chief priests wanted to kill him. We might safely assume that he saw life somewhat differently than he had before. Certainly he did not fear death. His knowledge and love of Jesus was firm as he became a living testimony to Christ. But we do not know of difficulties he may have experienced with family or friends—or with his religion. The truths about eternity he discovered for himself may not have been exactly what his religious leaders had taught him to expect. Today, there are many of us who know from personal experience that it could not have been easy for Lazarus. Coming back presents many challenges as well as giving new perspective and an inner peace.

Upon returning to life we are faced with the problems of telling our experience to loved ones. Some of us have family members who are open to spiritual things and trust what we share with them. Others do not believe us. One young woman writes: "I told my mother and she told my entire family of my incident, and some refused to believe her. Maybe you could tell me how to let go of my fear of telling people about my experience, and whether or not I should even talk about a spiritual experience with others."

Wisdom dictates that we wait for guidance before sharing sacred things. Some people simply do not have faith enough to accept truth that cannot be proved. Acting in fear, some people ridicule us, even cease to be our friends. We have to ask ourselves should we enlighten others with the truth as we know it, or should we consider the revelation as meant privately for us? I believe the answer may lie in recognizing that a war is raging on mortality's battlefields for the souls of God's children. Satan, the destroyer, and God, the Creator, stand as exact opposites—one seeks our captivity and downfall, while the other seeks our freedom and eternal progression. Each of us is part of this war. We can help build up either side. When we refuse to share universal truth for fear it is too sacred, we give Satan the advantage of all the ammunition. He is spreading lies each fraction of every second, and we must be willing to stand against his lies by spreading sacred truth. We must witness from our private lives what truths we have received and thus open ourselves to whatever consequences lie ahead. This is a holy war between darkness and light, and just as darkness remains in the absence of light, ignorance and fear remain in the absence of truth. As long as our spiritual experiences remain fearful little secrets, people will continue to live in darkness for the lack of them. They will remain skeptical that God can and does perform miracles.

What does plain wisdom dictate? It dictates that truth is powerful and can heal or can damage depending on how it is used. When I came back from my experience I knew that I was to share it with others. Initially I told my family, then later close friends. When I was guided and directed by the Spirit, I shared it with the world. I know with all my heart that I followed the Spirit's voice in writing *Embraced By The Light* and in sharing it with those whom God had prepared. I have never once been anything but confident in sharing it. Nevertheless, each person who has been given eternal knowledge must individually pray for wisdom in knowing when to share it. No advice is more meaningful or powerful than God's—even if it seems to go against what you have traditionally been taught.

Through the ages, millions have experienced death then returned to talk about it. In their experiences are found common elements such as seeing a tunnel-like opening that draws the spirit into the next world, or feelings of extreme peace and love. But there are also differences from one experience to another. Instead of a tunnel, some see darkness with a point of light in the distance. Others make the journey in a type of elevator or walk up a beautiful staircase. Some people return before reaching the end of the journey. One person wrote: "All I saw when I arrived in what I call a tunnel was darkness, except for my father at a distance in a dim light telling me the time wasn't right for me to be there, and that I had to go back."

Many people simply hover above their bodies observing and listening to those around them, and some never fully leave the body at all. The woman who writes the following had been in the hospital for an angiogram. Doctors were looking for blockages in her heart when she began bleeding internally.

I was in a great deal of pain. I felt as if I was losing consciousness as I heard someone say, "We're losing her! We're losing her!" I was so exhausted, and even though my body felt as if it weighed a ton lying on the bed, I felt the top half of me begin to rise up. The heaviness of my body was still lying flat on the bed, but part of me felt as light as a feather. I no longer felt any pain. Before I could enjoy this feeling, I felt an injection in my neck and it was painful. At lightning speed, I felt as though I had been slammed back into that heavy, painful body. I was extremely afraid. I screamed twice very loudly and begged for someone to help me. At this moment I was terrified of dying. I believe my spirit or soul, if you will, was preparing to leave my earthly body at one point. It concerns me that I was so terrified at this moment. And when I related to my husband how you had felt free and happy when your spirit left your body, he said perhaps I did not go to the level you did, therefore I was afraid.

I can fully sympathize with this woman. When I returned from my experience, I felt confused and agitated. Existing half in and half out of the body is distressing, even if it lasts only a short time, but it doesn't mean that something is wrong. This woman simply didn't complete the transition from mortality. Had she fully separated, she probably would have felt the same serenity and freedom that most feel when free of the restrictions of the body.

Some people return from a near-death experience, or NDE, aware that much had happened but unaware of the details. This letter comes from a woman who had her NDE during childbirth:

> Immediately upon coming out of the anesthetic I began to remember the tunnel with the light at the end, and how when I reached the light it burst very brightly around me. And then I must have had a glimpse of God, because I came back thinking or sensing I had been with God and had learned all the answers to everything, and I knew God was real. And even though I could not recall any of the answers, I had more faith in him than ever before.

This NDE may have become both a blessing and a trial to the woman—a blessing because of her expanded faith but a trial because of its tantalizing but sketchy details. But such experiences, whether fully remembered or not, are meant to help us grow closer to God. We will recall only that which is necessary for us to remember from our NDEs. Because of our individuality, each of us needs different experiences. Some have had multiple NDEs in their lives, and each has been unique.

The diversity of NDEs can be explained partly by the analogy of people traveling to a foreign country at different seasons of the year. Each would come back and report on their individual experiences, and we would hear different details about the same country. Each would have visited different people, experienced different weather, gone to different cities, seen different sunsets, heard different voices. Some may have experienced paradise there, others may have spent time in jail. In a limited way, you can see why NDEs can be so varied.

I was told that most of what I saw and heard would be removed from my memory, that what remained would be necessary for me to remember when I returned. I was also told that over time it would serve a greater purpose for me to begin recalling some of those things that I had forgotten. This seems to be a common factor in many NDEs: rather than dimming with time, the knowledge gradually illuminates, expanding and clarifying. In some cases, the details and clarity come back all at once and at unexpected moments. One such experience is related in this beautiful letter:

I saw you on the Oprah Winfrey Show that aired on January 3, 1994. As I watched the show, a similar experience I had some years ago came back to me. I had forgotten some of the facts until you started talking about the garden. Then it all came rushing back to me.

I had been sleeping and was dreaming a very frightening dream. I don't remember what the dream was, but knew that I didn't like it. I felt a pain in my chest over my heart, and it was then that I felt the air leave my lungs and I floated into a sea of blackness. I knew that I was moving but did not know where or in what direction. There was a light, but I can't honestly say it was at the end of a tunnel. I was totally surrounded by blackness. There was no doubt in my mind that I had left where I was, and that I was going somewhere.

In the distance I could see a little pinpoint of light. As I drew nearer to the point of light, I could see clouds and a huge castle-like city that was bathed in brightness. I was approaching the light and was near the city when a man appeared floating on a cloud. I can remember his clothing as an ivory-colored robe with a wine-colored sash. He looked just like the traditional Jesus figure we in Christianity have come to know. He was the source of the light, and I noticed that he spoke to me without moving his lips. His words were gentle, almost a whisper, and they were heard but not with my ears. He wore a big smile, and I was totally at peace the instant I saw him. He was the obvious source of all the universe and somehow I knew it. He wasn't, however, demanding that I bow before him, or mean or judgmental in any way. I was totally in awe.

He told me it was not my time and that I would have to go back. I was concerned that if I somehow screwed up my life in the meantime, I wouldn't be able to return to this beautiful place to be bathed in this wonderful light and fantastic peace. I wanted to stay so badly. He said that no matter what happened that I was saved and that I would return to him someday. He smiled and my heart melted. He took me into a garden and I remember the color of the place and I, too, saw the river of life and saw the fruits on the trees. I was told to take some fruit and eat it, and I did, and it was the most delicious thing I ever put in my mouth. I was touched by his kindness and most of all by his faithfulness to me. I am an insignificant little blip on the earth, and yet he knew me and loved me. He cared. He really cared about me!

Reports of NDEs have captured our interest and imagination because they help us to understand two things that concern us most—life and death. Many people fear death and are looking for something to ease their minds about their own inevitable passing or that of a loved one. They are searching for something to remove the uncertainty and fear of the unknown.

The following provides some details about death. The man involved experienced his death almost as an observer at first. Then he was taken from his body before feeling the pain of death. Brought into a heavenly place, he was given information necessary for the healing of his physical body, then was sent back to mortality. God gave this man a precious gift. Although we may not know why he received it, we can be sure that there are reasons for all things. God's purposes may be mysterious to us, but they are simple and clear to him.

I was looking forward to going hunting on the 98-acre farm that my family and I lived on. My wife had already left for work. I usually called her before going, but being in a hurry on this particular morning I didn't.

I had about a two mile hike to my tree stand and arrived there around 10:15 am. My stand was about 20 feet high on the front side facing a thick patch of pines. The back side faced the river below and dropped off to huge boulders in the river below. I tied off my rifle to be pulled up after my climb to the top and began my upward ascent. I reached the top and positioned myself to pull my rifle up. Then without warning I heard a snap! I fell 80 feet into the river below.

I knew this was the end for me and though it was just seconds before impact, I felt as though the fall was in slow motion. Many thoughts raced through my mind. My wife, my daughter, my family, and no one knows where I am! Would I ever be found? Then, came total darkness. How long this darkness lasted I don't know.

Then something wonderful happened! I felt myself leaving my body. I was floating a few feet in the air above the river. I looked at my body with mixed feelings. I was bleeding from my mouth, nose, ears, and saw a trickle of blood underneath me on the boulder. As I reflected on the state of my body I felt a pulling and began to rise very fast! I began traveling at a high rate of speed upwards through the atmosphere.

I looked back and could see the earth. Such a beautiful site. It was so brilliantly lit. As I looked ahead I could see the planets. I thought to myself this cannot be. Where is Jesus? I was never told anything like this could or would happen when I died.

Faster and faster the speed was increasing! I saw other star systems and galaxies as I raced onward! I entered what seemed to be a hole of some sort. It was long and dark. However around me I saw streaks of light made up of every color in the spectrum. I saw a faint light growing brighter and brighter in the distance up ahead. As I entered the light I felt it all through my being. I was not afraid anymore.

Then suddenly I was standing before a massive set of steps. They led up to what seemed to be a bridge or walk of some kind. In the distance I saw a sight so magnificent and astounding! A city made up of what seemed to be glass or crystal. The lights were of many colors that radiated from it. Never have I ever seen such a sight. I began walking toward the city in a daze of unbelief. So many questions raced through my mind. I had to know where I was. What was happening to me?

I reached the front of the city and saw a double door that looked to be about thirty feet or so in height and width. It shined as if it was polished. As I stood there wondering, the doors began to open. I took a step back and looked inside. I could see what appeared to be people walking about on the inside, much like they do in a mall here on earth. These people though were dressed very different. For one thing they all seemed to be dressed in some sort of robes with hoods.

I entered through the doors in amazement at what I was seeing! The inside was massive. It seemed to be square in shape, with a balcony all around that led down to different levels. I walked up and looked downward over the balcony. It seemed to go on forever. When I looked up, I saw many people passing by me, yet no one seemed to notice me. Then one approached me and suddenly stopped. He slowly raised his head and I could see his face.

He appeared to be human in every respect but one. His eyes. He had no pupils. Yet they seemed to change colors in shades of blue. His hair was snow white. I wanted to speak but before I could he turned and pointed to a long hallway. Though we never spoke I knew I was to go down this hallway. Then as if nothing had ever happened, he continued on. Something beckoned me forward. I walked a long way down to the end of this hallway. I did not turn to the right or the left; I only went straight ahead. I knew somehow that my questions were about to be answered.

Again I saw before me a massive double door. It seemed to be of some type of metal—whether gold or not I could not tell. Suddenly the doors opened. I heard a voice, though not as we speak, but from inside of me; it seemed to say, enter. I did as I was told and the doors shut suddenly behind me! I was afraid for the first time. Total darkness. Total silence.

Then after a space of time the length of which I could not determine, a bright light began to glow in the room. Brighter and brighter it became. It was somewhat above me and in front of me. I tried to look but was almost blinded from it. I held my hands up in front of me and could make out the appearance of a figure sitting on some type of seat.

Then without warning it happened!

"What have you done with your life?" The voice penetrated my very being. I had no answer.

To my right I saw what seemed like a movie, and I was in it. I saw my mother giving me birth, my childhood and friends. I saw everything from my youth up. I saw everything I had ever done pass before my eyes! As my life played out before me I tried to think of good things I had done. I was raised in church and had been very active in church functions, yet as I pondered on this I saw a man in his car that had run out of gas. I had stopped and given him a lift to a local store, and bought him some gas because he had no money. I thought to myself, why am I seeing this?

The voice was loud and clear. "You took no thought in helping this soul and asked nothing in return. These actions are the essence of good!"

I saw all the people I had hurt as well and was shown how my actions had set in motion the actions of others. I was stunned! I had never thought of my life having an effect on the actions that friends, family, and others I had met would take. I saw the results of all I had done. I was not pleased at all.

I looked on until the events came to an end. Indeed I had done so little with my life! I had been selfish and cruel in so many ways. I was truly sorry that I had done so little.

Then again loud and clear I heard the voice speak again. "You must return!"

I did not want to return though. I was content to stay and longed to stay even after the things I had seen and heard. "I have so many questions," I replied, "things I need to know but don't understand."

"You must return and help others to change by changing your life. Physicians will want to perform surgery on you. Do not let this happen! If you do, you will never walk again. You will be visited by one who will bring you answers to the questions you have. When I call, you will come again. You will recover from all that has happened if you do these things. Look and see what lies ahead!"

I turned and saw the earth in a turmoil! Wars and death, terrible sights! Cities fell and new ones were built! I saw the United States and a volcano exploding covering many cities in darkness! I looked on and saw the collapse of our government as we know it. People killing for food and water, horrible sights! I saw what seemed to be a giant explosion in the earth's atmosphere and much land was destroyed! I looked on and saw a new type of people, younger and of a peaceful nature. The cities were few that were left, but these people seemed to be content.

"It is time for you to go," I heard again! I wanted to see more but the doors opened and I felt myself almost being carried down the hallway. I passed through the doors of the city and felt myself shooting through this hole I had come through. Faster I went, unable to stop! I entered the atmosphere of earth and saw the river below. I saw my body still lying there motionless!

Then it was like an electric shock so tremendous I felt my body jump! I opened my eyes and saw the trees above and the skyline. Then, Oh God, the pain! I was struggling for every breath, choking on my own blood.

I managed to roll onto my stomach. This pain was all I could bear. I looked at the sky and saw that the sun was lower than I remembered. I looked at my watch. It was 5:30! My only thoughts were how could I get help. I noticed my rifle was not far from me, still attached to the rope I had tied around my waist. I began pulling it toward me. I managed to grab hold of the barrel and pulled it up to me. I fired a shot about every ten minutes hoping someone would come.

It was getting late and I knew I would not make it much longer, so I began crawling on my stomach, pulling myself with the stock of my rifle. I managed to crawl up a trail that ran down to the river. It was thick with brush and briar patches. As I crawled I became tired and wanted to give up, the pain was so great I passed out many times. I knew though I had to make it, at least to where I could be found—I hoped! Finally, I saw the road that I lived on, and I could hear sounds in the distance.

"Yes, thank you, God," I thought to myself. I began a feeble cry for help, but being too exhausted I just lay there in the road.

My father-in-law was returning from work and found me lying there. "It's all right," I heard him say, "help is on the way."

That was the last I remembered until I saw the lights inside the ER. A doctor stood at my feet.

"Can you feel this?" he said.

"Feel what?" I asked. He had been sticking my feet and legs. I was paralyzed.

"We cannot help you here son," he said. "We are sending you by ambulance to a hospital that will be able to handle your injuries."

Whether from the pain or medication I went out like a light, until the next afternoon I awoke to find two doctors standing at the foot of my hospital bed. They introduced themselves as my attending physicians and proceeded to explain to me I must undergo surgery at once. The broken bones in my back were putting pressure on my spinal nerve causing paralysis.

Then I heard the warning I had heard before: "Do not let them perform surgery, or you will never walk again!"

I understood completely, but knew they would not. I told them I must see my wife and daughter first.

My wife arrived with my daughter shortly after the doctor's visit. I told her what they had said. She advised me I must realize they were doing what was necessary to help me. I did not know how to tell her what I had experienced. I told her it was my "belief" that I should not be operated on. Although she disagreed, she honored my wishes.

When the doctors returned and I told them of my decision, they were very upset. I listened to lecture after lecture.

"OK," one of them said, "if you never want to walk again that's up to you!" Then they left.

That night I lay upon my bed and wept sorely. Was I insane? What was I doing?

A light began to fill my room. "You will be well," I heard a voice say. Then it was gone. I composed myself and dosed off to sleep.

Months passed, then one morning I felt a tingling in my feet. I was overcome with joy! I told the nurse I wanted to get up and walk. She stared at me and said, "We'll see, we'll see." I knew I was healed without a doubt.

The nurse put a call into my doctor and the next morning he stopped by. "So you think you can walk?" he said.

"Yes," I replied.

"Well, we will see."

A few hours later I was taken down to the physical therapy room. They carried me down and raised me up to a vertical position. The nurse helped me in front of a set of parallel bars. I gripped the bars and placed my feet firmly on the floor. One step. Two steps.

"My God, he's walking!" the nurse said to the other nurse who had brought me down.

The next few days were hard. I took many trips to physical therapy and had numerous X-rays done per my doctor's orders. My wife and family were all amazed, yet, I knew! I had been told! The rest had to be true as well.

My doctor was more amazed when he found no bones pressing on my spinal nerve. I quote him: "This is not normal. It seems a higher power has done for you what we were going to try and correct with surgery. I have never seen anything like this before."

Since that day my life has changed and I have been able to help others in ways I never dreamed. I wanted to share this, as it is what has led me onward in My Quest for Truth!

The power of our Creator confounds the wise and opens the hearts and minds of those willing to receive his truth. He comforts us with the knowledge that he is in direct contact with us, even when things appear bleak. He prepares us for our future, and he loves us so much that he will not allow us to experience more than we can bear. "O death, where is thy sting?" (1 Cor. 15:56).

Another experience confirms that death need not be frightening or painful. At the age of thirteen, this young lady went with her family to a lake. While swimming, she got caught by an undertow. She called for help and struggled to get free, but the undertow finally pulled her beneath the surface. As she went under for what would be the last time, she was in a full-fledged panic—until something surprising happened.

Minutes before, I had been frantic to get out of this cold, dirty water, but now I floated downward with no desire to struggle. As I slowly sank into the dark water I felt completely at peace. I had no fear. I am unsure if my eyes were actually open, but I could see. I looked upward and saw what appeared to be floating green leaves and a bright light almost like sunlight, even though it was a very cloudy day. Still, I was seeing this bright light and it made me very happy. Then my aunt rescued me, and just for an instant I felt really angry with her for having disturbed me. As I reflected on that moment later, I thought how odd that I would feel my aunt had "disturbed" me rather than rescued me.

Similar stories are common to those who go through NDEs. During my experience, I was told that in the process of dying, our bodies release our spirits before the pain becomes unbearable. Our physical shell might appear to be in pain to those watching, but the spirit is free and already at peace. In bringing this knowledge back with them, those who have experienced death bring a peace to others. This knowledge of freedom from ultimate pain allows many of the rest of us to live life more abundantly, without fear of dying. This is only one more reason those who have been to the other side need to continue sharing, letting truth ripple into the lives of others. Each of us needs to open our hearts and minds to the beauties beyond this life. The woman who shared the following has found a way to use these truths into her everyday life:

When I was fourteen years old, I experimented with drugs and was rushed to the hospital after having a bad reaction. I can remember having a hard time breathing and the doctor yelling at the nurse to get something. Then the next thing I knew, I was in the corner, up by the ceiling, and I was looking down on myself lying on the table. The doctor was yelling to get the crash cart, and they put paddles on my chest. The next thing I saw was my father standing next to the table behind the nurse, and he was crying. I never saw my father cry before. Well, this made me extremely upset! It didn't bother me that I was dead, although at first I didn't know that I was dead because I didn't feel any pain or fear. As a matter of fact, I felt great!

I can remember the room getting very bright. I also remember I wasn't alone in that corner of the ceiling. Behind me there was a woman with a pale blue robe on. The only thing I could see clearly was her hands; they were older hands, maybe of a woman in her fifties or sixties. She put a hand on my shoulder, and I could tell she was telling me to go with her, but I didn't hear the words. All I could do was look at my father crying. I knew I couldn't leave him like that.

I can remember that warm, safe feeling of being in that bright, soft light, and that I was so happy that the woman was with me that I didn't want to stay in mortality. I wanted to leave that room and not look back, but since my father was crying, I was so torn.

The next thing I knew, I woke up with tubes down my throat, and my father yelling, "She's back," and crying, "Thank you, God!"

Before that point in my life I never really believed or disbelieved in God or Heaven or Satan. I guess I believed when you die you get buried and that's it. I thought earth was Heaven and Hell, depending on what you made of it. I do not believe that anymore. I believe there is a Heaven.

I, like you, believe there is now a reason for me to be here. I don't know what it is.

I am now a nurse and work with the chronically ill. I try to help them in their final moments by holding their hand and letting them know they are not alone and never will be alone. With most of them, just being there holding their hands and talking calmly with them gives them a great sense of peace. Some have told me that they were scared, and I tried to reassure them that the journey they were going on would be the most beautiful, comfortable journey they could imagine.

For the ones who could comprehend what I was saying, I would briefly tell them my own experience. I would tell them I know it sounds crazy, but I truly believe it to be the truth and that when my day comes I would hope they'd come to receive me, because they were special in my life here on earth and I'd like to see them again when I leave here. They always promise they will come see me again.

As this story beautifully reveals, the most valuable blessings of a near-death experience are not in helping us understand death, but in helping us live life more completely and lovingly. As one reader said, "I expected *Embraced By The Light* to be about death. Instead, it gave me a profound understanding of life."

We are here to learn how to love, and it is not surprising that love is the essence of most NDEs. As another nurse relates:

I can still cry to this day when I think about how I felt when I was going towards the light. I have never experienced such love and warmth. It was as if I was surrounded by peace and the most wonderful love anyone could ever experience. To be engulfed by that kind of love is the most beautiful experience that I can imagine.

Another woman writes:

The light was the whitest thing I had ever seen in my entire life. It was brighter than looking into the sun. The light was so beautiful and peaceful. I felt free and warm. I felt as if a ton of bricks was taken off my body. I felt like I was floating and there wasn't a worry on my mind. I felt peaceful and free in spirit, and nothing could ever make me unhappy. I felt like I could never be hurt or be unwanted.

A veteran policeman who experienced the light after being shot in the line of duty describes it this way:

I had a feeling of such great peace that I never want to forget. It was like the greatest day you ever had, the most exciting instant, the greatest moment in your life. Now multiply that feeling by the largest number you could possibly imagine—even infinity—and then imagine having that feeling forever. Wow, what a feeling.

But, of course, feeling immense love is only a part of these experiences. Many also learn how the Spirit works with us as it shows us the way to help others.

A little over a year after reading *Embraced By The Light*, I had my own out-of-body experience. I had a reaction to

175

some medications that ended up knocking me unconscious. I went into a place of total peace. Indescribable peace. A place of humor. And ultimate knowledge.

It seemed to me that I was in some kind of white room, with my guides surrounding me. I think there were three. They made it known to me that I had not really died, that I had just fallen asleep to the reality of the earth. They said that the reaction to the medicine was not an error but a preconceived plan made long ago in order to impute in me knowledge necessary for the rest of my journey on earth. I then was able to ask them questions, and they would not only reveal the answers, but also their source. I found out about things I had no interest in before, but somehow these things would be revealed to me while they were answering my other questions. To this day when I hear someone ask a random question, something that they wonder about, out of nowhere I blurt out the answer, not knowing previously anything about the subject.

I learned about my family, why I had to go through the hell of my childhood, why I had depression and why God let me go through them. It was amazing. I heard heavenly music that made the music we hear on earth sound like two notes going up and down repetitiously. I learned that music is one of the greatest sources of communication that we have here. Music acts as some emotional translator that enables us to experience and prepare for emotions we may have not quite experienced before.

One of the most fascinating things I learned was that there are experiences that happen to us every day that are necessary to prepare us for experiences yet to come. For example: My whole life I have always noticed single shoes lying in the middle of the road. Have you ever seen this? You're driving along, and off to the side of an esplanade you might see a tennis shoe, a boot or some high-heel shoe. I often wondered how these shoes got there, and where was the other shoe, not to mention the owner? After my experience, I saw a shoe in the middle of the road and instantly remembered being told about "everyday experiences preparing us for things to come." I also remembered that one of the things that has always been "a clue" about life for me, was that single shoe.

The purpose for me is simple. When I see that shoe, my spirit is instantly being prepared for someone who is about to walk into my life, someone who needs some kind of encouragement. In other words, I am to hand them the lost shoe in the form of a word or words that will benefit them. Now that I am aware of this, whenever I notice a shoe now, I prepare myself by praying that God will help me to purify my spirit and give me energy to do the "special encouragement session" I am about to encounter. I then look for the person, and sure enough within a day I find that person. They can be anyone from a stranger, to someone I work with and even someone in my family. If they have a soul, that's all that I need to see. My holy spirit alerts me and the conversation somehow, just happens.

Now it is almost a game for me to look for the everyday clues that life brings to each of us. I always get a kick out of it. The other benefit to this realization is that I can always tell when I am spiritually regressing. The clues are less evident and the people sent to me come to me less in number.

There was so much more made known to me, but I think a lot of it was stored somewhere in my subconscious mind. I was not allowed to remember because God knew that I still needed to experience my own personal growth as long as I am bound to the earth. The most important thing I know, I guess, is to remember to constantly be looking skyward and not to be deceived by the binding ability earth has on us in the form of our egos.

Weeks after my experience, my feet didn't touch the ground. I was so incredibly happy. I was loving with everyone that I had contact with because I COULD SEE THROUGH THEIR PROBLEMS and often know just the right thing to say to get them to a higher place. It was amazing. I felt as if I was acting out Heaven on earth.

Being in the Savior's indescribable love banishes all fears, all heartaches, all pain and suffering. There is no greater desire in the hearts of those who have experienced it than to do everything possible to experience it again.

When I returned to my mortal body and the challenges it brought, I also returned to the many challenges I had faced before.

Spiritually, I had grown beyond any previous understanding, but this spiritual growth had created new and greater challenges. Since then I have learned that many with NDEs have suffered the same fate. We all know that returning to mortality means facing the adversities of life again, but also it means facing the challenges of new faith and new knowledge as well. This new faith and knowledge often comes without any instructions or parameters. Questions we never considered before now float through our life daily. And as we seek the solace of our experience, letting the reality of it fill our mind again and again, we may begin to feel guilty for having had such a life-changing experience. Feelings of unworthiness begins to creep in when one has experienced God. We ask ourselves, why me? But answers don't come. What comes is just the unyielding reality of the experience itself.

I fully empathize with people who suffer these feelings. In continuing with a letter quoted earlier, we can see how deeply the feelings of unworthiness can become.

> I am an insignificant little blip on the earth, and yet he knew me and loved me. He cared. He really cared about me! The question that bothers me most is, why me? I am really not worthy. I am a non-entity with a really bad job and no self-worth. I am not particularly good-looking or dynamic in any way. I don't have a lot of friends, or for that matter, relatives. I was a poor Catholic and have done some things in my lifetime that I regret. That is the question that bothers me most—why me? "Why" eludes me. Why he chose me to take this marvelous journey is a mystery to me.

Over the years this is perhaps my most persistent question as well: why me? Since no answers have readily come, I used to wonder about my usefulness to God. For years I reflected on my NDE, learning how to accept it and how to live with it. Sometimes, during depression—my darkest hours—I became convinced that I had let God down and that he should have given the experience to someone else, someone who could speak more eloquently, someone emotionally stronger or perhaps more admired and known in the world. Instead, he gave it to me. Although I came to accept his will in this, I will not fully understand his reasoning until I go home to him again. Until then, I will always do my best to live up to the promises I made to him, because nothing could pain me more than to return to him knowing I had let him down. No hell would be hot enough to burn away the pain of that disappointment in me.

As one wrestles with the enormous questions of an NDE, depression can set in. You feel isolated and almost helpless with all the knowledge—both of this world and the next. And at the same time, there can seem to be no apparent purpose for your experience. In 1973, I didn't know that an NDE was possible. Later I discovered others who had been through similar experiences, and I began to feel less alone. Just knowing there are others is healing. Here is a woman who describes her depression and her yearnings to feel heavenly love again after her NDE:

> After reading your experience, I feel we share the same bond, as I also had a similar experience. I, however, was not as fortunate to come back with the recall of the experience as you did, but I could relate to a lot of the same type of "feelings" you had. The most important part of your experience to me was the depression and the "not wanting to return." What you said about it helped me enormously and, in short, this is why:
> I went into the hospital for an operation and the operation which was to last only four hours instead took six. During this time I had the life/death experience, but it did not end with me waking up after the operation, for I was in a "waking-coma state" (as it was explained to me) for at least two more weeks. I was in the "light" during most of this time, with only a few brief waking moments. When I finally came out of it, I was depressed and very angry that I could not stay on the other side. I have carried this depression and anger with me now for almost five years and I kept wondering what was wrong with me and how was I going to get my life and feelings back to "normal."

Then I read your book and saw that you also went through similar feelings, and that I was not alone, that I was not lost. I have realized that there must be many of us who have had this experience who are depressed, who are angry and/or sad, and who did not want to return.

I came back a stronger individual. But why I came back, well that is still a mystery to me. I would have preferred to have stayed "Home."

Right after coming back to my body, the love I felt in heaven still surrounded me. As time passed, nothing else in my life gave me greater joy than to recall this love. Soon, because I lacked the ability to draw my memories of it back to its fullest strength, I fell into deep depression. I needed to discuss these things with someone who understood, but no one was available. Then it became impossible for me to live each day in a normal fashion. I almost felt rejected by the light—as though it were trying to shake me free as I tried to cling to it with all my might. I learned that the light is life and that its absence is death. I continued to draw on my experience for comfort, replaying it over and over in my mind, bathing in the love I remembered, trying to absorb again all I could. But soon it was not enough. My spirit desperately wanted the fullness of that love again, the tangibleness of Christ's embrace. But no one on earth could fulfill that. Frustration settled upon me. I felt isolated and so sorrowful of heart that I could hardly bear it. As waves of grief swept through me, I would weep alone for hours. My prayers became lamentations of desolation, and I wondered, "Why, God? Why have you abandoned me with this? After awakening me to you, to the love, what am I to do without it?" God knew my longings and heard my prayers, but in his wisdom, he allowed me to learn patience and solidarity in my own convictions. In time, I became strong— stronger than I had been before. And now in the confidence of my knowledge, I share the truth of God without fearing its loss, without feelings of abandonment. As this message of Christ's love ripples out, I know that waves of joy and peace will follow.

I've never written to an author before, but I felt such a strong need to share this past week's experiences.

My husband is a truck driver, so he is not home often, in fact, so little that I pine for him. Our love will get us through this rough time. My aunt is chronically ill and lives with us. Her days are very numbered. This past week my husband's elderly parents, my sister, and my father and his wife came for a week's visit.

Anyway, it was crowded and we had the best fun we could ever have. The second day my sister mentioned hearing about your book and wondered if you wrote it just to make money. I had a near-death experience in 1984, but talked of it only lightly to her. I went and bought her the book. She would read a page or two and stop to talk about it, so I picked it up and read some, and then went back to the store and bought them all the book.

While together, we didn't all finish it, but we spent hours discussing it. It was a comfort to me—I knew you really had the experience—so many today just want to be on TV and make money by copying, not experiencing. In discussing your book we learned that our father had an experience but could not talk of it until then because of extreme fear. He found an inner peace that we literally watched come over him. If nothing else wonderful had happened, this would be more than we could ever have hoped.

But the ultimate is how you touched my sister. She has a lovely seventeen-year-old daughter, who has not been well from conception. Doctors wanted her aborted from the beginning, and her illnesses have been heart-wrenching. She is dearly loved, and we have always wanted her. As a small child she would tell us she played with us in heaven, that she chose her mother and father, and while most children have imaginary playmates, she played with God. When you have such an ill child this is very frightening—she was never dissuaded from her beliefs, but she was given counseling and guidance by doctors and psychiatrists as a measure to satisfy us that she was not also slightly unbalanced by so much happening to her body. She also told us of angels taking her on trips—it was a long list of things—and we now know how special a child she really is. We knew she was special before, but your book confirmed that belief and gave us a new understanding.

But my sister is healed, finally. She was always a very religious person but by the time her daughter was about ten years old, she stopped going to church—stopped her teaching, even stopped discussing her religion. Well-meaning people caused this who kept insisting that if she prayed hard enough and long enough, her daughter could be healed. Since her daughter could not be healed, she felt tremendous guilt that she was not a good enough person to have her prayers answered. If her prayers couldn't be answered, she wasn't good enough for heaven, therefore she wouldn't be with all of us in our later times. I never knew of these depths of loneliness, of how truly bleak she was until we read your book. Now she is healed! You gave my sister her life, her greatest peace. There are no words to tell you how much I love you for that. I can think of no greater mission in all the world than that in one week you touched seven people right here in my home. You gave us peace.

My own near-death experience was because of my attempted suicide. I found peace in the experience, but was told by others that I was mistaken because God could not forgive suicide. I did doubt my experience a little because of this. Now I know it was as wonderful as I remember it.

Thank you, my dear woman, for so much love and peace. I wish we had before and after pictures—I do believe it was something you could physically see, like a sparkle or lightness or something.

I apologize if I sound crazy. I don't think I am—I'm just overwhelmingly happy.

I have never doubted my experience. It is truer than anything else in the world to me. If I had to draw a comparison—life on earth compared to my experience in heaven—earth is like death. We are like shadows of what is real, vapors of a greater reality just outside our reach. For us here, life has yet to be experienced.

In Chapter Two, I quoted a letter from Joanna Camp, the widow of paleontologist, Charles Camp. She spoke of three

NDEs he had before finally departing from this life. These experiences brought him closer to God while revealing his true mission in life. After these experiences, he revealed to her the higher or greater reality of life on the other side, as opposed to life in the flesh. Another excerpt from Joanna's letter speaks of this:

Charles was taken to Paradise, just as you wrote in your book, Mrs. Eadie. In fact, he described it almost with your exact words. He saw majestic mountains there, too, a river, and such gorgeous flowers that there are no proper words to describe their beauty, he said. A large golden-colored poppy caught his eye. He bent down to look into it, and it appeared to have a glowing liquid flowing through its petals, like liquid gold that flowed. Everything in this paradise vibrated with life, he exclaimed. As he walked there, he could actually hear the "life" in every plant, tree and flower. Their sounds were crispy, exciting to the senses—and these sounds of life caused him to feel even more alive. The air itself seemed to nourish him, healing his soul until he felt whole in every way. An invisible, loving presence was at his side through Paradise, he said. This presence explained that this paradise was not far from earth—that it was in another dimension and was a healing place for souls that have gone through a long, painful illness here and for those souls who had suffered great, traumatic events on earth. Each one was allowed to remain there for as long as they desired and needed to be there. He learned also that love is the greatest force in all of God's universes. That love is the "key" that opens up heaven for us.

Charles was also given knowledge of God's plans and purposes behind all he is doing. He learned that everything God has ever done and is doing makes perfect sense! His works are indeed totally perfect in every way. He also said much, much more.

As we enter the Awakening which takes place before the coming of Christ, more and more people will be filled with knowledge of the truth. People with and without education will come to see that faith and love are crucial components to any healthy soul. In the years to come, a polarization will occur. Those seeking spiritual truth will be on one side, and those fearing its consequences will be at the other. Many have written letters to share knowledge from their own experiences. One woman even claims to know the end of *my* story. Perhaps she's right.

I couldn't wait to get to the word processor and tell you the end of your story.

Like you, I had two near-death experiences. Both last year. While I was in the hospital receiving chemotherapy I left my body twice in three days. I will try not to bore you with the details, just a short description of what happened and then I will open another door for you and give you information you were either not told or have not remembered.

I was lying in the bed watching the fluid drip into my veins, when all of a sudden I felt the hand of God rip me from my body and throw me to the ceiling of my room. I was startled to say the least. A booming voice yelled at me and said, "I have no time to explain, the host is dying and we must leave now!" I found myself looking down on what I perceived to be the ugliest thing I had ever seen. It was like I was looking at a slimy piece of debris that had washed up from the ocean's depths. I kept saying to myself how repulsive this thing was, but still my curiosity got the best of me and I got closer to it. I couldn't believe my horror to find out it was my shell of a body I was looking at. Well, it was right then and there I decided nothing in Heaven was going to make me return to that repulsive thing.

The voice returned and it was very soft this time. It said, "follow me." I don't remember how we got out, but everything in both your books happened to me just as if you had read my every thought and prayer. I wanted to tell you, and I am elated and goose pimply in typing this, the end of your story. Here goes and I hope as a part of God you believe me.

The last thing I was told and shown was: God told me that he was awakening all of his oldest followers to help the others prepare for what was going to happen soon. Do you know anything about the big bang theory? I know enough to tell you that God is going to do just the reverse; he showed me he was going to take back everything good into himself and repel what was left. I don't think anyone was excluded from being taken back into the oneness. I saw it happen and suddenly I remembered being told we are all a part of God. We are literally tiny fragments of the whole and it is getting ready to reform itself.

I hope this door to the future helps you in some profound way. Just like you, I am so homesick, I can't stand most days. I don't know why I am here either. I was given the choice and shown what would happen either way. I chose to come back, but the reason was taken from me. I pray every day that God will reveal his reason to me or that I will just achieve it on my own. I want to go home and be one with God again.

Who knows, maybe this is why I came back—to refresh your memory!

We are fragments of God! Yes, this new friend has refreshed my memory and my spirit. If we do nothing else with the rest of our lives but learn about God and how we can return to him, we will have accomplished a pure mission.

The greatest miracle of an NDE is not the restoring of the body to life, but the restoring of the soul to life, to remembrance. Christ restored Lazarus to life after four days, but the greater miracle occurred later. Lazarus was simply a type and shadow of something even more wonderful yet to happen. He became a reminder of eternal life, which God promised all who live in him. In speaking with Martha, Lazarus' sister, Christ hinted at this greater miracle: "I am the resurrection, and the life: he that believeth in me, though he were dead, yet shall he live: And whosoever liveth and believeth in me shall never die" (John 11:25-6). This is the great secret, the great miracle, the great truth. Real life does not exist in the body, but in the Spirit. Yes, we may live in mortality, but life, as God defines it—as he lives it—exists in the Spirit. Christ is not just the resurrection of the body, but of the soul as well, lifting us when we are down, healing us when we are sick, raising us when we are dead. He is our life and light, both here and hereafter, and if we will live in him, we will truly never die.

Earth and all that lives on it was meant to be terminal. We all live here in that condition. It is not how or when we die that is important, but how we live. Our expression of life determines our state of being in the hereafter. To fear life is to fear God. And there is no reason to do that when you understand the truth about him. In the Bible it states that "The truth shall set you free." Freedom to live life abundantly and with joy can be a reality when we live *in truth*. As many have learned from their near-death experiences, we are here to become more like the Creator, to learn to love as he does, and to prepare for the eternities yet to come.

The Eternal Connection

My beloved husband of twenty-six years died twelve years ago. The day he was cremated, he came to me—just a flutter that I felt late at night as I was trying to get to sleep. He kissed my forehead and said, "I'm okay," and was gone. That gave me immeasurable strength.

My beloved mom died three months ago, and I'm devastated and broken-hearted. She, like your mom, died after a very courageous battle with cancer. Her incredible strength, bravery, zest for life and most of all love is what now carries us through this excruciating time.

Which brings me to why I am writing. I am so interested in knowing what Mom's life is like now since we can no longer physically communicate with her and what her experience with death was like.

Loving families lay the foundation for our eternal progress. They help us build strengths, identify and overcome weaknesses, and bring challenges of their own for us to overcome. They significantly influence us in our earthly missions and affect how we influence others in their missions. Every family bond—with spouse, children, parents, grandparents, grandchildren, in-laws, aunts, uncles, cousins, etc.—can play a crucial role in teaching us how to love and be loved.

In the pre-mortal life we bonded with those who have become our family members and friends. Heavenly Father helped us select husbands, wives, children, and friends. Our spouses were precious to us in eternities past, and our marriages were made in heaven. Some of us experience love at first sight here, while others take longer to make the connection. But our spirits recognize our eternal mates at some level and they compel us to complete our promises to join for life. Agreements of trust made in the pre-mortal life are thus fulfilled here.

We enter mortality individually at birth, and most will leave it individually at death. Our time of returning to our Creator was known and agreed to before we came. But from the perspective of life on earth, our season with loved ones is shorter than we desire. When a loved one departs, the loss can devastate us. We feel suddenly incomplete, as if part of our being, has been torn away. When a friend's mother died, her father said, "Bury a part of me, because a part of me just died with her."

No emotional trauma distresses us more than the loss of a dear one, and so a proper understanding of death is vital to our emotional and spiritual well-being. Loneliness tests us to the breaking point and can lead us into despair if we let it. However, knowing where a loved one goes after death is important to our healing. It comforts us, as does the knowledge of an eventual reunion on the other side. Loss is natural and important to the growth of our spirits.

Knowing the truth surrounding death liberates us from fears which can hinder our progression. Sometimes we are concerned that a loved one suffered or was afraid at the end. We may feel guilty because of our helplessness in preventing the death or the suffering. But grief and guilt are alleviated by knowing that suffering is part of our plan and that God does not let us endure more pain than our spirits can withstand. When we reach the other side we will learn that each death experience is an important factor in our spiritual development.

Death is a divine event and is attended by angels and guided by our loving Father. Prior to the moment of death, the dying one's spirit is in contact with God's love. The release into death is made when the spirit is ready to leave the body and move to the next realm of development. This transition is like a birth into the next life. As we pass over, we will be greeted and welcomed joyfully by loved ones waiting there. Knowing this, helps ease the transition for everyone.

> About two months before my husband died of prostate cancer, he woke up one morning, and the first thing he said was, "I didn't want to wake up. My dream was so special and beautiful. I was near a thrashing machine—instead of rice coming from it, music came from it, the most beautiful music I have ever heard. There is not or never has been anything like it."
>
> I used to sit near him and cry because of his condition and because I could not even help him, other than do the best I could to make him comfortable. I would tell him I didn't want him to leave me. I didn't want to be left alone. This was his answer: "I will never leave you. You will never be alone." These are the words that keep me going.

He was right, we will never be left alone. Never. Sometimes we distance ourselves, but when we are ready and if it is needful, we can feel the presence of departed loved ones.

The question which people ask me most about death is whether our departed ones can hear us and see us. A woman who lost her brother and nephew in a car accident writes, "Can my brother still see us—see how his family is suffering? Can he hear me when I talk to him? How do I know?" Another reader writes: "Can I talk to my mom either mentally or out loud and have her hear me, or must I send messages through God or angels? Does she know how much we think of her daily and how greatly we miss her? Can she know or see everything about us and what we're feeling or doing?"

Our bonds with loved ones continue after death as they began long before birth. The love between us is eternal and does not cease simply because we cannot see the departed. Those who have passed to the other side are very much alive—more so than ever—and they are able to comfort us and send us their love. But they are also bound by laws which govern our lives and which limit their free contact with us. Yes, they care about us, about our lives and our welfare, but they must not interfere with our progression in life. Fulfilling our life's mission requires exercising our free will. Those who have returned to heaven cannot meddle with that. Only when deemed necessary through Godly wisdom can they come to comfort us or to prepare us for events in our lives. For our part, we can pray for them, just as they might pray for us. We can speak to them too—either verbally or in thought—and our words will be heard by them or be relayed to them. They have their own work of progression and are just as occupied with it as we are with ours. They do not remain continually in our presence; rather, they busy themselves with important and engaging activities that are known only to those on the other side.

Many ask if the deceased can help us cope with their loss, and yes, they can remain nearby for a time. They stay to give comfort and sometimes are called to serve as guides or guardian angels to those left behind. Many, as related in the following letter, simply come to give an assurance that all is well and then return again to their heavenly home.

> After Mom's death I prayed for her to let me know if she was happy. After a few days had passed, she did. She appeared to me glowing and appearing to be quite happy. I was so glad to see her in such joy because she suffered deep pain upon her death.

Many letters offer evidence that God often allows the departed to speak peace to those who remain. Sometimes these precious spirits speak words which help a loved one prepare for the future. On occasion they may even touch us physically as is beautifully illustrated in this letter from a mother who lost her infant son.

I was blessed with a spiritual experience I will never forget. The room began to grow lighter and lighter, until a brightness surrounded the room. I was aware of the feelings of warmth from the spirit and an overwhelming feeling of love.

As I gazed in the light I noticed a gathering of people around my bed. Standing before me were hundreds of people, all wearing white robes and smiling at me. A voice from above their heads called down to me, "Mammy." I listened carefully, and the voice again called, "Mammy." I was curious and questioned the significance of such a voice.

I was then reminded of the day my son, who at six months old, had lay dead in his cot. With a broken heart I wrote his obituary and had misspelled mommy as "mammy." I knew that this was indeed my son who had left me six years previously.

He "floated" down until I recognized a distinct shape of a young man, in his early twenties, who knelt before me upon my bed. As tears rolled down my face he spoke to me, through our minds. No words were used, I mean there were no spoken words; his lips did not move nor mine.

He went on to tell me that he had been given permission to come and visit me. He told me of six children that were yet to come to me. He told me I had been given three of them as special gifts, given to me to love and cherish and teach. He praised me as he was happy for the choices I had made and reminded me that he loved me dearly. He comforted me by saying that we would be together again one day, and that the spirit world surrounded us, and I was to take comfort in that fact knowing that he was always with me. He smiled and told me he had to go, that he had work to do, and that he was very busy. Pointing to the people who stood around my bed, he said they would come back and visit me and he would also, but that he would not always be able to come with them.

I cried at him leaving me again, and tears began to roll down my face rather quickly now. He reached out with his hand and tried to wipe the tears that rolled down my face. I could not feel his hand, but I did feel something. I tried to touch it and it felt as if my hand was a glove over his, but I knew it was not a physical hand that I could feel, it was spiritual. He began to "rise" upwards and I reached out for him. My grief was reborn. I did not want to be without him. It was then that I felt the most amazing feeling of love ever. His hand touched mine again and as we joined hands, our fingers entwining, I felt the warmest feeling overcome me. The feelings of love intensified and I felt complete. I have never felt love that strongly before, and I felt happy at the thought of him leaving. It was the brightest, most glorious feeling ever, and for that moment I thought, if this is what it feels like for two spirits to be united, then what rapture must we feel in love when all the spirits of our brothers and sisters are united together.

The memories this letter evokes in me! I weep again while reading it, remembering the oneness available to us on the other side. The sweet oneness we feel here is but a dim candle to the bright, warm feelings of unity and love there.

Sometimes departed ones communicate with us through dreams. One woman who suffered anxiety over her brother's death shares this experience:

At the time my brother died, he was starting to question Christianity. He had always been such a gentle soul that his new opinion of religion really shook me. And then he died so suddenly. So I was so worried about his afterlife.

Then one evening I had a dream about him. The only one I ever had. I had gone to heaven and was standing in front of elevator doors. As they opened, there stood my brother. He was never one to smile much here on earth, but now his face just glowed with such peace and happiness, and his smile is something I have always remembered. He told me there were many levels to heaven and that because he had just slipped in—which I took to mean he had called out to God in the last moments of his life—he was to work there in heaven. He said not to worry, he was very happy. He told me the more good you do and the more love you show earns you higher levels in heaven. I never dreamt of him again.

Another way beloved spirits communicate is by sending small but significant signs. This letter gives a touching example of how departed spouses can assure their mates that they remain in their thoughts and hearts. Some might say the sign this widow received is hardly dramatic proof of her husband's love—but her husband knew it was all the proof she needed.

After twenty-nine years operating a wrecker, my husband's left hip and knee were causing him a great deal of pain, and even after getting some relief from his doctor, he decided he'd had enough. He said, "I'm going to take an early retirement at sixty-two and draw my Social Security."

The last day he worked was in May. In June he had a heart attack. In July he had a stroke. And in August they found out he had lung cancer. In October he died.

After his death I would go out to his grave and say, "Oh Lord, if I could just hear him say one more time, 'I love you, and I'm happy and I have no more pain,' then I feel like I could go on with my life." But one evening while I was standing at his grave, I said, "Lord, please just give me some kind of sign that he's happy and that he loves me."

And, Betty, this sparrow flew in and landed on top of his monument, not one foot away from me. It turned its little head and looked right at me, then flew off toward the hills.

I said, "Thank you, Lord," and left with happiness in my heart.

I went home and told my oldest daughter and her husband about it. Two weeks later my son-in-law and I went out to mow my husband's grave and cut the grass around his flowers. My son-in-law had taken his camcorder with him, as he wanted pictures of the grave.

While he was taking the pictures, this little sparrow flies in, lands on the blue artificial flowers, and I said, "Bill, do you see that?" He said, "Yes. I'm filming it." The bird hopped off the flower, hopped all around my husband's monument, back on the flowers, then flew off toward the hills.

When we got back, my son-in-law told my daughter what had happened and that he had filmed it. But when he put the tape in the TV, we could see everything he filmed, but not the sparrow!

Jesus said, "Are not two sparrows sold for a farthing? and one of them shall not fall on the ground without your Father. (Meaning without God's will)... Fear ye not therefore, ye are of more value than many sparrows. (Matthew 10:29,31).

What a wonderful and appropriate way to let his wife know that he still lived and loved her. Signs can come in infinite ways and often draw upon the joint memories and experiences of those involved. Special music boxes may play without being wound. A favorite chair may rock. A lost picture may suddenly reappear. In special ways known only to the loved one, departed spouses reassure their wives or husbands that they are remembered and that all is well on the other side. Signs or symbolic tokens offer comfort without the difficulties associated with visual manifestations. Direct contact with departed spirits may frighten some in the midst of grief. It may also intensify their longings to the degree that they refuse to let go. God wants us to move on, and our departed loved ones want the same. They want us to live every moment of life to its fullest using every opportunity to grow to our fullest potential.

Sometimes communications come to us through promptings and inspired thoughts which may come from the Spirit of God or from our loved ones acting under God's influence.

> My father's death was a great loss in my life. He had a massive heart attack at home. As they were taking him in the emergency room from the ambulance, I recall holding his hand. Before I released him to the doctor I whispered in his ear, "Follow the light, Daddy, it will be OK." I knew at that moment that while Daddy was with us physically, his spirit had passed.
>
> His comfort is still on my mind, and I miss him deeply. I became extremely depressed and lonely. I neglected my family as I grieved. Three months later, I began getting out of the house.

I truly believe that my daddy felt my grieving for him because I received a message from him to study about angels. That lead me to the library. I looked in the index and came across two references regarding angels. One of the references happened to be *The Awakening Heart*. That was the book that brought me back to life.

We are never alone. God or his angels are with us, attending and guiding our daily lives. But their efforts are usually imperceptible, and for people who desire obvious contact from a loved one, the apparent silence can be frustrating. One woman writes: "I wish my mom would give us a sign that she's okay. Why doesn't she? I pray for it repeatedly. I know she would if she could. What does her silence mean?" Another woman asks, "Why can't I dream of Dad? I miss him so much, but he doesn't come to me."

Prayer is always the best form of communication with the spirit world. God hears us and sees that our messages are conveyed to loved ones if necessary. To receive his answers requires open minds and hearts as well as faith in his will. Likewise, to receive a message from a departed spirit may require openness and faith. Grief can block the channels through which divine or spiritual communication comes. Powerful emotions such as anger or confusion deaden our spiritual senses and prevent words, thoughts, or visions of spiritual beings. Our motivations may also prevent spiritual communication. Do we want the communication for reassurance, or for other more prideful reasons? Perhaps we doubt the reality of life after this life. Or perhaps we doubt that God exists and require a sign before we will believe otherwise. The Bible says that signs "follow them that believe" (Mark 16:17), not them that doubt. Since God knows exactly what we need for our learning and growth, we should ask for nothing without praying also for his will to be done in our lives.

Sometimes we simply need to ask God for help in letting go. By clinging to a loved one, we may prevent him or her from moving on. That spirit is held back from its transition to the spirit world. The woman who wonders why her mother will not give her a sign, also writes this:

> We're all devastated by her death. After three months, could she still be here in spirit, helping us get through this excruciating time? Do I need to reassure her we'll be all right, so she can go on to the loving welcome awaiting her? A minister told me I was the reason she was experiencing such a lengthy death—because I was holding her back by not accepting her death and not "letting go." Is this true?

People who love us are usually willing to do anything to lessen our pain—even while they are dying. A spirit may choose to prolong the experience of death—though this may also prolong its suffering—in order to give loved ones more time to prepare. After death, the spirit is keenly aware of the grief in family or friends. It may choose to linger in its transition until after the funeral in order to comfort those left behind. Once the funeral has passed, the spirit usually feels a great need to move on, and we should let it go. We should accept our new circumstances as best we can, praying continually for comfort and guidance. God will grant us all we need.

When I experienced my death, I wanted to be with my family one last time before leaving this earth. My spirit traveled from the hospital where my body lay dead, and I entered my home. As I viewed my husband and children, I felt love for them but no concern. They were not aware I had died, but I had no desire to speak to them. And I knew they had no need for me to remain— alive or dead—because God showed me they would ultimately be fine without me. They would mourn for me, but since mourning was natural, this did not bother me. In time they would go on with their lives, and I wanted this for them. I felt free to go on.

God grants to each departed soul the experiences which will serve them best as they make their transition through death. Our Father's goal is to help them move on, to bring them home to him. Though their departure brings us pain, we should consider their needs above our own, and perhaps a sense of their joy will come through to our hearts.

But even when we are able to let loved ones go, we still care and are desirous to know about their new circumstances. "If I were to see my deceased dad," writes one reader, "would I know him by his looks, or would I feel inside that it was him?" Another asks, "How do relatives find one another after spiritual changes in appearance?" And a fourteen-year-old girl whose mother is fighting a crippling disease asks, "When someone dies with a disease or is crippled at the time of death, do they stay crippled when they're up in heaven?"

These questions are common when people believe in an afterlife. Our deep love for deceased family members prompts a natural curiosity about their conditions there. Picturing them as they might appear now, brings us comfort and lends hope for a loving reunion. Some people live their entire lives in crippled or handicapped bodies, and many look forward to an existence without these limitations. But I believe everyone has imagined what life is like without the restraints of the flesh. I can personally promise you that such a time is coming.

Immediately after my death I learned that our spirit bodies are composed of light and are filled with energy and love. As more love enters us, our spirit increases in brilliance. Some spirits have internalized so much love that they radiate enormous light. Spirits are easily influenced by thought, allowing them to change appearance. When loved ones appear to us, they usually take the form we last recall—in some cases even wearing the same clothes we last saw them in. In other cases— as with the mother who saw her infant son—spirits may resume their original adult stature from before this life. In the case of the crippled mother, she will not be crippled still. The flesh may have been handicapped, but the spirit is whole. Some who see Jesus see the wounds in his hands and feet, reinforcing in their minds and hearts the truth of his sacrifice and divinity. Others see no wounds. When I saw him, I did not look for the nail prints in his flesh. But when I questioned Jesus, he told me I did not need to see the evidence of his pain to know who he was.

As spirit beings our loved ones are not subject to gravity or aging. They can move at the speed of thought, and their thoughts can take them anywhere. As they release thoughts that bind them to earth, their spirits quickly recall their divine nature, and they are filled with love and become more youthful and radiant.

Of course, no two spirits are exactly alike. Even on earth identical twins have distinct spirits and personalities. So it is in heaven. Each spirit has its own expression, its own unique disposition and character. Our loved ones recognize each other not by physical appearance alone but by the "countenance" or "aura" that emanates from them and projects their true nature and identity. The daughter of the crippled mother would have no problem identifying her mother. Even if her mother's spirit body appears younger and in perfect form, the daughter would recognize her instantly, and I am sure with great joy.

My father passed away one year before I wrote *Embraced By The Light*. In a vision of him afterwards I saw him scoot across the floor with his walker, much as he had done before dying. He glanced at me, smiled, then set the walker aside and began walking. I was filled with joy as he communicated to me that he was doing well. In a later vision I saw him running, and again my soul leapt as I saw him laughing, carefree and joyous. In reflecting back on my life with him, I could not recall seeing him run before. A third vision came during the time I was writing *Embraced*. I was cooking dinner one afternoon when I turned and saw Dad standing in the hallway. He motioned for me to follow him, so I did. He led me down the hall into my bedroom. He looked young and handsome, about forty. He was no longer bent with age but stood erect at his full height of six-foot-three. His face beamed with excitement as he pointed at the computer I used for my writing. Cheerfully he said, "Betty, I love what you are doing here!" Then he was gone as quickly as he had arrived. His appearance gave me all the strength and encouragement I needed to complete my book.

I think back on that vision from time to time, just to feel close to him. The feeling he gave me remains to this day—a feeling of hope and anticipation, of missions being performed and completed. I treasure the knowledge that he was still with me, and that others I have loved are mindful of me and are available—at our Heavenly Father's bidding—to help me when the need arises. I know with perfect clarity that they are *back home*, helping me, praying for me, anxious for me to finish my mission and to complete my promise to God.

You too can take comfort in knowing that your family members—perhaps from many generations back—are aware of you and are guiding you at times with unseen hands. God shares out the work of raising and watching over his children. His work occurs at many levels to ensure we are never alone. Knowledge of his plan tells us that our deceased loved ones are indeed our loved ones still. Though our mother, father, child, sister or brother may die, our love for them does not. By this we know that the bonds of love do extend between earth and heaven. By this we have hope and even assurance that family connections are enduring, even eternal.

Yes, families *are* forever.

Suicide

I grew more and more despondent. . . . I had to die. It was the only way.

Over the years since the release of *Embraced By The Light*, I have received letters beyond number from those who have wished to end their lives. The heart-breaking pain in these tear-stained pleas for help has opened my eyes to the extent of suffering in the world. And it makes me marvel at the Creator's power to heal the deepest wound when people turn to him for guidance. Remembering God's immense love, I am filled with conflicting desires when I read these letters. I want to gather the writers into my arms, hoping that if they cannot feel God's love for them, at least they might feel mine. I would tenderly hold them until they felt a portion of that heavenly, healing love that I felt in the arms of Christ. On the other hand I also want to shake some sense into each one, like a loving mother or sister with mixed emotions, jarring them into understanding that suicide is not the answer. God never gives up on us—and neither should we.

Our Father sent us to earth that we might develop our spirits and learn to express them in this strenuous, demanding world of flesh. We wanted to come even though we knew there would be trials. God set the stage by allowing our adversary, Satan, to frustrate us. His efforts test our endurance and our faith. He places fear, guilt, and despair into our hearts by whispering lies to us in an attempt to weaken our hope and resolve. We give place to these lies when we listen to them. If we listen long enough, we begin doubting our own divinity or God's reality. "There is no God," he might say, which is one of his favorite lies. Or, "God does not care for you now that you are a sinner." Or, "You have nothing to live for. . . . You don't deserve to live. . . . You can't take it anymore. . . . There is no way out." He surrounds us with these lies, and in this environment of negativity, his words begin to sound reasonable. We start believing them and allow them into our minds where they accumulate, and soon, dark desires for death enter our hearts. Nothing could please Satan more.

The thing to do is not to listen. Regardless of the troubles we face, we should ignore these lies. This way, our spirits grow stronger, our faith deeper, and we reach the next higher level of growth and ability to endure. But each level has its own exam. And only God knows what it takes for a person to endure the test of a mutated and wounded spirit whose imbalance produces a driving force toward death.

I think often of the valiant soul's that have come to earth during our most troubled times. These spirits were selected by God because of their level of development and closeness to him. To them the veil is kept thin, that they are more aware of truth that all too many have forgotten here. These elect spirits are prepared from the beginning to administer to the earth, to bring it new life and energy, hope and love during the time we need it most. They are more sensitive to love—or the lack of love—because they retain in greater measure the experience of being loved by the Father's unconditional love. Their sensitive souls yearn for this love and for the peace and acceptance they experienced in heaven. While the pain of this loss can be devastating, it can actually strengthen their beings if they will let it. But unfortunately, because of their sensitive natures, these souls, more than others, are sometimes tempted to take their own lives. Their feelings of despair go deep because of their passionate spirits. Earth's treasures mean little to them and they become depressed for the lack of heavenly surroundings. They crave the love that they recall subconsciously that cannot be found here, although, they desperately seek it from people who surround them. Not finding the quality of love they seek often drives them into despair and brings them to take their own lives. These sensitive souls are our youth—the best, saved for last—who innately are stronger than most. We need them, and so we must warn them that it is not God's will that they die young. But rather that they endure the hardships of life— as they surely are able to do—and rise up to meet the challenge of restoring to earth the love they are so willing to give their lives in search for.

I speak to the youth, yes, you . . . *The* Elect. You must mature to your calling. You must help bring about the changes that are so necessary in healing this world. The older generation is steeped in tradition, but with love, *your* love, you can make a difference. Little good it does for your families to bury you. You flee from pain only to reap more of it on the other side as you face the disappointment of having quit before you began. Our world needs you, you are our hope. You can bring about change.

What God creates and nurtures, it is Satan's nature to diminish and destroy. His effect is to make us feel worthless, to get us to enter the cycle of self-destruction. When we feel worthless, we remove ourselves from God. When we remove ourselves from God, our reason to live weakens. As our reason to live weakens, we succumb to despair, then eventually we may join with those who made us feel worthless in the first place. Thus, the cycle spins ever downward. In effect, negativity claims its own—those who give it and those who receive it, both parties embracing misery and self-hate.

A sixteen-year-old girl perfectly describes the effect of lies in her life as she writes: "I almost took my own life away because of its worthlessness. You see, Betty, all my life I have been told that I was no good. First, by my family, and now by my friends." Though the adversary did not personally speak these lies, his energy plainly produced them. His energy opposes God. Sadly, this girl's situation is a common one. Those closest to her—her own family and friends—created this negativity, paving the way for despair and possible death. Tragically, they can only give what they themselves have internalized from their own lives. But this young girl does not have to accept the ridicule. No one does. Our divine worth remains untouched by lies no matter how discouraged we may feel. I saw clearly that each life is precious in the eyes of God. Each soul, weak or strong, humble or proud, worldly or pure, is treasured beyond compare by our Creator. I also saw that every spirit, no matter how deeply deceived by lies, has the ability to reject the lies. This girl will overcome and will grow again when she finds God. So it is with everyone.

But not every despairing person finds God, and too many make the irreversible choice to end their lives. When they do, they affect more than themselves with their pain. Families and friends grieve with the tragic question of guilt, wondering if they could have prevented the suicide. The ripple effect can be devastating. One woman whose brother-in-law killed himself writes: "We've all had a million questions about why it was his time, why it was God's will that his own mother find him, and how could he have been so close to his family and yet hurting that much, and was it us who failed him?"

We come to mortality with a mission in life and with our days known and agreed to. However, our free will is held sacred and inviolate. God will guide us, but he will never force us to follow the plan we agreed to. The choice is in our hands to pursue life to its natural end or to sever it prematurely. We should never consider suicide as part of God's plan for anyone. Suicide is the result of a mind or a spirit that has become ill. It is the ultimate act of one who has already withered and died inside. God always provides the means for healing, but some—when in the right mind to accept help—tragically choose against it. We should recognize that both physical and emotional factors can combine with a dysfunctional spirit to allow negativity to grow in a person. In most cases we will never perceive all the factors that lead to a suicide. God alone knows the secret parts of each soul.

The writer of the letter above wonders if it was God's will that the victim's mother find the body. When I was in heaven, I was told that there are no coincidences, that certain events are orchestrated for reasons known only to God, but that they are always for our ultimate good. Knowing this, and recognizing the traumatic effects of finding the body of one's own son, I can only believe that God's will was involved in the mother's painful discovery. It is part of her mortal experience now, part of the struggle she must work through in learning something for herself, or, in teaching something to another.

The legacy of a loved one's suicide is a heavy burden. It encumbers the spirits of those left behind with grief and guilt and may poison the memories they had of the one who died. The person taking his life blindly disregards God's precious gift, the gift of life, as well as the love and the needs of those left behind. One woman whose husband committed suicide writes: "I kept on blaming myself, and never once did I forgive myself or my husband for leaving me like this." The person who commits suicide lashes out in pain as if to say, "I don't care what God or anyone else thinks or feels. I don't care about life, I don't even care about me." Family and friends are not considered, sometimes not even thought of. A suicidal person becomes myopic, caring only about the pain that he is eager to flee.

The factors which compose these spiritual and emotional illnesses seem to be increasing in the world, especially among our youth. This teenager found life so unbearable that he prayed for God to take his life:

When I was fifteen, I became suicidal. The only time I found some relief from life was when I was praying—it was peaceful. After a time the only thing I prayed was for God to take me. Well, he didn't. I became angry at him and more desperate for relief and decided I would just do the job myself. I was in my room one night when I made the decision to go into the bathroom and swallow many bottles of pills followed with alcohol. I felt very calm, feeling that at last I would be with God—no more pain. I never got that far. In fact I never got to leave my bedroom. As I walked toward the bedroom door I collapsed on the floor and immediately felt surrounded by warmth and light. I was lying on a white marble floor surrounded by very tall people that seemed to glow from within. They never opened their mouths when they spoke— they just smiled as they "talked" with me. At first I thought I was home free! They told me that I was not dead but resting in my room. They said that they did not want me to kill myself but that I had the freedom to do so if I chose and they could not stop me. However, I would not "escape" like I wanted to—that none of us can run away from our problems. They said it was like a school here and that if I didn't want to finish certain lessons this time here, I would eventually have to learn them somewhere else and that it would be better not to run but to call on God for help. I was very angry and upset. They said, "We won't lie—things aren't going to get better anytime soon but they will eventually, and you should hold on." I knew absolutely that they were telling me the truth. I wasn't angry anymore, just a little sad. They told me that I was not alone. Once again, they projected such a pure honesty and love that I knew they were right. As things turned out, they were right. Things did get harder, but in my heart I felt very strongly that I had companions watching over me and that God was truly with me. Over the years, life has continued to get better and I live in the world with less fear and more faith everyday.

There is no escaping our problems—as this boy learned— because they arise from the needs of our spirit. Our "problems" are actually gifts. They are opportunities for us to understand and to overcome the weaknesses in our souls. By leaving this world prematurely we do not leave the problems behind; we instead take the source of them with us. In the eternal march of progression, we put off the chance to overcome adversity until another time and place—a place we may have originally dismissed in favor of this one.

We should view each problem as a tool for refining and furthering our growth. In doing this, we embrace life to its fullest. By seeking lessons for good from every trial and by wanting to endure, God will turn our weaknesses into strengths and make of our lives miracles of growth and ultimate joy. However, to fight this process, to seek to end it because of our problems, is to fight God's efforts, which only increases pain and despair.

What awaits those who have given in? Or as one writer puts it: "What happens to souls that have died by their own hands?"

I learned that some who commit suicide realize their mistake as soon as they die, and that when they call out to God for forgiveness and help, they will receive it. As they accept God's will and learn to forgive themselves and others, God's love penetrates them more deeply, bringing them to a higher degree of heaven where they will continue their progression. During this process, our prayers help these people by adding our love to their environment, which aids them in accepting the love and truths of God. And, of course, our prayers are beneficial to our own healing as well.

Sometimes in the course of life we make wrong choices, and in the wisdom of God, he may arrange the circumstances to let us try again. His love is unconditional. This is the greatest, most prevalent truth in existence. We did not come to earth to earn our way back to him. We came to experience and develop that which had existed in us through the "eternities." But the right to make mistakes, even the right to discontinue our development lies within our own hands. God knows the limits of our ability to be tried, because he knows each of us perfectly. In his justice and wisdom he may even grant to some who take their own lives another chance to make better decisions. The near-death experiences of those who return from suicide have a profound impact on their subsequent lives. Our Father has determined that these people can endure more, and that their torment in having "failed" in life would have proven detrimental to them in heaven. Or, perhaps he knows they would be more useful to the rest of us by being given a second chance. In any case, God blesses them with exactly what they need when they return. Angie Fenimore's book, *Beyond The Darkness*, and Sandra Rogers' *Lessons from the Light*, relate many such experiences and give great examples of God's higher plan for those who return from suicide.

For those who prevail in taking their lives, we must accept that God's will was not to give them a second chance, or that they refused it. In this case, God has accepted their right to die prematurely. In doing this, he also allows greater challenges for those who are left behind.

Our Creator understands the pains of this life. He lived it too. Through his omniscient knowledge, he makes perfect judgments. He knows who we are and exactly what we need at every moment of existence. His love is so complete that the only souls who do not receive it are those who do not want it. But, eventually all will accept God and his Son who paved the way of life by bringing back the teachings of love. We can endure in this life because he is with us, caring for us, helping us to realize our potential. Asking for his help is a sign of strength that our spirit wants to live. Asking for his will to be done is a sign that our spirits want to live in him again. When we feel alone and have lost *our* will, we can turn to God, and wait for *his*.

A woman wrote who had endured seemingly every challenge imaginable and had come away stronger for them. But then her youngest son died and her marriage fell apart. It was too much. She felt she could go no further. After several failed attempts at suicide, she decided to jump from a hotel window. She describes what happened next:

> I took the screen off the window. Below I could see the cars going by and people walking in and out of the hotel. The lights were twinkling, and it was a warm spring night and the breeze felt good. It would be good to die. I crawled through the window, sitting on the ledge five stories up. In my mind I imagined myself falling. I knew I could do it. All

I had to do was push away. I put my hands on the ledge and rocked back and forth.

As I shut my eyes to jump I suddenly visualized my remaining son. I opened my eyes. What would happen to him if I died? He had been through so much. I thought, "Did I have the right to do this to him?" I had to live. I had to live for him. I came back inside the window and fell to the floor crying, until I exhausted all my anguish.

I began going to church every morning. I prayed to God to help me. I told God that I couldn't continue to live like I was and begged the Lord to help me. I said, "God, I've really messed up this life you've given me. Please, Lord, take it over. I'm ready to let you be in control."

It took a succession of tragedies before this woman turned herself over to God. Then her life began to change. She eventually found wonderful love and joy—not in others—but in God and in herself. Once she completely accepted God's will for her, she freed herself from the effects of her misfortunes—the sexual abuse of her youth, an abusive marriage, failure to provide a "normal" life for her son before he died. Guilt and perceived failures had smothered her spirit, but now they were gone. Vanished. God's help had been there all along of course—all she lacked was to need it bad enough to allow it into her life. She concludes: "I found that as long as I am still alive I have the opportunity to change, to be forgiven and to live life as God intended: happy and fulfilled. God forgave and healed me, a manic-depressive, suicidal, scarred, bitter, and very lonely person."

The road back from darkness is seldom easy or quick. Daily effort is required to stay on course, but a whole new world awaits at the end, if we persist. As we pray for help and stop thinking so much of our own misery, seeking instead to serve others, we will find peace in our souls. This service, combined with self-forgiveness and faith that God has already forgiven us, will renew us in spirit and grant us more energy to pursue the opportunities before us. God is never away. We can reach him. And when we accept all he intends for us, we find new beginnings of personal happiness.

While working on this chapter, I received the following e-mail from a young woman who was happy to allow me to include its message here. It perfectly demonstrates God's movement within our lives and how he uses the most unusual ways to bring us comfort and understanding. The chapter, "David Stone," in *The Awakening Heart* is a favorite of many readers. David's life moves people and helps them understand God's strength and love. This letter about another David offers a different perspective on that story:

My brother David committed suicide in 1994. After David took his life, I began to receive "signs" that puzzled me at first, then later they comforted me. Things actually began to happen a couple of months before he took his life. David's wife was killed in an auto accident. Then my best girlfriend's brother died the day I was told about David's death. It was then that I started looking for and asking David for signs. Any sign that he was okay. I was on my porch and when I saw a black shadow of a bird, I felt that to be a sign, although I questioned this because of it being black. Then I saw a puddle of water, and in the puddle was a reflection of a bird, again, a black shadow of a bird. Hoping to figure out what kind of bird it was, I was patient. Later, I was walking down a hall where I work as a teacher's assistant, and right in front of me was a wall covered with pictures the kids had made. Each picture had two birds cut from black construction paper and underneath it read, "Brother Eagle, Sister Sky." I then believed the type of bird I saw must have been an eagle. Later I had a few pictures of David I borrowed from my sister. I looked close at them and noticed his belt buckle had an eagle on it.

Next, driving home after David's funeral, a song began to play on the radio that told almost in detail the circumstances of my brother's death. I pulled over and listened to it closely. I really felt that David, and also God, were actually helping me through my pain by using this song. David had shot himself under a highway bridge near a river. The song was also about a river and death.

I had a letter that David had left for me to pass on to our Reverend. And though I didn't really want to go to the church, I was compelled to go. I had some feeling of premonition, which I thought of as a sign. I felt David was going to tell me something. When I sat down in the pew, I noticed that they had begun a play from the Bible. The introduction to the play began by them explaining, "We're going to talk of a young man who has won his battle. His name was David." I was stunned. I took this to mean that my brother David no longer had a battle going on in his head.

One thing I had a hard time with was I wondered if I could have changed David's mind about taking his life. I kept this question in my head, realizing that only David could tell me. I always felt someday I would get an answer to my question. That day came for me when my mom and I went shopping at K-mart. My mom said, "Look, another book by Betty J. Eadie." When I picked up *The Awakening Heart*, I "knew" that finding it came by inspiration from David, and that he was going to tell me something through this book. That night, I didn't want to read it until the kids and my mom were asleep. I wanted it to be still and quiet. I began the first chapter and I thought I would finish reading it the next day. Before I closed the book, I read the table of contents to see what tomorrow's reading would be. That is when I got the shock of my life! I saw the chapter titled "David Stone." Not only is my brother's name David, but his last name is Stone! His story was very similar to this person in your book. It could have been my David. And as I read about your David, the part that really stuck out to me was where he said he didn't call you on the phone for you to change his mind about killing himself, but that he just wanted to say good-bye before he did it. I felt by reading this in your book, that it was my David's way of letting me know that I couldn't have said anything to change his mind!

One might believe that it was David's sister's desire for signs that led her to find them. This might be true, or it might be her openness that allowed them to happen. In the end it doesn't matter. David's sister is a happier person and has found her answers. She knows there was nothing she could do to prevent her brother from taking his life. She is also comforted by feeling her bother's love reach her in her time of need through signs that only she would know and accept as being true.

God can and does touch us individually, personally, by any means he can and in any manner we are capable of receiving. He uses "what is" to create what will be.

What of assisted suicides? Are assisted suicides wrong if the patient is terminally ill?

In many things our motives may be noble, but our deeds can still be terribly misplaced. This is true with assisted suicides. The saying, "The road to hell is paved with good intentions" may never be more applicable. Only those who do not understand God's love would consider euthanasia an appropriate act. He intends to lift us, to perfect us to a point where we can create eternal love and universal joy of our own, independently and in our own spheres of influence. The way he does that is by giving us experience. We grow in patience, humility, faith, love, long-suffering, tolerance, and in other virtues through the things we suffer.

Death is a crucial part of life. It's an event we agreed to, with a time set aside to test and strengthen our spirits in ways unattainable except through travail. For those who suffer long painful illnesses, there is much to learn, though exactly what, may be kept from us in this lifetime. As we reach the other side where angels and loved ones wait to meet us, we will realize that our deaths and the way we met them were precious experiences, perfectly calculated to improve and strengthen our spirits.

For those who remain, however, watching a loved one linger in pain can cause immense personal suffering. The agony we observe becomes torture to ourselves, and we find ourselves willing to do almost anything to end it. But we must not succumb to the temptation to cut the experience shorter than God *naturally* intends it to be. Doing so is to cheat the loved one and ourselves.

Each person involved in the experience can grow through it, but to assist in a suicide is to place one's own mercy over the mercy of God. It makes God an observer rather than participant. Simply because we don't see the mercy of God does not mean it is not there. As with so much in the realm of the spirit, his mercy and wisdom are often mysterious to us, requiring exactly the kind of faith we are here to develop. Euthanasia, in my opinion, is a medical term giving license to kill, and its ripple effects will continue on both sides of the veil, affecting many in negative ways.

I have worked as a hospital volunteer specializing in the care of cancer patients and attending many on their death beds. I have witnessed the thinning of the veil and the glorious reunions as patients "graduate" and meet precious loved ones from the other side. I have whispered my love to them and have encouraged them to go to the light. I have heard them breathe final words of awe and joy as the veil melts away and they see the outskirts of their heavenly home and the brilliant faces of loving spirits gathering near. I have felt the joy of what we call death, the silent perfection of a spirit mastering the transition with dignity, and I would never ever consider cutting it one second shorter than what God intends.

He is our Home and our Master. Whether the issue is suicide or assisted suicide, let us leave the method and moment of our homecomings to the one who gave us life in the first place.

In situations where we must decide whether to let our loved ones go, whether to allow them to die naturally or to prolong their lives artificially beyond what their bodies can sustain, we must seek the wisdom of God. Only he knows if the patient's life on earth is over. Make God your partner in all things. Be willing to let go, and let death come naturally, but do not be the cause. When we work with the Creator of life, we will hear his sweet, still voice guiding us, and it is my promise that as we become his partner, he will bless us in all areas of our life.

Fearing Death

I never had a near-death experience, but I believe in God, a kind and loving God, not a fearsome one. Your books confirmed that belief, and also my belief in a wonderful heaven to go to after we die. Now I know not to fear death, but to embrace it when it comes.

God gives each soul the instinct for self-preservation. This natural protection motivates us to care for our bodies, shielding us from taking excessive risks. But if taken too far, this instinct can also prevent us from preparing for the end which must come. Because this life is familiar to us and is the only life we currently experience, most of us try to preserve it at all costs. Death and what happens afterward can seem frightening and mysterious. For some, even the process of dying is cause for concern.

Fortunately, we can take comfort from facts brought back by those who have been there. Death is an end, but not *the* end. Today through scripture, whisperings of the Spirit, and accounts of near-death experiences, we have more knowledge about the afterlife than ever before. As we open our minds and hearts to

213

this knowledge, we can learn to live life richly and embrace the next world willingly.

Some, however, fear the continuation of life after death. They have been taught to fear God, and they assume he will be angry because they have not lived a perfect life, and so they dread the thought of entering his presence. These fears are unfounded. God's mercy and love are magnificent and irresistible. If there is suffering, it will be of our own making, but as we call upon him for help, he will quickly rescue us if it is for our higher good. When God is involved, there is never a reason to fear.

> After reading your book, I know I will never fear death again, which is a fear that has, at times, been almost paralyzing to me. Like you, I was raised to fear the wrath of God. Your recollections of being in the all-encompassing, boundless and unconditional love of Jesus Christ filled me with hope and longing for the day I meet Him, too, face to face.

Our Heavenly Father wants to meet us in joy. As with all parents, he wants to be loved and respected, but not feared. The phrase, "to fear God," found in the Bible, might be better translated as "to honor God," which, I suspect, better convey's the prophets' meaning. I know it conveys what I experienced in his presence. In returning home, we will find that God's love is so complete that fear has no place in his house. Unconditional love and fear cannot coexist. As we accept the reality of his love, including the realization that death is a part of his plan for our growth, our view of death takes on a different light. We are able to see that graduating to the next level is something we have looked forward to for some time. Also, recognizing that our challenges are our teachers, and recognizing that death is often the ultimate challenge, we realize that death can also become one of our most powerful teachers. This truth answers many questions, including those asked by this woman who lost two loved ones:

From as far back as I can remember, death has frightened me to the point of terror. It has only been in the last five years or so that I have come to understand that everyone must die at some point in their lives. I guess the part that baffles me the most is "why at that particular point in life."

My brother was only thirty-seven years old and his son would have been eleven the day after they were killed in a highway accident. Over one thousand people came to the funeral, and during the forty-mile procession to the cemetery the line of cars was at least three miles long. I guess this tells you a little about how many people he knew and how well he was liked. That is the reason it is so difficult to understand why. Why would God take their spirits back so soon?

Recognizing that these spirits had chosen the time and circumstances of their deaths before coming to mortality helps us to accept the "rightness" of their passing. We may not understand all the reasons, but we know that the deaths of these two were allowed and approved by God.

Many of us chose the method of death we would experience, selecting its circumstances according to the type of growth we needed. Some have chosen to die in ways which strengthen their courage or faith or love. Others, to learn selflessness, compassion, and charity. Some deaths bring broken families back together, and others expose hurts and difficulties that need healing. Some deaths teach lessons to those who remain which might not be learned in any other way. Each soul's mortal plan contains their perfect completion to mortality. Death—like life—is all about growth.

The timing of our passing was also chosen in the divine plan. Death does not come at a time other than that planned, it occurs at exactly the right moment. The plan can be changed though, but only as our spirit and God act in harmony to effect other divine purposes. King Hezekiah in the Old Testament (II Kings 20:1-7) was granted an extra fifteen years because of his faithfulness. Whether this was part of his original life's mission or not is unclear, but we can be sure that God was involved in the change.

Sometimes God gives us a premonition or "knowing" in preparation for our leaving. As our time on earth draws to an end, God grants this knowledge to prepare us for the transition, to ease our fears, and to open our hearts to his light and love. The following demonstrates how God might use our current belief system as a reference point in preparing us.

Betty, I want to share my mother's experience with you, as it confirms your experience. Since you were raised in a Roman Catholic environment, you'll understand the theology behind what I'm going to share with you. My mom died in 1982, and this was "our" experience. I say "our" as I was included in it, too.

My mom was diagnosed with pancreatic cancer in April of 1982, and I assumed the responsibility of caring for her. The usual treatments followed, and it was awful, just horrible!

The Franciscan priests in my parish were very good in allowing me to keep the Eucharist at home. I kept it in a little gold container called a pyx, on top of a chest of drawers in the bedroom, which had a small altar on it. We, as Catholics, believe that Jesus is truly present in the Eucharist, and so a votive candle is constantly lit. Each day, I would give my mom Communion and pray with her. When things got bad at home, I would go into the bedroom, take the pyx, kiss it, hold it to my heart, and ask Jesus to be with me and to give me a sign that everything would be all right. This gesture was so comforting, to hold the Lord to my heart, and having Him present with me throughout the ordeal. This went on for about six months. I have to mention here that I did not tell my mother she was dying. It was too painful for me, and I knew that she was terrified of dying. I felt, too, that she would have died sooner, just knowing, and that her quality of life was more important.

On October 16 she woke me up several times during the night. My cot was pushed up against the chest of drawers in her room. As we had to go to the hospital that morning, my mother and I got up early and I mentioned that she had woken me up several times during the night. She got very quiet and said that she couldn't sleep because of all the people in the room. She told me they had been talking to her, but

216

she hadn't paid them any attention because of the light. I knew what had happened, and since she was reluctant to talk, I began to gently question her about the experience. Finally I asked, "You mean the little red votive candle?" She shook her head and said, "No, it was a white light, and it came from the chest of drawers. It was so bright that it filled the whole room and it even covered where you were sleeping, so much so, that I didn't see you anymore. You were gone!"

Tears filled my eyes when I realized that the Light had come from the Eucharist. When I composed myself (I was trembling), I said, "Well, who was it? Was it St. Francis? Was it Jesus?" She just shook her head and reluctantly said, "It was just a light." "What did it say?" I continued. She responded, "Nothing. It was just there." So, trying to put some humor into the intensity of the conversation, I said, "Well, Jesus said that He is the Light of the world. Since you were in the presence of God, what did you do?" She was very reflective as she responded. "Nothing. I just got out of bed and prayed." Betty, my mom could not get out of bed without help. She moved about in a wheelchair.

I was excited about her experience, as the Light had touched me, too. It had absorbed me into It. Believe me, her experience was what gave me strength in the months to come. That night, after we got home, she had me mail two letters. I told her that I would mail them Monday, but she said, "No, mail them now. I'm having a Rosary sent for you." I misunderstood, as I thought she said that she was having a Rosary "said" for me. I got all choked up and said, "Gee, Mom, that's so thoughtful. You didn't have to do that." She then answered, "It's to thank you for everything you did for me." I had to go into another room and cry it out.

The next day, October 17, I asked her if she wanted to receive Communion or wait until I came home from church. She said she wanted to receive it then, so I gave her Communion and prayed the Our Father with her, tucking her in. As I left for church, she said, "You go play your music. I'll see you later." (I played the guitar in church.) During the prayer of petitions at Mass, her name was omitted from the sick list. I thought this was strange and approached one of the priests about it, kidding him about efficiency and sharing my mom's experience with him. He invited me into their kitchen to have coffee, and while we talked, my uncle came and rang the rectory doorbell, telling me that my mom had died. Her name not being mentioned on the sick list was the Lord's way of telling me that she wasn't sick anymore.

And so, Betty, when I read your book I felt comforted knowing that I, too, had been embraced by the Light. The experience helped me to keep on going. I felt that I had to share my story with you, as you have shared so much with all of us.

May the Lord continue to bless you in all that you do, and in all that you are.

This beautiful experience not only prepared the mother for her passing, but also the daughter and others for their own ordeals and, later, for their own future passings. In the following letter we see how death can actually bring joy, peace, and understanding to loved ones who remain behind, if they open themselves to the rightness and beauty of the transition they are viewing.

My father steadily got worse, and eventually we brought him home to my sister's house to live out the rest of his life, which he did with the help of a hospice that helped us get medicine and taught us how to give it to him.

About a month or two before he died is when the visions started. Because of the morphine and extent of the cancer he had started to hallucinate. When that happened he seemed to be in a daze, not really with us. In between these episodes he would have what we called visions. In these visions he wasn't in a daze, but knew exactly where he was. He would be completely peaceful and happy. In the very beginning he was frightened of the people in these visions, I think because he was afraid to die. And because the visions happened while he was in bed, he eventually refused to sleep in it. He would only sleep in his chair.

He was just refusing to die. At first he was seeing people at the end of the bed, people he knew were dead, and they were calling to him and telling him they were waiting for him. This frightened my dad, and it wasn't until he saw a woman—who I feel was the Virgin Mary—that he began to calm down. She told him that these people were there to help him make the transition from earth to a better place, and that she was sent to lead him to her son. She would then point to a corner where a light would appear, and within that light was a very good man. My father loved this man, but was frightened of him just the same. This man would beckon to him, telling him that it was time, that his life here on earth was over. My father would back off and start yelling for help.

When he told us what he was seeing, we tried to calm him down by reminding him that the man in the corner was a good man, and we told him that when this man called to him, he should go. We told him not to hesitate, and that we did not want him to suffer anymore. He told us he understood and that he liked this man a lot, but it didn't change the fact that he was frightened to go with him. This went on for days, until about a week later, when we noticed that my father was no longer afraid of the man in the corner. He was starting to want to go with him. This is when the visions started to change. He wasn't just seeing Jesus anymore. Now he started to say the light was all around him and that within this light was the sweetest music he had ever heard. He also saw the whitest doves he ever saw, holding streamers of white ribbon.

I'm sure it will come as no surprise to you that within days of these visions he passed away. On July 2, we asked him if he would lie in his bed, where he'd be more comfortable. After a month of being told no, we were shocked when he said yes. I knew right then and there that my father was going to die by the end of the day, and he did. He died peacefully, with no pain or regrets. It was the most wondrous time of my life, and it gives me hope for my future and my daughter's future.

Deathbed visions can be rich blessings to the loved ones left behind. They offer hope that the departed one's spirit has gone to a place of love, serenity, and beauty and that their transition was assisted by loved ones on the other side. Although many people choose not to share their visions before death, those who do, often bless the lives of many others. This moving experience was sent to me by a nurse:

> I would like to share an experience I had when I worked in intensive care. We had a seven-bed unit and only had two patients, which was very rare. My patient that evening was a young man who had been in an automobile accident. He was dying, and he knew it and was scared. He cried and wanted me to sit by his bed and hold his hand because he was so afraid. I'd sit and hold his hand till he was asleep, and let go while he was resting. When he would wake up, I'd go back and hold his hand and comfort him. He would cry and sob because he was so scared. And then, one time when I was holding his hand, his tight grip started to loosen, and all of a sudden he became so peaceful and calm. He let go of my hand and looked at me and smiled. Then he reached up towards the ceiling and said, "They are here for me now," and died. All of us in the unit just wept for days after our experience, remembering the total calm and serenity that came over him. I know now the angels came to take him home. It was an experience I will always cherish.

What a beautiful gift. The power of this experience not only touched the spirits of trained professionals, but it rippled out— as the nurse writes further—to affect family members and friends. Now it affects us all. Death is the opening of a doorway back to heaven, our original home. Many nurses have written to share their precious experiences of watching others pass through that door. Another nurse shared this powerful experience:

> I worked the night shift, and on this particular night another aide and I were on our rounds. We had just cared for an elderly lady in her nineties who had suffered a stroke two days before. We were just leaving her room when something occurred to cause us to look back. Looking toward her window, I saw the most radiant light go through it and upwards.

The light was magnificent, in the center emitting an inten-sified glow. There I saw a likeness of this woman's face, yet it was childlike. She was smiling radiantly, twirling freely and happily. The room was still, there was no noise; it seemed filled with peace. She passed through the window. A few seconds later, without saying a word, the other girl and I went over to this lady's bed. We touched her and in quiet voices both said, "She's gone." We got the head nurse who was in charge, and she verified that the woman had indeed passed on. This other aide and I never exchanged verbally what had happened, not then or ever.

The nurse shared with us what this woman had done earlier that day. Right after her stroke, she had become totally unresponsive, not even opening her eyes. Earlier that evening, she apparently woke up full of energy and life. They brought a phone in to the room and hooked it up. There she conversed with her son who lived miles away on the east coast. They said she was happy and was very coherent throughout it all. After the phone call, she slipped back into being unresponsive. Hours later she was gone.

I share this with you because you have shown you believe in the Light. You have experienced it. I envision the eternal beauty of your experience. I haven't shared this but with a few, and of those, I don't know how many understood, really. It was an experience too big for words.

Our way home is paved with love by a living God who cares for us. Yielding to the enticing of his Spirit will always lead us to the light. By embracing the change that comes at death, we open our arms to receive all those who come to escort us home. By opening ourselves to Christ, we will find ourselves in the bosom of eternity, experiencing a love we didn't know was possible, filled with meaning and light and life. As we learn his truths and internalize them in our lives, we will begin to look forward to our homecoming with him, to the celebration of joy that awaits us in a home long forgotten by our minds but now awakening in our hearts.

Saying Goodbye

Sometimes the pain and loss is so great I don't think I can take another day.

Watching my mother suffer and die before my eyes made me question a lot of things about God and life here on earth. But after reading your book, I now realize my mother's purpose and that she is in a much better place, a place I will be in due time. But for now, I've got work to do and I must allow her to do her work as well. Thank you and God bless you.

About two weeks before Christmas, some very good friends of mine lost their dad in death. He had a severe heart attack. After getting him to the hospital, the attending nurse told the family that the damage to his heart was quite severe and he would not have long to live. This gave the family members time to say good-bye to their dad and husband. He died the next Wednesday—three days later.

After a loved one dies, grief may overwhelm us no matter how prepared we think we are; a relationship once taken for granted is suddenly stripped away from us, and an awesome void enters into our lives. We are left with sorrow, uncertainty, and a sense of helplessness. Often, vulnerability replaces confidence, and simple decisions become unfathomable matters of confusion. Regrets over love left unexpressed may consume us and perhaps threatening our sanity and faith. We may worry over the fate of the loved one: Are they happy? Are they suffering? And what awaits *me* on the other side?

Profound mourning grievously afflicts those who do not understand the purpose of death or the opportunity it affords us to grow. Here, a young man describes the grief his family felt after the death of his mother:

> When my mother passed away my sisters and brother freaked out! They do not want to talk about it. Every holiday is spent at the cemetery crying over mom's grave. They feel it would be disrespectful to continue celebrating holidays and her birthday without her, and since she is not present it is customary to mourn. I have, and am, trying to teach them the things I have learned through your books. Sometime in their life they will have to say good-bye to our mother and let her go so that they may move ahead in their own lives.

This young man is right. His family members will have to learn how to say good-bye. But they will do this in their own time, and he must have patience. His teachings, if given in kindness and love, may help them learn. But if given in the wrong way, he could set them back. Recognizing the value and purpose of death requires faith in God and in eternal life. Such faith comes only when people are ready to let go of fears and to accept new truth. The reality of the final good-bye can test us to our cores. For some, as with the next writer, the test may even last for years.

> I didn't think much about dying or death. I sympathized with friends, but one can never know how deep it goes until it happens to you. You see, my dad died unexpectedly.
>
> As I write this, I hold back the millions of tears. I'd give anything just to hear my dad's voice again, get a hug from him, anything. My life has not stopped, but it is basically

meaningless. My mom, brothers, and sisters are the same way, and unfortunately we are struggling silently. We have always been a close family, but not very talkative when it comes to religion, etc.

I've always been very emotional, sensitive. It hasn't been easy for me since Dad died. I have become disabled because of diabetes and can't work, so you can probably guess my every thought is about all of this. My heart aches so bad. I tell myself he is in a better place, but I don't think I really believe it. Not that it couldn't be a wonderful place, I just can't make myself believe it. I tell myself that Dad was so tired, he was ready. I tell myself he doesn't have any more worries, and I am happy for that, but yet I am not. I guess the base of all this is that I want him back so badly. I know I won't get him back in body. I just want assurances he is okay. But then again, why don't I believe it? I wish he could tell me he is okay, maybe that would do it. But I know this isn't possible.

To be the one who dies in faith and love, is to be set free. But to be the one who remains in the loneliness of this world, is to face a new death each day. Until we let go of a loved one and return to embrace this life, our agony and loneliness persist. Sometimes our torment ceases only after a witness or sign is given that the loved one is well and happy. Sometimes a simple indication that life continues is all that is needed. In the following letter, two sisters experience a joint witness that their dying brother loves them and would continue to love them after he is gone.

In my dream I was with my brother in his bedroom, along with his friend and our sister. Now, my sister had told me a little bit of how bad he looked recently, but when I saw him in my dream you could actually see and feel his suffering.

But when he looked at me, when our eyes met, the feeling of love that filled the room was the most powerful feeling I believe I have ever experienced in my entire life! It wasn't just between us, it was around us, it was in us, it was connecting us, it consumed the entire room.

The only time in my life when I have felt anything remotely close is when I looked at my children after they were born. After my brother looked away from me, my sister and I suddenly had an urgent need to buy him some flowers to brighten his room. The problem was we had no idea what kind we wanted to get him, we just knew they had to be special!

Well, I called my sister a few days later to get the most recent report on our brother. Of course, I told her about my dream and the incredible feeling of love that filled the room when my brother and I looked at each other. When she asked what else happened, I told her about the flowers, though they didn't seem as important to me as the incredible love I had felt. She then asked how long ago I had the dream and I told her just a few nights ago. She then informed me that three days previous to my call she had called a tele-florist to order some flowers for our brother. When asked what kind of flowers she wanted, her reply was, "I don't know what kind. I just know they have to be special!"

This powerful event prepared the sisters for the difficulties of the brother's suffering and of his final parting. They still feel his love with them.

On occasion, the departed one may return with messages of love and encouragement. Not all survivors will receive this kind of powerful communication, but those who do will never feel the same about death again. Such an experience came to this woman, who is part Native American:

My mother loved her parents very much and spoke of them often, though they were both deceased by the time I was born. She often told us this story.

When mom was ten years old, grandma became very ill. One day on her return from school, Mom came into the house and found the doctor there, along with her father and several friends, all of whom were crying and in disturbed states. Grandpa told Mom that her mother had died. He allowed Mom to go into the bedroom where her mother lay on the bed.

Mom fell upon her mother, crying in anguish. Then, my grandmother awakened as though she had been sleeping, and she stroked my mother's head. She told my mother that she had been to heaven, and it was a beautiful place with lovely flowers and beautiful people. She asked my mother not to be afraid, and told her that she would go back to visit heaven but that she would be staying here for three more days, and that at five-thirty on Friday evening she would leave again, but this time forever. My mother said that as Grandmother had promised, she lived for three more days and died at five-thirty on Friday.

I do not know if the heaven my grandmother described was true. I do know my mother lived until she was eighty-two and never feared death.

This near-death experience allowed the daughter to prepare for her mother's passing and to learn of heaven in some detail. The daughter discovered that death truly is an awakening into a greater, more beautiful world. Here is another story of a family who received a similar message of the beauties of the spirit world:

In the past year my mother was told she was dying of cancer. I never wanted to accept it. I watched her go from one hundred and sixty-five pounds down to seventy-five pounds. She didn't want to die in a hospital. She wanted to be at home. Two days before her birthday, she was back in the hospital. We were told she would die before morning. She was on a No Code status.

We all went in—all thirteen kids—to say our good-byes. We waited in the ICU waiting room all night. The next morning, to the doctor's amazement, my mother woke up like she never had been sick, and we took her home a few days later. She told us of a beautiful place she'd been, where the meadows are full of flowers and animals roamed around free. And how she petted a deer. And how she was at peace and didn't fear death. Before this she didn't want to die. She would get angry if anyone told her she was going to die.

Well, our hearts were ripped out six weeks later, when our brother who lived with Mom and helped take care of her died in a car crash. We had to go to the hospital Mom was in and tell her he had died and to bring her home for the funeral. She never cried or mentioned his name.

Two weeks before her death, while at home again, she got up in the night without us knowing and fell in the bathroom. She crawled to our brother's bed and got on it. She had no strength to climb up, and we couldn't figure out how she got on there without messing up the covers. Three days before she died she called us into the living room and told us we weren't going to believe her, but that our brother had picked her up and put her on the bed.

That night after she told us this, she sat straight up in bed, reaching for something. She hadn't been able to talk very well since the cancer was in her throat. But she called our brother's name and told us she was going to be with him on Saturday. She wanted to die in her own bed, not in a hospital, so we moved her to her bedroom. Mom died Saturday night, just like she said she would.

I got so depressed over our brother's and Mom's deaths that I wanted to die, too. Then one day, out of the blue, I saw your book and bought it. I've been wondering about life after death, and now I understand what Mom saw. And I believe they're happy and at peace.

Most people who glimpse heaven lose their fear of death. The reality and power of what they see produce a desire to become more in tune with heaven, that they might enjoy it fully when they get there. Once a person has experienced the full love of God, that person is willing to do almost anything to obtain that love again. God blesses many shortly before they die by giving them a taste of his love. His love is always present at the moment of death, preparing and healing us as much as we will allow. He also surrounds us with familiar and loving spirits to guide us through the transition. The experience is similar to a homecoming party after being gone for a long time, but far more joyful and loving than we have known on earth.

As we have seen, God may grant spiritual experiences to surviving family members in order to ease fears and to leave a legacy of hope and faith for future generations. He usually shows only an exciting taste of things to come in his larger plan, but through these experiences he reveals some of his sacred purposes, allowing the knowledge of them to ripple out to the world. Faith, knowledge, hope, and love increase wherever these experiences are shared and believed. In many cases they produce greater faith in Jesus Christ. One woman, raised in a Jewish home, saw the spirit of her deceased father. He told her he had met Jesus on the other side, which changed her perspective. Now she writes: "His coming back to me let me know he does still exist in a different realm and he had not become nothing. And I was then able to go on with this existence here, and I've now left most of my problems of my day to day life in Jesus' hands. Imagine that."

Placing our lives in Jesus' hands requires faith in him. The knowledge and power that came into this woman's life because her father appeared to her, may bless her and her children more than any act of his in life. Through the unifying power of love, our Creator does not cut us off from our loved ones. Parents who have died often contact their children and reveal that they are alive in God's presence. Many do not recognize these experiences for what they are, or shrug them off as imagination or coincidence. When we do this we short-change ourselves and our departed loved ones. When these spirits attempt contact they do so because they want to reach us. When we fail to notice, they sometimes resort to creative means.

My mother was diagnosed as having lung cancer, and for the next three weeks or so we lived at the hospital. She was doing very poorly and we expected her to die very soon. The doctors advised us to let her die peacefully when the time came and not to let anybody revive her when her heart gave out. We agreed.

When we went to see her on her birthday, she had never looked more beautiful. She was glowing, her skin color was rosy instead of the sickly yellow color she had been lately. It gave us hope that maybe she would live. I know now that she was trying to tell us she was happy. She was not afraid to die. When we came back in the evening we found that she had a stroke and would probably die before the night was over. Well, she did. At 8:30 p.m. she stopped breathing, but her heart was still beating, although extremely slow. We told the doctors not to revive her, but her body clung to life for another half-hour. I felt such guilt that she may have been alive and feeling everything for that half-hour. I cried for myself and I cried for her. I didn't want to think she was alive for that half-hour.

Later that night all of us went back to our parents' house to talk about her death. We all felt the same way—wracked with guilt. Did we make the right decision? That's when my father asked what time it was. Even though he had his wrist-watch on, he looked at the clock on the wall, which was my mother's favorite clock. What we found was that the clock had stopped working at 8:30 p.m. We were shocked and over-joyed at the same time. My mother was telling us when she had actually died, and it was not when her heart finally stopped at 9:00 p.m. This is when I truly started believing there was something beyond this life.

What a wonderful message from beyond the veil. The mother not only comforted her family but also taught them valuable truths.

Sometimes spirits of loved ones contact us through somebody else—someone who is in tune or open to them. Often, these are little children. Still open and accessible to the Spirit, children sometimes receive marvelous gifts of knowledge through the veil. "Out of the mouth of babes," said David in Psalms 8:2.

Six months ago my father was diagnosed with brain and lung cancer. The last two weeks of his life were bad. He lived a good distance away in New Mexico, and I was worried I wouldn't be able to talk to him in person before he died. I couldn't fly because I had pneumonia. So on April 3rd, I called. He was still in a coma, but my mom held the phone up to his ear on the chance he could hear what I wanted to tell him. An important fact is that she and I were the only ones who knew what I said to him—my six-year-old son wasn't home. "Dad, I love you more than life itself," I said to him. "You mean everything to me. I am trying to get to you, so hang in there. I'll be there soon, and when I get there I'm going to give you a big hug and a kiss."

Four and a half hours later, he died. I found out about it after midnight. My son was sleeping, and I shut the door to his room, then got my dad's photo off my wall and hugged it and cried. I said, "I wish I could give you a hug and a kiss," and then I went to bed half an hour later. I didn't sleep very much that night.

I hurt for my son and my dad so bad. My son had been having a hard time dealing with my dad's illness. He had been acting out and crying all the time. He and my dad had planned to go fishing, but my dad got sick very fast and was too weak for the trip. Nor did they get to say good-bye to each other. So when I said my prayers in bed that night, I asked that my dad could come back to talk with my son, so that they could say good-bye, and so he could help him understand he was okay and to be happy for him.

The next morning when my son woke up, I called him to me and told him Grandpa had died last night. He said, "I know. Grandpa came in my room last night and told me the most wonderful story. Grandpa told me he died last night, and not to cry for him but be happy because he didn't hurt anymore, and he was in heaven, and God and Jesus were both there. They have wonderful lakes there and you can ride the sharks because they won't bite, and the land animals play with the people and they won't bite either. They live peacefully together. And when I come to heaven, we will go fishing. He said to be a good boy and mind you and not hurt you anymore, and I am to mind you no matter what at all times." My son said, "Mom, you said he was sick and didn't look like Grandpa, but he looked wonderful to me. He looked young and handsome. He said he would watch over us, then he told me he had to go back. I told him I was scared, and asked if he would lay with me until I fell asleep. He said he would lay on the floor next to the bed. He did, and put his hand on the bed. Then, when I woke up, he was gone."

Later that day my son came running outside to me and said, "Mom, Mom, I forgot the most important thing! I was supposed to tell you that Grandpa wishes he could give you a big hug and a kiss, but he can't. But he will when you get to heaven, and he loves you, too."

It was my dad's reply to what I said to him when he was in the coma, right before he died. It was like he wanted my mom and me to believe my son, so he gave him messages for us so there would be no doubt in our minds.

What a beautiful experience. Like this boy, I, too, look forward to riding on sharks that don't bite and playing with the animals. We cannot imagine what glories and joys and beauties our Creator has prepared for us. And we cannot comprehend the love between us and God, and the love between people there. It is tangible, permeating. If we truly knew what awaited us, saying good-bye would be a joyous event, a celebration rather than the mournful experience we often make it. But here on the dark side of the veil, we go on in ignorance, not quite knowing where the loved one has gone. And our loved ones know how we feel. They perfectly understand our ignorance and sorrow, and they want to help us through their passing. They want us to realize that one day our turn will come, and it will not be so bad. When it comes, we too may desire to comfort others. Ask yourself: When you go, will you want others to mourn your passing, or celebrate your awakening to new life?

Life goes on—eternally. We expand and grow through new experiences, constantly learning, strengthening, becoming.

Letting go of loved ones when they pass into the next life is natural and right. In letting go and praying for their continued growth, we share our love for them and open ourselves up to the power we need to move on. We need not insist that they return to comfort or calm us. God is able to do that as his spirit works among us, guiding us to the full and rich lives he intends for each of us.

And when our journey is through, and we too slip from this mortal state to see and hear and feel for ourselves the truths of eternity, we will know for certain that our lives were perfect expressions of our identities, that the things we suffered were perfectly matched to our needs, and that life in mortality—that most mysterious and marvelous gift—was exactly what we needed for our eternal development. We will know then, as we never knew here, that all this was from God. And this larger truth we will also know: that God, indeed, is Love.

The Miracle Baby

God works in mysterious ways which are sometimes surprising, too; just when we feel we are on the right path, he seems to change it. Not that he actually changes his mind (he has no reason to) but our lack of faith and understanding of a higher plan might lead us to believe he does. I have experienced the unsettling effects of this recently. Looking back, I see two of God's ripples in my life, along with their effects. One gave me the opportunity to expand my love and faith, and the other blessed me as a result of this growth.

My son Tom works as an agent in the book industry and has represented many authors. One, Roy Mills, happens to remember details of his life in heaven before coming to earth; the veil was never closed to his memories. This fascinated me from the moment Tom told me about him, and I knew I had to meet this man. We eventually visited for hours as I listened to his descriptions of heaven and of God. What Roy described affirmed what I saw during my near-death experience—things I have not shared publicly—and I knew he was telling the truth. My heart leapt with joy upon meeting yet another soul who knew by personal experience many truths about heaven. I encouraged him to write what he knew from his perspective and to share it with the world. Roy agreed.

Much time passed without contact between us as Roy became busy in his work and I, in mine. One day Tom phoned me, and I immediately heard disappointment in his voice. He had sent Roy's finished manuscript to twenty publishers who all had turned it down. In their opinion, books about spirituality and particularly books about the spirit world were now a passing fad. They were looking for other types of books. This infuriated me. I knew that God had only just begun to awaken people to their spiritual roots and that sincere interest in spirituality is actually increasing. Books like Roy's serve a great purpose in illuminating our aware-ness of spiritual reality, and many people *are* interested in them. The world needs more books like Roy's.

For days after Tom's call, every time I thought about these publishers dismissing God for supposed lack of interest, I felt a fire kindle within me. That fiery passion grew, and I ranted and raved to all who would listen—including God. But then I calmed myself and began to pray for wisdom and understanding. I asked him to soften the hearts of the publishers, to open just one door for Roy's valuable book.

God did open a door, and when he did, I was stunned.

Sometimes our Heavenly Father allows things into our lives just to awaken us to a higher calling. The passion we feel about a matter might be the first clue that the job was ours all along. When we need to be brought to an understanding, the recognition of a need does just that. I called Tom and asked him to bring Roy's manuscript to me. Burning with Spirit, I read each simple and powerful page, reliving again the glories and wonders of life in heaven as I remembered them. I immediately called Roy to discuss his manuscript in greater detail, probing him for more memories of home, asking him to go further, to be more clear. Occasionally he asked me questions, then we talked as if we had known each other for ever—which by now we felt we had. We discussed things I have never shared publicly and perhaps never can, except with those who have seen for themselves. My heart beat with excitement, and I knew that this humble, soft-spoken Southern gentleman was filled with the love of God. I knew his book had to be published, and I knew that the inspiration I had received concerning Roy's dilemma had come straight from God: I was to publish his book, *The Soul's Remembrance.*

This would be a huge step for me. It would require boldness and great faith, and I wanted to shy away from it—at first. But it was a step laid out by God, and I could not back away. Over the next few weeks, confirmations came, more doors opened. I knew it was right, but I also knew I needed help. Writing a book is one thing, but publishing and marketing and running the business behind it is another. On the back cover of *The Awakening Heart* I had written, *"Embraced By The Light* was the plow; *The Awakening Heart* is the seed; Our harvest . . . Unconditional Love." I had not truly understood the depth of that statement until now, the nature of my commitment, the need for my time and energy. Over the years, people had asked me if I was going to start a new church. The idea seemed silly because God's gift to me is not a new theology but merely his message of love. Besides, I felt there were already too many churches. But a publishing house . . . Yes, I could do that and share the message of God's love as he was now directing me.

I began to feel more excited as I thought about this. Each detail lined up in my mind and then lay down in an order which I knew was right. Without hesitation, I reached for the phone. "TOM," I screamed when he answered, "I KNOW HOW WE CAN GET ROY'S BOOK DONE! WE WILL PUBLISH IT OURSELVES!" I expected him to be shocked at first and then to express resistance to the idea, but instead, I heard excitement that matched my own. "Mom, that's a wonderful idea. Let's get started!"

Suddenly there were interviews with *The New York Times* and *Publisher's Weekly.* I told them that not only would I publish my own books from now on but also other inspired books which I could personally endorse.

The timing had to be perfect. *The Ripple Effect* would go out first, followed by Roy's book, and then others. It would require long hours of work to put it all together, but the excitement of these days helped pull us through. It always invigorates me to share the knowledge and the hope I had discovered on the other side. I wrote late into each night on *The Ripple Effect*, taking only brief breaks to read the guest book at my web site or to drop into the chat room . There, I met many who had powerful experiences to share and others who simply wanted to say hi. Their encouraging words made me more determined to do everything in my power to continue my work. One inspired person e-mailed me to say, "Betty don't quit, please don't ever quit." Another wrote, "Ripple On," and this note is still posted in my office.

Through the support gained in prayer from friends around the world, I grew in strength and found energy to continue. Then God allowed me another surprise.

My son Jeff and his recent bride Lucy came to visit one evening. Jeff had been married previously, and during most of the nine years after his divorce he and his darling son Zachary lived with Joe and me. During that time, Zach became more of a son to me than a grandson, and I worried over who Jeff might marry, should he eventually remarry.

Jeff has a great capacity for love, and when he met Lucy he found someone who could honestly share that love in return. They dated for a year and then married, uniting a beautiful new family which included Zachary and Lucy's daughter, Lauren. They were very happy, and several months later Lucy shared the exciting news that she was expecting. Jeff walked around in a state of bliss, and Lucy glowed with happiness. Zach, now nine, was thrilled at the idea of having a new brother or sister. But life has a way of changing, sometimes crashing, and the bliss ended.

One day Jeff and Lucy came home in a daze from the doctor's office. Lucy had been ill for some time and the diagnosis was grave: lupus. Lucy's body was rejecting the child, and the medicine she needed to maintain her own health could not be used while she was pregnant. The doctors made it clear that if she did not abort the fetus, Lucy's health would deteriorate to a life-threatening status.

Lucy was three months pregnant when she brought home ultrasound pictures of her baby boy. As we gazed at the pictures, the baby became much more than a fetus, more than a baby; it became family—a son to Jeff and Lucy, a grandson to Joe and me, a nephew or cousin to the others. One picture showed him crossing his legs and sucking his thumb, and we laughed at his emerging personality. He was perfect, whole in every way, already endearing himself to us. Jeff and Lucy chose the name Jonah for him, a name that seemed more apt with each passing day.

But the medical decision had to be made, and only Jeff and Lucy could make it. My husband's heart condition worsened with the stress, and he spent more time in bed or resting. My own work began to suffer. Instead of writing for hours with great energy, now I could barely write for a minute or two before my thoughts returned to Lucy, Jonah, or Joe. My son Tom and his wife Mabel learned that they too were expecting a baby, incredibly on the same due date as Jeff and Lucy's. Mabel had been the first of my daughters-in-laws to ask me to use my knowledge of hypnosis during the birth of their first baby. Her doctor had said he wished all births could be as easy as hers. Mabel and I had become close, but now a cloud of anxiety engulfed her and Tom too as they watched and prayed for Lucy and Jeff. Sadly, as Mabel's belly swelled with Jacob, her child, Lucy's began to decrease . . . Jonah was losing weight.

Tears flowed easily as tensions mounted. Lucy and Jeff's decision had to come soon, not only for Jonah—who, as one doctor said, lived in an "unfriendly environment"—but for Lucy, whose own life was put in jeopardy by the pregnancy. Our nightly prayers were for our entire family, as Joe's health continued to deteriorate as well. But I knew our prayers were being heard as our faith and trust in God helped us to accept his will. Still, anxieties remained over the plight of our loved ones.

Finally, I had to stop my writing. I busied myself with housework to release the stress my body felt. I found comfort in doing things which came automatically, things I didn't have to think about. The pain I felt for my husband and children was just too deep, and I began to feel helpless to do anything but pray and wait. Each day seemed longer than the last.

Then one afternoon I was in the kitchen when BJ, (little Betty), came home from work. This lovely high-school senior had suffered as much as the rest of us, and I could see from her swollen eyes that she had been crying.

"Sweetheart, what's wrong?" I asked.

BJ had never been one to express herself openly but tended to keep her feelings inside. Now she sat on a stool, lay her head on the counter, and sobbed. I wanted to rush to her and wrap my arms around her, but I remained still. I knew her well enough to know that she needed space and time.

Then a final whimper, almost inaudible, came from her, and she looked up. "Mommy,"—which she calls me only when she's hurting—"I don't want Lucy and Jeff to lose Jonah. I have been thinking . . . if it were possible. . . well . . . if the doctors could . . ." Her voice became stronger and her jaw more firmly set. "If they could, I would have them take the baby out of Lucy and put it into me. I would carry it for them. I know that's impossible, but I don't want them to lose Jonah." Her eyes locked onto mine. "If they do lose Jonah," she continued. "I want to carry their next baby for them. I read about that possibility somewhere. I will do anything I can for them, or anyone in the family, I love them so much."

Tears fell from her chin, but the strength of her conviction shone in her face. I marveled at her. My little baby girl. My special angel . . . now, a young woman. She didn't just want to help in some small way, she was willing to give all that she had, to give—herself, her body. I couldn't speak. There were no appropriate words. Tears bottled up inside for weeks now flooded my eyes and I let go. I did not fight them any more, nor did I want to. Still, I could not move toward her, neither was I able to speak. With tears of love falling from my eyes, I marveled at this precious, precious spirit. I was in awe of her willing sacrifice, one she alone had contemplated and had brought to the altar of love.

I remembered back to my time in the spirit world when I first recalled BJ's and my connection. I had glanced at my features in a pool of clear water, and I saw another's face appear beside mine. That face was my "special angel's," BJ's, and I loved her. We knew that our love for each other would always transcend what would become a mother-daughter relationship here. We still remember our friendship . . . beyond this earth. We know each other's thoughts sometimes, and anticipate each other's feelings. Now, facing each other, we realized that our emotions combined would be too great for us to endure, that we could only bear them alone. It didn't matter to me that transplanting Jonah was an impossibility. What mattered was that my precious daughter had sought to save the lives of those we both loved, even at great personal sacrifice. "Dear Father in Heaven," I silently prayed, "thank you for giving me this wonderful spirit to be my daughter, my friend. And thank you for the strength and hope she brings me now." Thoughts of a verse from the Bible filled my heart, and it, too, gave me great joy. "Greater love hath no man than this, that he lay down his life for his friends" (John 15:13). Finally, we embraced, then granted each other the space we each needed.

Looking back, I can see that I was brought face to face with the message of unconditional love. Seeing it so perfectly revealed in my daughter, I wondered why I had not considered what I could do personally for Jeff and Lucy... besides pray. Yes, deadlines loomed for completing *The Ripple Effect*, the new business and especially Roy Mills and other special authors God was sending to me needed my attention. But did my family perhaps need me more? I had hardly been able to concentrate on the business. God had opened that door, but now it seemed he was closing it. I have learned that when God closes a door, it does little good to butt your head against it. He never misdirects his children, but he uses "what is" to teach us more. He offers choices, and when our strength and faith are tested and prove us capable, he uses us in greater ways. His timing is always perfect, and while we wait for his "answers," other lessons are learned.

I began to see that my book and my business would have to wait. It was time to give more than prayers for Jeff, Lucy, and Jonah. Even prayers of great faith often require our own action for God to use in blessing us. BJ had offered herself as a solution, now I sought to do the same. I went on-line and downloaded everything I could find about lupus. I went to my chat room and asked for help in the form of medical knowledge and prayers. Within hours new information began flooding in. Friends bought books and pamphlets about lupus and gave them to us. Many people e-mailed to share their concern and prayers. The ripple effect of love and practical help almost swamped us, and we accepted it gratefully.

What we learned about lupus helped our understanding, but also found that it is an extremely complex condition. Jeff and Lucy decided to take things one day at a time, choosing not to abort unless the crisis suddenly became critical. At five months Lucy went to the hospital in labor, and we feared again that Jonah would be lost. But the doctors were able to stop the contractions and to stabilize Lucy. They said that only continual bed rest offered any hope of keeping both Lucy and Jonah alive. Here was something else I could do. I took it upon myself to find a nurse, a sitter, and a housekeeper for their home. Unfortunately no one person could assume all three duties, and it quickly became apparent that three people would be needed. This created more tension and stress. Then Jeff called: "I'm sending Lucy and Lauren to her mother's. I can't sit here and watch my wife in all this pain day after day. At night I hold her until she stops crying and falls asleep, but then I'm no good for the kids in the morning or for work. Her parents are only an hour away, and I can keep Zach here in school." My heart broke for him and his family as he finally said, "All we can do is try."

Lucy went to her parent's house but within days entered labor again. Being away from her new husband and son only created more stress, as she needed to be with them and they with her. This time the doctors were able to slow but not stop the contractions and became adamant about taking the baby. Lucy's health had grown extremely precarious. We needed some answers, fast.

I prayed more fervently, and this time the answer came that I was to invite Jeff and Lucy home to live with me and Joe. At first the idea seemed awkward because I had not gotten to know Lucy well. We all loved and accepted her completely as the newest member of the family, but I hadn't yet thought of her as a daughter. Lucy needed a stress-free environment, and I had never considered staying with a mother-in-law as stress-free. But the answer, if surprising, was also plain: bring them home. As I contemplated this, everything began to sink in: Jeff and Zach were half of Lucy's stress. I was used to caring for these two, and if they all came here, they could be together to support one another as a complete family.

The next day I called Tom and told him that *The Ripple Effect* would have to be postponed indefinitely. He understood and agreed. All the speaking tours, radio shows, and television interviews were canceled. The investment made in the company would be sacrificed, gladly, as we did everything in our power to save Lucy and Jonah.

I recalled the hypnotherapy clinic I had owned before writing *Embraced By The Light*. That was another door God had opened for me to walk through in faith—a doorway which blessed me greatly. But with the release of *Embraced*, I had to leave it behind and walk through yet another door. How long this doorway to my new business would be closed, I didn't know. But it seemed irrelevant in the face of the greater truth my daughter had shown me: If we truly love somebody, we will lay down everything, including our own lives if necessary, to save them.

Since God uses what already exists to create miracles, I knew that I had to be in tune with him so he could use me. I had to access every skill I possessed, which meant not only being a mother again, but to the best of my ability, a nurse, protector, and friend. I realized that, for Lucy, living with in-laws would be difficult at first. She was aware of Joe's condition and didn't want to compromise his health, and so we tried to alleviate those concerns. Joe welcomed her with open arms and let her know that she was no burden, that he and everyone else would soon be just fine. Lucy needed to rest, so we immediately put her into bed.

The doctors permitted Lucy only four contractions per hour. Any more and she would have to go to the hospital for Jonah to be removed. We prayed greatly that the contractions would cease and that her body would begin to heal. When I was with Lucy alone, I used knowledge I had been taught in the spirit world to promote healing. I lent her my strength and energy.

A week or two passed and Lucy and I grew quite comfortable together. She told Jeff that she felt somehow serene and peaceful in our home. I was encouraged that my healing efforts were being effective and that prayers for her well-being were answered. A few days later God blessed us more fully. Lucy's labor ceased entirely, and she began to gain weight.

In the coming months my days began early and ended late. But it brought so much joy to see Lucy healthier and happier— and her tummy bigger. At night when all were finally sleeping, I would go to the computer and respond to e-mail, praying that the questions and special needs of readers and friends would be answered. There were so many questions; I could not possibly answer them all. I knew that *The Ripple Effect* would one day answer the more common questions and offer guidance and inspiration, but for now the book lay unfinished. Each night, I asked God to show me still other ways to share his message of love with so many who deserved it, needed it. I felt his peace, but no answers came at that time.

At eight months Lucy's health deteriorated again and both mother and child lost a considerable amount of weight. The contractions started again but were ineffective as Lucy grew weaker. It still wasn't time for Jonah to be born. He needed more time to gain the necessary weight that would ensure complete health. However, after two weeks of contractions and weight loss, we went to the hospital, and Lucy's doctor immediately induced labor. The rest of the family arrived and we all waited anxiously, but the labor was slow and difficult. After six hours Lucy had only dilated to four-and-a-half centimeters. They gave her more medicine, and even broke her water, but she ceased to dilate. Her doctor suggested a Cesarean birth, but Lucy wanted to have Jonah naturally if she could. The doctor reluctantly gave in and, since she lived only ten minutes away, went home to get some sleep.

Besides feeling exhausted, Lucy felt discouraged and helpless. Her body was betraying her again, preventing her from doing the only thing she needed to do: give birth. She asked me if I would consider using hypnosis as I had with my other daughters. I said yes. Normally there had been time to prepare the mothers, but with Lucy, I would have to rely upon her faith in God and her trust in me to help. Gratefully a "knowing" came to me that she was ready.

Using skills developed through years of practicing hypnotherapy—skills God had blessed me with to nurture and strengthen others—I began helping Lucy to relax. It didn't take very long. In ten minutes she was dilated to nine and a half centimeters, and the nurse's emergency call to the doctor reached her just as she entered her house. In another ten minutes the doctor was back in the delivery room, and moments later Jonah was born.

Relief and joy flooded my heart, but as the doctor placed Jonah on Lucy's stomach, a voice of warning told me to take the baby quickly and hold him close to me. It startled me but I knew it was God's voice, and I acted immediately, sensing something was wrong. I lifted Jonah into my arms and pressed him to my heart. This took everyone by surprise, but I hardly noticed as I held him tightly. Then, focusing all the power of my love upon him, I felt a burst of intense energy explode from me directly into Jonah's body. This energy was love, unconditional love. Love that I experienced only one time before. Love that is so pure, so divine, so Christ-like that it heals and perfects. It swelled to include Lucy, then the entire room. God was using my love to heal and strengthen this family.

The doctor examined the placenta which she said did not look normal. "He's a miracle baby," she said more to herself than to us. "This placenta is ruptured!" She placed the placenta into a container and asked one of the nurses to take it immediately to the lab. Sensing concern in the tone of her voice, we knew that Jonah had indeed come close to danger. Our attention went back to the baby. He was breathing fine, and color filled his body. "A miracle baby," the doctor said again. Before I gave Jonah back to his mother, his eyes pierced mine. For just one moment we had a secret, a knowing, a recognition of a bond that will always keep us close—a bond of love that predates our earth lives.

Yes, the doctor called him a miracle baby, but little did the doctor know that the miracle went far beyond Jonah. The miracle of this experience had filled our home with love for months. It had blessed Lucy with strength and peace, had blessed Jeff and Zach and Lauren with Lucy's presence, and had blessed BJ with a new awareness of the gifts of life. This experience had blessed Joe with new vitality for serving our family as our pillar of strength. And in no small way, it had blessed me. For I had been given the gift of practicing unconditional love and selfless service. And in doing this, I learned that a sacrifice offered in love is no sacrifice at all, because it does not diminish oneself; instead, it enlarges everyone involved.

Thanks to many people and their prayers, Jonah weighed over six pounds at birth. He grew so quickly in a few weeks that he outgrew his clothes and his bassinet. His body was strong and his lungs so powerful that each time he let us know he wanted a bottle or a new diaper, he thrilled us all. We grew to love our miracle baby more than we imagined possible when we first pleaded for his life—when in our minds he was only an image, but in our hearts, we knew him as a special child of God.

Tom and Mabel's angelically dimpled son, Jacob, arrived one week after Jonah. Both families were blessed with healthy, beautiful sons. These spirits, I knew, had chosen to be born as family, bonded to my wonderful sons and daughters, to me and to Joe. I marveled at this and even wondered about the spiritual connection between them, what their missions were, and how this experience would mold their foundation for life. In years to come I will understand it—if not on earth, then in heaven where all truth is known openly.

When Jonah turned three months old, Jeff and Lucy and their little family were ready to be back on their own. When they moved into their own home, it left an eerie void and silence in our home. The sounds of children playing and an infant's soft cries are melodic to me as a mother. They had comforted me. I missed my loved ones and eagerly baby-sat when Jeff and Lucy sought to reacquaint themselves as husband and wife.

Sadly, Lucy might never become completely well. But the strength and beauty of her spirit amazes me, and her ability to withstand the pain and depression of lupus is phenomenal. Our relationship as mother and daughter-in-law ceased to exist when we bonded *as friends*, and our experience together created a powerful love and respect for each other.

Joe's health improved enough that he could continue recording his family and ancestral history. This is his gift to his children, a gift that will remind them of the strength of their heritage, a strong breed of Scots-Irishmen. Gratefully, he also has the opportunity to share precious moments with his new grandsons. All of our grandchildren bring joy to his life, but it's the babies that spark something deep within him. What Joe and the babies share is a delight to behold.

Now I paused to think back on that door of lost opportunity. Was it closed forever? The new business, my next book, Roy and the other authors: were they all gone? Or were they waiting still for the door to open again? Tom had valiantly supported me while he cared for Mabel during her pregnancy, but now crucial decisions had to be made. He and I had continued to pray for guidance about the business. We knew we could not decide alone. We needed the same divine help now which had caused us to create the business in the first place. All things are possible with God, and without him every decision is difficult, every task, monumental.

I gathered my boxes of mail and tried to catch up. I read faithfully each day, but every letter reminded me painfully of work still undone—a work which extended beyond family and home. And so many letters closed with this fateful yet inspiring phrase: "Betty, please don't quit."

I wondered at God's perfect timing. My grandsons had been safely born, my time was my own again, and God was placing in my heart a desire to continue my work. So, at my computer once more, I followed directions to finish *The Ripple Effect*.

Doors began to open to greater opportunities, and as they opened, a clearer picture of my work began to emerge. Ironically, what had appeared to be crises and setbacks were now shown to be the basis of a strong foundation for individual and business growth. These personal challenges helped bring forth not only a miracle baby but other miracles of God's making. Perfectly timed opportunities for sharing his magnificent message of eternal love are suddenly opening everywhere. We are finding them in the media, and in new books and authors. As we move forward into this expanding work, we invite all to share in it.

Yes, as the saying goes, God works in mysterious ways "his wonders to perform." And what wonders! As we watch for them in our lives, practicing faith and patience, Heavenly Father awakens us to what he intends our present and futures to be. Then, when our eyes are fully opened, we will see a clear vista of his love for us, a love so wondrous and great that it causes everything we experience, everything we are, to become a source of never-ending joy. Our Creator is constant. And though our trust in him may waiver, his love for us never does. We must let it ripple into our hearts, then send it rippling out again—for a love so great cannot be contained. When we give love to others—as I learned in giving love to Lucy and Jonah—we join with God in becoming givers of life. Love *is* life, and one day in the eternities, we will have life in beautiful and perfect and loving abundance— which is the greatest Ripple Effect of all.

No, I won't quit. I can't. There is much work to do, and the Spiritual Awakening has only just begun.

Index

The following index is meant only as a tool, and not as an exhaustive exploration of the subject matter contained in *The Ripple Effect*. Indeed, many of the indices not listed here were excluded precisely because their prevalence throughout the work made them too large to be useful. The very nature of *The Ripple Effect* is to share the message of God, the message of unconditional love. Thus, the book in its entirety is a reference to faith, hope, and love.

If you would like to subscribe to
Betty's newsletter, *Onjinjinkta*,
or if you would like to write to Betty,
write:

Betty J. Eadie
c/o Onjinjinkta
P.O. Box 25490
Seattle, WA 98125

or dial:

1 (800) 433-8978

or log on to:

www.embracedbythelight.com

Available this fall from Onjinjinkta Publishing:

The Soul's Remembrance - Author Roy Mills writes of his experience with God before his mortal birth. He came to earth without the 'veil of forgetting' and recalls his previous home in heaven. Roy Mills' intimate and amazingly detailed prebirth existence reveals answers to some of the most profound questions that we have: Who are we? Where do we come from? Why are we here?

He explains that he was given a mission to share his memories that others might gain insight into their lives and understand God's love and desire for them.

The Soul's Remembrance recounts moments during Roy Mills' heavenly and earthly existence that taught him the divine nature of life, the great worth of every soul, and the eternal connection we all have. With sparkling clarity and humor, *The Soul's Remembrance* encourages us to develop unconditional love for everyone, and to learn of our individual self-worth.

The Adventures of Caterpillar Jones - by J.J. Brothers. A story of transformation and growth through the battles of everyday life. *Caterpillar* teaches life-lessons while it makes you laugh and cheer. Experience the wisdom of the Great Owl, the slither of E. Phil Snake, and the challenge of Ponder Rock.

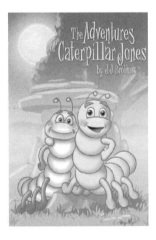

Caterpillar Jones is a children's book that tells a charming story of how one caterpillar found his way to becoming a beautiful butterfly. This tale, sometimes whimsical and sometimes sober, has a message of universal truth and application for anyone in any circumstance. A wonderful book for parents to help teach their children about life and the transformation to a higher existence.

If unavailable in local bookstores, additional copies of these titles may be purchased by calling **1 (800) 433-8978** or you may order on-line at www.Onjinjinkta.com

Read by   DATE 8-2012

Mary Fahy Boegler Clarkson

Sandra McGuire   Sept. 2012
    a Keeper - to be read again
    (Betty is Morman - Embraced By the Light
    first came out with LDS & Morman
    things in the book - then she scrubbed
    all Morman stuff from her next
    editions so non-morman's would
    read her book.